The Role of Roman Gladiators in Shaping Civilization

Jason F. Morrison

Abstract

This book takes Foucault's statements regarding political strategies of historical discourse in modernity, from the Enlightenment to the present, and through this lens reads the historiographic study of gladiators as a text which reveals deeper truths about the modern west's self-image as the seat of 'civilization'. In *Society Must Be Defended*, Foucault claimed that the modern discourse of history is essentially structured as a 'discourse of perpetual war', which narrates a permanent state of conflict between history's speaking subject and a constructed figure of the barbarian against which 'civilized society' defines and defends itself. The construct of civilization exists in a complex and perplexed relation to the 'barbarism' of violence, and successive strategies of historical writing have, in Foucault's terms, applied different models of filtering such barbarism. Within this discursive framework, classical historiography, particularly with respect to ancient Rome, performs a foundational function as a myth-history of 'western civilization'. This dissertation takes the historical image of gladiators, especially insofar as this image signifies the intersection of violence with pleasure, as a particular barbarism which troubles the myth-historical narrative of western civilization, and critically examines the shifts of scholarly opinion surrounding three linked dimensions of the practice: its origin, the 'nature' of the crowd of spectators, and the concomitant interpretations of the meaning of both the violence and the pleasure of gladiators in terms of the sub-discourses of race and class struggle. The persistent imperative to account for the anxiety invoked by gladiators as a 'barbarism within civilization' reveals a deeper discursive structure of power and legitimacy surrounding the linked constructs of nation and State. A selection of scholarly texts from the mid-eighteenth to the early twenty-first centuries tracks the course through which the interpretation of gladiators, in the context of changing strategies of historical discourse, has shifted from violence to non-violence, from illegitimate to legitimate pleasure, and from barbarous to civilized.

Table of Contents

Introduction

The problem of gladiators: violence, pleasure, and civilization

The image of Roman gladiature[i] – violent armed combat, blood on the

sand of the arena, and the massive amphitheatre with its roaring crowd – is utterly

familiar. The Grand Tour made much of the Colosseum, in both poetry and visual

art; gladiatorial combat was a favourite trope of historical romances of the

nineteenth century, and made several famous appearances in canonical literature

as well. In the twentieth century it has been the subject of novels both

philosophical (Arthur Koestler's 1939 *The Gladiators*) and pulp (Philip Wylie's

1930 *Gladiator*). It is a recent mainstay of English-speaking historical television

programming, and the history of its representation in cinema is as long as the

history of cinema itself, ranging from lauded epics such as Spartacus and

Gladiator to dubbed B-movies and pornography. Modern tourists to the ruins of

the Colosseum in Rome are met by a fully unionized troupe of actors in

historically inaccurate costume, who for EU5 will hold a plastic sword to one's

throat for souvenir snapshots. They do, by all accounts, a brisk trade.

Less familiar is the academic question of gladiature's origin. The

historiography of gladiatorial origin has its roots in the classicism of the

eighteenth century, although it was not explicitly articulated before the nineteenth,

and the lately subdued debate continues into the present. Scholarship on the

subject traditionally rests heavily upon surviving written texts, but refers also to

material and visual evidence, architectural history, and at its best integrates

broader historical circumstances to increase the coherence of a historical picture which has always been ambiguous. A brief glance at over three centuries of academic labour, however, immediately reveals two arresting points. One, the origin of gladiature has long been constructed in terms of an originating cultural context: the question has long assumed the form of asking 'who' first developed gladiature, and for most of the relevant period of historiography, the answer has located the origin of gladiature outside the boundaries of Roman society itself. Two, the question of 'who' originated gladiature has always simultaneously evoked a following question of 'how': how it initially appeared in its original non-Roman context, but more importantly, how the practice of gladiature was able to traverse the boundary of Rome, how it was able to find purchase within Roman society, and how it was subsequently able to reach such staggering proportions of mass spectacle under the Empire. Thus, the origin story of gladiature has been consistently deployed in classical historiography to provide some rationalization for the subsequent bloody history of gladiature at Rome. These two linked questions of origin and subsequent social meaning – the first inscribed as a matter of race in a broad sense, and the second as a matter of class – have shifted in tandem over time, and together have formed a remarkably unchanging foundation upon which the historiography of Roman gladiature has been written and rewritten throughout the modern period.

The definitive historical problem of gladiature, the factor which constructs and constrains its interpretation far more comprehensively and perniciously than any surviving (or lost) historical evidence, is modernity's imperative to account for gladiature in its appearance as an irruption, an aberration, and a deviance: the possibility that violence, which is the perceived (and contested) essence of gladiatorial combat, could function as a highly developed institution of mass spectacle in the Roman world invokes an anxiety and a rationalizing imperative in modern responses. The object that is subject to rationalization within this historiographic discourse is precisely that whose cartoonish and banal echo can be bought for EU5 at the Colosseum: the cathexis of violence with pleasure, along with an entire discursive framework surrounding the locus of violence in social order that springs forth at the moment this particular intersection is encountered. The problematic intersection of those two elements frames, for modern scholarship, the 'what' of gladiature – the *a priori* basis for the interpretation of its possible meaning and function within Roman society.

Ancient Rome holds a particular significance that is more than merely incidental to the question of the origin of gladiature as a specific incidence of socially embedded violence. It may be asked why classical scholarship does not simply 'accept' the notion that the violence of gladiature could have been an object of pleasure for Rome, in the way that scholarship 'accepts' the structural position of violence in, say, pre-conquest Mesoamerica (to whom the Romans have more than once been analogously compared; see, for example, Futrell 1997.)

There are, arguably, two closely connected reasons for the specific significance of Rome. The first is ancient Rome's status as one of the dominating *topoi* of the myth-historical foundations of the west. In many ways, Rome is a major key to the existence of 'the west' as a numinous entity with an historical sense of itself; beyond the influential and often celebrated inheritances of Roman law, the Latin language, Greco-Roman aesthetics, and elements of historical writing itself, the broad idea that the roots of the modern west can be traced back to the socio-political organization of the Mediterranean world two and a half millennia ago is partially constitutive of the image of 'western civilization' as such, and further is integral to the west's historical articulation of the construct of 'civilization' itself. Within this grand mythopoesis, gladiature has appeared to post-Enlightenment classical historiography as a deviant element within an otherwise august tradition, and further as a violent, chaotic space situated at the centre of the Roman social order which western modernity identifies as its ancestor. It is a deviation which, whether explicit in classical scholarship or not, necessarily raises specific questions regarding socio-political structure, class conflict, and the legitimization of violence within social order. Therefore, when we write the historiography of gladiature with respect to the rationalizing force accorded to stories of its origin, we are undoubtedly constructing and working within a deeper discourse about violence, power, and social structure in modernity; the push to fix a point of origin may be partly explained by the suggestion that, at a deeper level, the historiography of gladiature formulates a broader, more generalizable myth-history for violence within socio-political structure, and of state control of the means of violence. The myth-historical position of Roman antiquity entails that the re-inscriptive function common to all historical writing is even more imperative than usual.

Secondly – and leaving aside, for the moment, the plastic swords – modernity has a specific issue not simply with violence, but with violence as pleasure: both in a more general sense, and with gladiature as a particular form. For the latter, aside from referring back to Rome as a foundation, gladiature appears to modernity as an uncanny spectre: as a social institution of mass spectatorship, the amphitheatre is something that modernity holds directly in common with Roman antiquity, with nothing comparable to be found in the intervening centuries. Moreover, modernity's broader difficulty with violence as pleasure relates in part to the extent to which the construct of civilization presumes the exclusion of violence from social order which is called 'civilized', and the correlating extent to which, in the wake of that exclusion, that which is defined as violence invokes a response of abhorrence.

Statements of such abhorrence of violence are abundant within gladiatorial historiography itself, and will be a major area of investigation in this dissertation. In most recent work on the subject, the aberration which gladiature presents has even inspired an explicit (but, as will be examined in Chapter 6, strategically invoked) anxiety over the possibility of an affinity on this point between the Romans and 'ourselves', two millennia later. This recent anxious perception of an uncomfortable or uncanny affinity with Roman gladiature, however, is the latest stage of a long line of historical thought which can be traced back to a radically different place. In the centuries between the Enlightenment and the present, the academic interpretation of gladiature at Rome has moved between two very different extremes. Put briefly, whereas the scholarship of the eighteenth century held a general consensus that the particular violence of gladiature was cruel, bloodthirsty and uncivilized, the present academic climate is marked by a demonstrable tendency to disconnect gladiature from violence in various ways, including the striking claim that the practice was in fact always nonlethal for the combatants.[1] A reader who examines a passage from Mommsen's definitive *Romische Geschichte* (1855, vol. III:13), for whom gladiature was simply "revolting" and "demoralizing", is presented with a much different picture than a reader of Barton's "The Scandal of the Arena" (1989), who sees the gladiator as "a living symbol of redemption and self-vindication, [and] the 'moment of truth' in the arena [as] a focused and intensified 'reality' beyond anything experienced outside" (23). Although the recent spate of scholarly writing on gladiature commonly does rehearse the traditional attitude of abhorrence towards this particular violence, such statements often appear to be, in fact, strategic, given how frequently these are joined with analyses of gladiature which, like Barton's, shift gladiature's 'meaning' away from violence, thus doing away quite neatly with any cause for anxiety over the possibility of an affinity or resemblance between ancient Roman gladiature and anything in the modern world (cf. the introductory chapter of Kyle's *The Spectacle of Death* for an excellent example).

This dissertation explores the possibility that the key to understanding these numerous long-term shifts in gladiatorial historiography – shifts of gladiature's origin, of contemporary attitudes towards the intersection of violence and pleasure, and shifts in the discourse surrounding modernity's relationship with antiquity – is, in fact, yet another dominant element of modernity's image of gladiature: the crowd. The arena crowd effectively functions as a double signifier of two closely associated and ultimately opposed ideas, which together form a

---

[1] *D.S. Potter*

disjunction that arguably has driven much of the relevant scholarly work of the past three centuries. On one hand, the Roman arena crowd is frequently held as a representation of the *demos* as a chaotic social body, a many-headed mob whose potential for destructive force is indicated by its marriage of violence with pleasure; this sort of mob imagery has a long history, which will be examined in part, and which has provided a rich subtext for most of the novels and films referred to above. On the other hand, however, the crowd of the arena is distinguished by another dimension of meaning that sets it apart from virtually all other mobs: a crucial element of the complex semiotics of gladiature for modernity is its status as an unparalleled symbol of demagoguery, and ultimately as a grotesque perversion of democratic process, mirrored in the infamous image of the crowd presiding over the fate of an individual gladiator by a turn of the thumb. Consequently, what is concealed by moralizing discourses of abhorrence, and what an attempt at a reflexive, suspicious hermeneutics would potentially reveal, is the extent to which an entire political history, or a relatively unconscious history of political philosophy, can be excavated from the imagery of the crowd in gladiatorial historiography, and from the relationship between the sliding construct of the crowd and the equally mobile historical question of gladiatorial origin, as these tandem tropes connect back to a wider discourse about the proper or legitimate place of violence within 'civilized' order.

A close examination of historiographic scholarship of gladiature in the modern period reveals that this long-term repositioning of violence has been closely associated with similar shifts both in the question of gladiature's origin and in the changing construct of the crowd. As gladiature has become 'less violent' in scholarly opinion, it has also, on the one hand, become less 'other' in its origin; the once-prevalent notion that Rome acquired gladiature from some source that was either indescribably ancient or markedly 'non-European' no longer strictly polices the boundary between what are to be considered Roman and not-Roman. On the other hand, the withdrawal of violence from the historiographic image of gladiature has also coincided with a gradual transformation in the image of the crowd who attended such spectacles; its structural and political relation to the entire Roman social body has been interpreted as increasingly more integrated, and though the image of the gladiatorial crowd as a powerful symbol of social decay is still thriving in cinematic representations, it is no longer accorded the explanatory force in scholarship that it enjoyed two centuries ago.

Stories of origin: historico-political discourse

This dissertation is an attempt to read the modern historiography of gladiature as an exponent of what Foucault called a 'historico-political discourse' – a particular discursive field wherein historical narratives are constructed in the context of socio-political conflict and the contestation of the bases and distribution of power. In *Society Must Be Defended*, Foucault built upon his genealogical theory of knowledge and claimed that 'truth' was not only a socially and historically contingent construct within epistemic frameworks, but further, that since at least the end of the seventeenth century the construction of truth has taken place in the context of historical struggles between social groups, or sectors of society, contending for the authority to articulate the 'right to power' and using

historical narrative as a critical tool to that end. Foucault claimed that historico-

political discourse emerged in the late eighteenth century, and represented a

rupture from the preceding dominance of the 'juridico-philosophical' discourse of

history, represented by a form of historical narrative which told the 'history of

right' as a legitimization of the power of the monarch. In contrast, the emergence

of historico-political discourse is seen as a new historical narrative articulated

initially by the nobility, and eventually also by the bourgeoisie, to 'reoccupy the

knowledge of the king':

> "Up to this point [i.e. the end of the eighteenth century], history had
> never been anything more than the history of power as told by power
> itself, or the history of power that power had made people tell: it was
> the history of power, as recounted by power. The history that the
> nobility now begins to use against the State's discourse about the
> State, and power's discourse about power, is a discourse that will ...
> destroy the very workings of historical knowledge" (*SMBD* 133).

The 'destruction of the workings of historical knowledge' to which

Foucault referred was the development, within historico-political discourse, of a

new speaking subject: "someone else begins to tell the story of his own history;

someone else begins to reorganize the past, events, rights, injustices, defeats, and

victories around himself and his own destiny" (*SMBD* 133). This new subject is

"both the subject that speaks in the historical narrative and what the historical

narrative is talking about"; it is a "society, in the sense of an association, group, or

body of individuals governed by a statute (...) and which has its own manners,

customs, and even its own law. The something that begins to speak in history, that speaks of history, and of which history will speak, is what the vocabulary of the day called a 'nation'":

> "At this time, the nation is by no means something that is defined by its territorial unity, a definite political morphology, or its systematic subordination to some imperium. The nation has no frontiers, no definite system of power, and no State. The nation circulates behind frontiers and institutions. The nation, or rather 'nations', or in other words the collections, societies, groupings of individuals who share a status, mores, customs, and a certain particular law – in the sense of regulatory statutes rather than Statist laws. History will be about this, about these elements. And it is these elements that will begin to speak: it is the nation that begins to speak. The nobility is one nation, as distinct from many other nations that circulate within the State and come into conflict with one another. It is this notion, this concept of the nation, that will give rise to the famous revolutionary problem of the nation; it will, of course, give rise to the basic concepts of nineteenth-century nationalism. It will also give rise to the notion of race. And, finally, it will give rise to the notion of class" (*SMBD* 134).

In Foucault's analysis, another key element which signalled the discursive shift of the late eighteenth century was the exchange of the figure of the 'savage' for the figure of the 'barbarian' in historical and political thought. Pre-eighteenth century philosophico-juridical discourse rested upon the opposition of the savage to society: the savage, the "natural man whom the jurists or theorists of right dreamed up, (...) who existed before society existed, who existed in order to constitute society, and who was the element around which the social body could be constituted" (*SMBD* 194), was the extra-social and asocial figure who represented and defined the limits of 'the social' through his presence on the outside, and through the conception of his possible entry into the social body through the sacrifice of his imagined 'natural rights' to the sovereign. In these terms, society is founded upon the exchange of rights for protection, and through the act of dissolving a former identity, as "[t]he savage is basically a savage who lives in a state of savagery together with other savages; once he enters into a relation of a social kind, he ceases to be a savage" (*SMBD* 195). In contrast, historico-political discourse (as cribbed from Foucault's chosen exemplar, Boulainvilliers) hinges upon the opposition of the barbarian to civilization. While the savage defined the limits of the social (and signified its perceived essence) by his transformation into a social subject or citizen, the barbarian is defined by his permanent existence outside of civilization, and by his permanent desire to "destroy and appropriate" civilization: the barbarian "is always the man who stalks the frontiers of States, the man who stumbles into the city walls. (...) He appears only when civilization already exists, and only when he is in conflict with it. He does not make his entry into history by founding a society, but by penetrating a civilization, setting it ablaze and destroying it. (...) [H]e is the vector for domination" (*SMBD* 195).

> "The savage is a man who has in his hands ... a plethora of freedoms which he surrenders in order to protect his life, his security, his property, and his goods. The barbarian never gives up his freedom. And when he does acquire power, acquire a king or elect a chief, he certainly does not do so in order to diminish his own share of right but, on the contrary, to increase his strength, to become an even stronger plunderer ... and to become an invader who is more confident of his own strength. (...) For the barbarian, the model government is ... necessarily a military government, and certainly not one that is based upon the contracts and transfer of civil rights that characterize the savage" (*SMBD* 196).

In consequence, historico-political discourse since the late eighteenth century, in Foucault's view, has 1) turned upon the construct of civilization and 2) defined and constructed civilization according to socio-political narratives dependent upon the existence of the barbarian as a perpetual enemy, and upon permanent war and conflict. This results, in turn, in the presence of a political 'economy of barbarism' within historical writing (*SMBD* 198); the victors of any social struggle capitalize upon their political dominance to suppress a defeated adversary's version of events in favour of their own group propaganda, using historical knowledge as a weapon by 'filtering the barbarism' of their own ascent to dominance and re-configuring a barbaric image of their defeated opponents.

All of this leaves us, then, with a complex, interconnected set of critical questions, which this dissertation seeks to address from an initial, nested premise: that modern writing about Roman history is a centrally important medium for the discourse of civilization, and that, by extension, this particular historiography has functioned as a major idiom for the discourse of perpetual war. If modernity's historiography of Roman antiquity comprises a significant part of the articulation of the construct of 'civilization', particularly insofar as that construct has represented the west's definition and image of itself, can the presence of gladiature as an aberration or a deviance within the narrative of Roman civilization be read against Foucault's figure of the barbarian as civilization's hostile opposite? – or, in other words, if we examine the historiography of gladiature as a form of historico-political discourse, do we find that the origin of gladiature has been assigned in some way to the sphere of the barbarian? Does the image of the crowd also refer to the barbarian as the Other of civilization, and if so, how has classical historiography coped with the perceived presence of the barbarian embedded within the boundaries of the civilized social? If the post-Enlightenment western episteme sees 'the nation' as the speaking subject which constructs itself through a historico-political historiography built upon tropes of race and class, do the race/class tropes of the specific historiography of Roman gladiature express anything specific about modernity's discourse of 'the nation' as this has been inscribed upon and through the image of antiquity? Does the lengthy history of attempts to rationalize or reconcile gladiatorial violence within the larger scope of classical historiography reveal anything about the construct of the civilized nation insofar as that construct partially rests upon the exclusion of violence? Does the anxiety invoked by the cathexis of violence and pleasure manifested by gladiature, and the sliding interpretation of the nature and meaning of that cathexis, tell us something about how western modernity has 'filtered its own barbarism' through the inscription and re-inscription of Roman antiquity as a myth-historical, foundational narrative of 'civilization'? Finally, what does the moralizing discourse around violence and pleasure express about the rationalizing discourse around violence and power? – and what, if anything, does the overarching path of the shifts within these linked discourses reveal about modernity's 'self-image' over time?

'Civilization', I would argue, is a discourse which separates or distinguishes the nation from the State. If we take the State to mean something like the whole people, or something like the modern nation-state – a physical, territorially bounded entity with a political apparatus, a social structure, and a

cultural landscape that are all identified by a common name – then the 'nation',
when this linked construct is approached as a product of both racial *and* class
discourses, appears as a sub-group within the State – a 'something else' that
speaks of itself and claims its own power. As an entity which articulates its own
history of right, the nation identifies itself as the 'true' or legitimate power within
the State in part by virtue of its status as 'civilized'. As part of the language of the
history of right, the discourse of civilization is in part defined by the abhorrence
of violence – an interesting and critical contradiction, given that the nation, as a
speaking subject which narrates the history of itself, is defined *a priori* by
relations of conflict and is in fact constituted, in Foucault's terms, by the
discourse of perpetual war. What we begin to realize is that a critical reading of
the modern historiography of antiquity reveals this fact quite clearly, when we
focus specifically upon gladiature as the thing that troubles the myth-historical
use of antiquity on precisely the problem of violence and institutionalized conflict
within social and political structure. The historiography of gladiature focuses
upon the moral attitude of abhorrence, eventually culminating (by the end of the
twentieth century) in a kind of ideologically misrecognized self-reflexivity, but
this emphasis on abhorrence is a veneer which conceals far deeper issues, not
least the extent to which the myth-historical status assigned to antiquity is at base
an attempt to write out the 'history of perpetual war' by positing a continuity –
perhaps even a juridico-philosophical unity – between a certain image of Rome
and western modernity itself.

Modernity, mythology, and self-image: Elias and the auto-narration of civilization

To begin to address these questions, it is probably best to start on the surface at 'modernity's self-image' with respect to the construct of civilization. The essential function of civilization as a discursive entity emanates from identity formation and the politics of distinction on a macrosocial scale; a comparative, relative meaning is embedded in the most basic sense of the word, since civilization ultimately only signifies in its opposition to barbarism, in whatever way either of these is imagined (cf., for example, John Stuart Mill). It is this straightforward premise which underpins Foucault's claims surrounding historico-political discourse as a shift in the episteme of the late eighteenth century. Foucault's subsequent assertion that the oppositional pairing of civilization/barbarism is one of perpetual war, based upon conflict and the dynamics of conquest and destruction, grounds the construct of civilization in historical time through its association with the rise of the nation-state. This is the essence of the rupture between the philosophico-juridical and historico-political discourses: the structure of the historical speaking subject's ongoing articulation of its subjectivity as a civilized nation is represented through a relation of perpetual conflict with a hostile barbarian other.

This opposition and structural violence, however, is nowhere explicit within civilization's discourse of itself, which instead attempts to conceal or overwrite the 'perpetual war' with what has been called a 'triumphalist narrative' of its own legitimate dominance" (Burkitt 143).This is of course the political dimension of historico-political discourse, "in which truth functions exclusively

as a weapon that is used to win an exclusively partisan victory":

> " This discourse of perpetual war ... because it bypasses the great
> philosophico-juridical systems, this discourse is in fact tied up with
> a knowledge which is sometimes in the possession of a declining
> aristocracy, with great mythical impulses, and with the ardour of
> the revenge of the people. (...) It is a sombre, critical discourse, but
> it is also an intensely mythical discourse ..." (*Society Must Be
> Defended* 57).

The myth which stands at the core of the narrative of civilization in

western modernity - along with professional scholarship's potential for

complicity in defending and perpetuating that myth - has been concisely identified

by Bauman in *Modernity and the Holocaust*:

> "The ... myth deeply imprinted in the self-consciousness of our
> Western society is the morally elevating story of humanity
> emerging from presocial barbarity. This myth lent stimulus and
> popularity to, and in turn was given learned and sophisticated
> support by, quite a few influential sociological theories and
> historical narratives; the link most recently illustrated by the burst
> of prominence and overnight success of Elias's presentation of the
> 'civilizing process'" (12).

The 'civilizing process' mentioned by Bauman refers to *The Civilizing*

Process (*Über den Prozess der Zivilisation*), published in 1939 by Norbert Elias;

it is an excellent illustration of how the construct of civilization works to narrate

its own triumph. Elias' thought occupies a critically balanced intermediate

position between Freud and Foucault, although he took critical exception to

Freud's essentialist model of psychological drives, and he emphasized a general

continuity of sociohistorical 'movement' – inscribed as 'process' - in contrast to

Foucault's later assertion of discontinuous breaks between epistemic frameworks.

Like Foucault, Elias' model of civilization hinged upon a binary structure of social organization defined by two groups in perpetual conflict; however, Elias departed drastically from Foucault in claiming that the conflict underlying social order was to be understood not as a war, but as a game. The 'process' of civilization was the gradual expansion of the great social game into an increasingly democratic field which absorbs all players, subjects them to increasingly similar rules, and limits their scope for play, such that the structural potential for violence in group conflict diminishes and withdraws over time. Elias thus produced an uneasily critical model of socio-historical change which attempted all at once to confront directly the more mythical elements of 'civilization', and yet also tried to salvage the myth in some ultimate sense even while struggling to deconstruct it.

The Civilizing Process outlined a figurational, process-oriented sociological model whose central claim was that the historical development of the western nation-state could be seen to relate directly to parallel developments in individual psychology and social *habitus*, specifically with respect to violence; the critical indicator of this was the claim that, as western states have developed in part according to a process of centralization of the means of violence within the state apparatus, violence has simultaneously withdrawn from the sphere of daily public life, in concert with an increasing abhorrence of violence within both *habitus* and discourse.[ii] The 'civilizing process', therefore, is a directional model of social change, of which the primary index is the positioning of violence – violence within social space, as an element of interpersonal relations, and above all as an object of abhorrence, an attitude which, Elias claimed, intensifies as the directional process of civilization extends over time. Thus, the increasing withdrawal of violence from everyday life – correlated to a centralization of the legitimate means of violence at the state level as violent conflict is relegated to relations between states, and to the increasing refinement of an abhorrence of violence at the level of the individual as a dominant property of *habitus* – is seen as the defining characteristic of western social order as this has developed through historical time.

Elias focused the first volume of *The Civilizing Process* upon a survey of books of etiquette and manners from the sixteenth to the nineteenth centuries. Here he sought to demonstrate, through tracking consciously articulated rules of upper-class and bourgeois behaviour regarding table manners, body postures, modes of polite speech, and the proprieties of bodily functions, that there exists an observable long-term shift in attitudes and behaviour – 'civility' - between the late European Middle Ages and the modern period. Within the increasing suppression of aggressiveness in interpersonal relations of all types, Elias perceived an overarching patterned moulding of individual affect economy that he connected directly to a parallel series of shifts in the power dynamics underlying class relations. 'Civility' and its associated refinement of manners originate as a differentiating group identity strategy of sociopolitical elites, in a doubled response to both the dominant political authority of the ruler and the increase of social 'pressure from below'. Historically mobile redistributions of power among social groups, and ongoing productive tensions between emulation and further differentiation between groups, drive long-term shifts in 'civilized' manners, even though local and context-specific factors shape the finer details. Civilized manners are treated as a manifestation of, and a contested object within, the dynamic structures which locate and constitute social groups differentiated by what Elias termed an unequal distribution of power-chances. Civilizing, then, is the process whereby social classes, defined as groups with greater or lesser capacity to exert influence over other groups, construct, negotiate and adapt the local structure(s) of power relations that exist between them; a key element is observable in 'civility', which Elias read as a coded set of behaviours organized by attitudes towards violence in interpersonal relations.

This basic unit of 'figuration' – the group structure within which social groupings relate to one another – was the fundamental building block of Elias' construct of civilizing, and the source of the dynamism of social change which, in his view, entailed that civilizing was a diachronic process. 'Civilizing', in effect, reduces to the historical trend wherein western social figuration, broadly conceived, becomes characterized by the withdrawal of violence from the sphere of public life and an increased abhorrence of violence in the *habitus*; this dynamic of withdrawal and abhorrence is a key component of the ongoing process of social differentiation between groups distinguished by unequal power-chances; and the correlation, at the level of the state, between the withdrawal of violence from social group relations and the process by which political authority becomes increasingly centralized in state formation, leading to a rationalization of conflicts between states and an internal pacification within them. All of these factors add up to a generally more integrated sociality, and a relative equalization of power-chances over the long term, which Elias summed up as a 'process of functional democratization' which is the civilizing process. Elias' thought thus occupies a critically balanced intermediate position between Freud and Foucault, although he took critical exception to Freud's essentialist model of psychological drives, and he emphasized a general continuity of 'movement', in contrast to Foucault's later assertion of discontinuous breaks between epistemic frameworks.

When it came to specifying the competition over 'civility', Elias grounded his concept of process by invoking the primacy of the 'established-outsider' relation as the central mechanism of social change. The established-outsider relation is a tool which attempts to generalize relations between groups as 'positions within a game' rather than reified designations of, for example, class; the distinction between established and outsider is ultimately based upon each groups' differential control of power chances relative to one another, and the group 'playing' the position of established or outsider is contingent upon factors inherent in any specific social figuration and subject to change through time. Further, Elias argued that what constitutes 'power' in such relations takes forms other than the control of economic or material resources, claiming that the control of magical and mythological powers of signification were equally or even more important (Mandalios 69).

Put briefly, Elias tabled three nested claims. One, both an established group and an outsider group will entertain fantasies about one another that are negative in character, and whose degree of negativity is a function of the degree of the imbalance of power between them within their common social figuration.

Two, the structure of an established group's fantasy of its outsider group will be based upon an image drawn, *pars pro toto*, from the anomic behavior of that group's 'worst' members. Three, the negative fantasy image constructed and upheld by the established group contributes directly to the established group's own self-image of its positive group charisma. In general, an established group will seek to affix the label of 'lower human value' to another group as a means of maintaining a position of relative social superiority. This labour of stigmatization, Elias felt, is a species of the collective fantasy of the higher-powered established group; it both justifies the aversion for the outsider group, objectifies the 'reason' for the aversion in a manner which exculpates the established group from the assignation of blame, and reciprocally reinforces the established group's image of its own superiority based upon the possession of different characteristics or practices.

Fantasy, if not logical in the strictest sense, is functional in the most general sense; it is "the social data *sui generis*, neither rational nor irrational" (*The Society of Individuals* xxxvi). However, beyond this most basic level, irrationality effectively reigns:

> " ... we often like to think that the element of fantasy, which plays
> an important part in directing a group's common actions and ideas
> towards its goals, is merely a blind – nothing more than an
> alluring, exciting mask of propaganda. We imagine that cunning
> leaders use it to conceal their boldly-conceived aims which in
> terms of their 'own interests' are highly 'rational' or 'realistic'. (...)
> But, on closer investigation, it is not very difficult to see the great
> extent to which both realistic and fantasy-laden ideas pervade the
> conception of 'group interests'. (...) The peculiar sterility of many
> analyses of ideologies largely stems from the tendency to treat
> them as basically rational structures of ideas coinciding with actual
> group interests. Their burden of affect and fantasy, their egocentric

or ethnocentric lack of reality are overlooked, for they are assumed to be merely a calculated camouflage for a highly rational core" (*What Is Sociology?* 28).

As Bauman summarizes, "[i]n the familiar controversy between Freudian and Weberian views of civilization Elias is firmly, and persuasively, on the side of Freud. Modern civilization is about control, not rationality" ("The Phenomenon of Norbert Elias" 123). Elias' hypothesis expressed a bias of interest in the established group; he felt that the established, with their greater corporate power of determination over the distribution of power chances, would generally exert correspondingly greater influence over the local content of inter-group fantasy images (*The Established and the Outsiders* xx). While an established group's negative fantasy of its designated outsider group is a product of specific historical figuration, not of rational calculation, nonetheless the power of a ruling group is dependent to a degree upon its capacity to harness signification within inter-group fantasies. Elias was even sensitive to local iterations of western modernity's 'morally elevating myth', and saw the various nationalist versions of civilization as high-level concentrations of social fantasy:

> "...the building up of collective ... fantasies plays so obvious and so vital a part in the conduct of affairs at all levels of balance of power relationships; and no less obviously they have a diachronic, developmental character. On the global level, there are for instance the American dream and the Russian dream. There used to be the civilizing mission of the European countries, and the dream of the Third Reich..." (*The Established and the Outsiders* 29-30).

In addition, fantasy functions within Elias' civilizing process as the source of civilizing's opposite, 'decivilizing', which is the space reserved within Elias' model to inscribe outbreaks of violence into the social fabric; such episodes are considered reversals or breakdowns of the civilizing process, wherein an unravelling of one or more of the primary sub-processes outlined above potentially leads to a reversing of them all. Thus the directionality which defines civilizing is inextricably bound up with violence - its control, its use, and its perceived meaning; in a very clear sense, the civilizing process as a whole unfolds from violence as its key organizing principle, and expresses a construct of the social which is itself ultimately defined by violence, and which is further shaped by Elias' implied image of history as a narrative of the withdrawal of violence from the social. Moreover, just as Elias equated civilizing with functional democratization, so decivilizing is characterized within his model as 'the transformation from democracy into tyranny, from civilization towards barbarism', and has been described as a spectre which haunts the discourse of political culture in the west (de Swaan 265).

Elias' 'civilizing process': violence, game, teleology

Elias' insistence upon labelling his model with the loaded term 'civilizing', teamed with the optimism of the claim that civilizing is an ongoing process of endless social refinement, has evoked considerable critique. Some supporters, such as Dunning and Mennell (1998), reiterate Elias' repeated claim that the civilizing model, although directional, was open-ended and anti-teleological (340). However, Lasch (1985) felt that "Elias takes for granted what many of us have come to doubt, that history records the triumph of order over anarchy. There is no irony or ambiguity in his account of the civilizing process. Even today, he retains an optimism increasingly alien to our age" (708). The more measured reading of Burkitt (1996), with reference to Bauman, sums up the question succinctly: "[H]as Elias become trapped in the self-definition of the West – that it is composed of 'civilized' societies – by accepting at face value the claim that monopolization by the state has led to pacification?" (138).

> "[W]hile Elias concentrated very explicitly on the processual meaning of the term, his work has some overlap with the notion of civilization as a complex ... [T]he overriding difficulty with Elias' work inheres in his apparent failure to recognize that what came by the end of the 19th century to be called the *standard* of civilization was a relatively autonomous, transnational norm. In other words, over and beyond Elias' *analytic* conception of the civilizing process there has developed a consciously known and recognized, prescriptive denotation of civilization. [...] In contrast to the processual conception of civilization, the focus upon civilization as a sociocultural complex, one that tended to be territorially bounded, is – at least, in an explicit sense - much older and probably much more familiar" (Robertson 421-2).

The 'overlap' between Elias' analytic conception of civilizing process, as he articulated it, and the 'autonomous norm' of civilization as a sociocultural complex is in fact more problematic than Robertson allowed. The dimension of the sociocultural complex of civilization that Robertson describes as 'territorially bounded' is, of course, the nation state, in both the historical and specifically Foucauldian senses; this dimension inextricably inheres within any possible attempt of Elias' to abstract and bracket out a conception of 'civilization' as an empirically demonstrable, objective process. In turn, the relation of nation and State (now speaking strictly in the Foucauldian sense) is the object constructed and delineated by histories of right which, in the west at least, form a long discursive history of which civilization is a central idiom. In essence, the construct of civilization – whether as a 'transnational norm', a 'territorially bounded sociocultural complex', or an 'analytic process' – functions within self-legitimating discourses of power. Therefore, even Elias' 'analytic conception of civilizing process' is ultimately such a perfect expression of the functionality of civilization within a broad conception of modernity's history of right, as Burkitt states, that it deserves to be examined as a clear embodiment of several elements that Foucault's notion of historic-political discourse seeks to critique.

In terms of the discussion at hand, the most critically significant aspect of Elias' model is the extent to which the long-term refinement of civility in the civilizing process encompasses a generalized withdrawal of direct interpersonal violence from the sphere of public life, and the entrenchment of a relatively increasing abhorrence of such violence in discourse and in social *habitus*.

This general continuity of movement – the linear directionality of the civilizing process – is evidently a process which correlates to a 'rise' in democratization, just as it correlates to a 'fall' or withdrawal of violence. Therefore, despite Elias' insistence that the civilizing process should be understood as inherently non-terminal, his model of social change implies a continuous progression towards an image of democracy as the inevitable structural outcome of western social order, and simultaneously defines the salient characteristic of such functional democracy as the withdrawal of violence. The implied inevitability of the interminable unfolding of a socially embedded democracy, bounded within internally pacified nation-states and marked at the level of the *habitus* by the abhorrence of violence, is the disavowed *telos* of Elias' model which stubbornly shadows his use of the term 'civilizing'.

The 'functional democratization' of the playing-field of social competition entails a generalization of conflict which dissipates its force. It is conflict, but it is also not-conflict; it is competition, but the imagining of the struggle for power as a massive social game in which no one player can see the entire field – the effective neutralization of power as 'power-chances' – represents a paradoxical refusal to critically engage with the social effects of structural inequality. Irrationality is omnipresent, but even when irrationality produces violent and destructive effects, 'process' remains enshrined as immutable, directional, benign, functionally democratized, and ultimately in the service of civilization. What Foucault critically described as a discourse of perpetual war, Elias, with his alien optimism, insisted was simply a game.

Elias as symptom: game vs. war

What we derive from Elias' writings, then, is a more or less direct representation of the very discourse of civilization that Foucault sought to critique. It is important to note exactly the point at which Elias and Foucault diverge in their respective analyses. As Elias had done with the civilizing process, Foucault grounded his approach to historical discourses in the Middle Ages; the 'violence' which Elias left largely undefined structurally corresponds with Foucault's referent of 'war', and Foucault described a historical process whereby the power to wage war withdrew into the hands of the State – and, consequently, withdrew from the sphere of private life:

> "... with the growth and development of States throughout the
> Middle Ages and up to the threshold of the modern era, we see the
> practices and institutions of war undergoing a marked, very visible
> change, which can be characterized thus: The practices and

institutions of war were initially concentrated in the hand of a central power; it gradually transpired that in both de facto and de jure terms, only State powers could wage war and manipulate the instruments of war. The State acquired a monopoly on war. The immediate effect of this State monopoly was what might be called day-to-day warfare, and what was actually called "private warfare", was eradicated from the social body, and from relations among men and relations among groups. Increasingly, wars, the practices of war, and the institutions of war tended to exist, so to speak, only on the frontiers, on the outer limits of the great State units, and only as a violent relationship – that actually existed or threatened to exist – between States. But gradually, the entire social body was cleansed of the bellicose relations that had permeated it through and through during the Middle Ages" (*SMBD* 48).

Elias and Foucault diverge, however, at exactly the point at which violence / the institutions of war withdrew from the social body and became a property of relations between states. For Elias, this structural shift corresponded with a withdrawal of violence from social *habitus* and a linked rise in the abhorrence of violence; as a whole, this process added up to 'civilizing' in a positivist sense, and any irruption or reappearance of violence in the *habitus* was consequently to be regarded as a reversal of this process. In Elias' model, 'violence', however imprecisely defined, is a stable construct, and civilization can be estimated according to the metrics of violence: its position in social space, the degree and intensity of abhorrence that it invokes, etc. For Foucault, in contrast, violence is subject to continuous discursive transformation; the 'definitive moment' at the end of the Middle Ages wherein the institution of war was structurally retracted to the level of the State represents not a positive withdrawal of violence from social life, but a fundamental transformation of its discursive underpinnings:

> "It is only at the end of the Middle Ages that we see the
> emergence of a State endowed with military institutions that
> replace both the day-to-day and generalized practice of warfare,
> and a society that was perpetually traversed by relations of war.
> [...] The paradox arises at the very moment when this
> transformation occurs ... When war was expelled to the limits of
> the State, or was both centralized in practice and confined to the
> frontier, a certain discourse appeared (...) a discourse on war,
> which was understood to be a permanent social relationship, the
> ineradicable basis of all relations and institutions of power"
> (*SMBD* 49).

This 'discourse of perpetual war' finds an apex of expression in the

construct of 'civilization'. Civilization carries with it a language within which

power has, historically, narrated and represented itself. The critical divergence

between Elias and Foucault, as stated above, lies in the choice between a sociality

understood as defined by perpetual war, with violence permanently inscribed

within power relations, and one which is defined as a game from which violence

has withdrawn to the margins; it may be fair to say that the representation of

power as free from violence, as rational and calculable, is a critical element of

civilization's narration of itself. The claim that Elias' game theory betrays his

position as convinced by the trap of modernity's self-image has already been

discussed. The question that this raises with respect to gladiature, however, is this:

if 'civilization' prefers to speak of the game, how then does it cope with

gladiature, which appears in the midst of its own myth-history as a grotesque

hybrid of both game and war?

A Foucauldian approach to Eliasian terms: abhorrence and decivilizing

Elias' theoretical work - the essential dichotomy of established-outsider

relations, the role of group fantasy in the construction and determination of social reality, or the identification of abhorrence of violence as an influence upon behaviour and (presumably) upon discourse - are all ultimately subordinate to a model of social change which, despite protestations of anti-teleology and an insistence upon 'historical empiricism', still propounds an image of society organized around a single dominant process of pacification whose very endlessness points toward utopianism. This dissertation, therefore, can best be described as an attempt to reorient Elias' conceptual toolbox to a Foucauldian critique. A certain amount of Elias' terminology will be retained and used, but this approach is intended to assist in objectifying the discursive underpinnings of gladiatorial historiography as a narrative of historico-political discourse, which is how it will be treated and critiqued from a Foucauldian perspective. Put another way, Elias' operative constructs – civilization, conflict, pacification, directionality and 'decivilizing', the diagnostic centrality of violence and the equally indicative language of abhorrence – can be seen and used as a kind of index of the tropes of civilization's discourse of itself. The directional tension between civilizing and decivilizing, for example, may not exist in an 'empirical' sense as Elias had claimed; however, civilization, the fear of its regression or reversal, and the deep post-Enlightenment association between civilization and violence have all enjoyed (and continue to enjoy) a robust existence on a discursive level, and classical historiography has functioned as a densely significant context for the articulation of such ideas.

The abhorrence of violence certainly does figure as a significant element of civilization as a main trope of post-Enlightenment historico-political discourse:

abhorrence functions as a key component of disciplinary speech, and of the modern west's account of itself as civilized. The attitude of abhorrence which circumscribes violence and proclaims its exclusion from civilized society is an important element of the 'standard of civilization' as a proscriptive, transnational norm; it is, in more Foucauldian terms, a recurrent trope of civilization's mythical discourse. Elias' blunder, perhaps, was to take the abhorrence of violence – legitimately understood in his own model as a specific and historically significant element of 'civility' within the we-image of an established group - and overextend its truth-value according to its own declaration of itself as empirical fact, and as denotative of a quantitatively greater pacification at a macrosocial level: thus accepting at face value western modernity's image of itself as composed of civilized societies.

The correlation of civilization with abhorrence of violence – which should be regarded as a component of the discourse of civilization beyond Elias' use of it within his model – gestures in turn towards a corresponding correlation of 'decivilizing' with violence; such dystopia is the 'spectre which haunts the discourse of political culture in the west'. Moreover, if pushed to its furthest logical extent, the dystopian opposite of the abhorrence of violence is the cathexis of violence with pleasure; thirdly, as discussed above, another face of the spectre is tyranny as the imagined antithesis of democracy. The historiography of gladiature is fundamentally determined by all three of these themes throughout the modern period. Consequently, 'decivilizing'– particularly as this notion functions as a species of social fantasy which revolves around the apprehension of violence – will be an additional plank of the following study. If we accept decivilizing as a legitimate spectre of the self-image or auto-narration of civilization in a Foucauldian sense, then it would be fair to say that gladiatorial historiography is a textual corpus which grapples with civilization's fear of the possibility of its own undoing, by apprehending the persistent connection between the gladiatorial violence and the 'fall' of Rome, and attempting to isolate what 'went wrong' with Rome as an historical mirror and mythical ancestor of western modernity. As will be seen, gladiature has been repeatedly identified by a long line of classical scholars as a critical symptom of a socio-political 'rot' in ancient Rome which has formed a key theme of historical writing since Gibbon; even the more recent attempts to depart from the 'decline and fall' discourse (which set in train the 'decivilizing' theme near the close of the eighteenth century, precisely when Foucault pinpoints the rise of historico-political discourse) still strongly tend to inscribe gladiature as an extremely significant and influential element, both sign and symptom, of Roman social structure and the dynamics of power. Thus it is possible to treat the historiography of gladiature as a form of historico-political discourse that, among other things, is driven by the spectre of what Elias called decivilizing in the midst of the ongoing narration of Roman history as an 'intensely mythical discourse' shared by the nation-states of the modern west, in their broad self-conceptualization as civilized societies.

Elias would have it that 'civilization', as a sociohistorical complex which he claimed to exist more or less independently of human agency, is haunted by decivilizing as the spectre of its own inversion; however, at least one part of

Foucault's distinction was to assert that civilization's discourse must always be traced back to a particular speaking subject, and that the barbarian(s) which civilization maintains in tension with itself is/are often equally specific. Elias' notion of decivilizing is potentially extremely useful when taken not as a legitimate critical construct in its own right, but instead as a descriptor of the idiom wherein the 'nobility', in its self-designation as 'civilized', speaks of its correspondingly designated 'barbarians'. Decivilizing can be read as that persistent trope within the historico-political discourse of the nobility which posits and constructs the relation that 'civilization' or 'civilized society' perceives as existing between itself and the figure of the barbarian. Thus we can read gladiature's historiography as an exemplary sample of the kind of historical writing that represents and defines western modernity's construct of civilization, and as an exploration of just how the 'discourse of the two races' (to be discussed in the next chapter) - even as it narrates itself to itself in the presence of only ancient, proxy, or otherwise imaginary barbarians – works to shape and construct the narrative of history, conceived of as the account of 'what happened' and what it meant. Although Roman social organization was far from crudely binary, gladiature as a particular topic tends to see scholars reduce Roman society to a stark contrast between an individual tyrant and a many-headed mass; this is especially true of the historiography of earlier gladiature as tied to the end of the Republic and the political shift to the Empire, as the historical writing pertaining to this period has frequently focused upon the emergence of individual tyranny from the more corporate republican political structures.

A Foucauldian approach to classical historiography: gladiatorial origin and the end of the Republic

To orient the ensuing study, one primary historiographic object whose genealogy will be traced is the shifting image of gladiature's origin; the periodization schema into which historical materials are arranged is organized around significant shifts in the various narratives of origin within the wider historiography of Rome. Origin narratives are a key object of interest for at least two reasons: firstly, because a central characteristic of the historiography of gladiature lies in the fact that narratives of origin are the site wherein we encounter the barbarian; secondly because, as suggested above, the accounts of gladiature's origin are associated with and, arguably, produced in response to anterior, more significant shifts in the linked concept of the crowd. As will be discussed in greater detail, there is arguably little persuasive reason within the historical evidence associated with origin for choosing between the various claims, or for choosing any of them; thus, although the precise dynamic between race discourses of violence/origin and class discourses of violence/pleasure undergoes its own series of structural shifts over time, it is clear that constructs of origin are invoked and deployed in relation to narratives of Roman social order, which themselves are a series of representations of contemporary discourse on 'civilized' social order and the (il)legitimate space of violence within it.

In light of this relation between gladiature's barbaric context of origin and its eventual civilized context of consumption or practice, the second primary object whose historiographic inscription will be followed here is the shifting narrative of the end of the Republic, specifically in terms of the struggle or conflicts between Roman social classes, the position and character of violence within that conflict, and the closely linked interpretation of the socio-political function and meaning of gladiature during this period of Roman history as a sign and a symptom of the structure of power relations between patrician and plebeian groups at Rome itself. The deeper consequences of the pursuit of this complex 'object' are difficult to summarize at a high level in advance; they will be discussed in greater detail in the next chapter, illuminated by example throughout the dissertation, and visited again in the concluding chapter. For the moment, the key detail to point out arises from the intersection of several of the propositions discussed above as inherent within historico-political discourse and the language of civilization in the modern west. If the historical function of Rome is to act as a myth-history for a certain construct of civilization, and civilization, in turn, defines or narrates itself in large part in relation to the structural and discursive position of violence within its construction and perpetuation, then we begin to see how the inscribed space of gladiature, as a particularly 'illegitimate' violence cathected with pleasure, within the shifting historiography of a pivotal point in Roman history wherein the character of its 'civilization' may or may not have fundamentally changed (and possibly either 'rose' or 'fell' at that point, to invoke the directionality familiar from both Gibbon and Elias) has the potential to reveal something about modernity's self-perception as civilized at any given time.

'There Is No Mention of Rome'

A significant characteristic of gladiatorial historiography, which should be always kept in the back of one's mind, is the arguable fact that the textual and material records from which it is interpreted have not changed significantly over time, and that consequently any shifts of scholarly consensus regarding gladiature's proper interpretation should be ascribed to shifts in surrounding discourse far more than to 'empirically-driven' or objective developments in research and academic commentary. Foucault spoke directly to this approach to history, by referencing a medieval legend which claimed that the French descended directly and exclusively from the Franks, and that the Franks, in turn, could trace their lineage back to Troy, thus eliding Rome despite a perfectly-well known Roman literature at that time. Foucault warned against the uncritical acceptance of anachronism, and spoke against the tendency to believe that the most current version of history was invariably the most 'correct', especially when dealing with origin stories:

> " ... stop regarding this tale of origins as a tentative history that is still tangled up with old beliefs. It seems to me that, on the contrary, it is a discourse with a specific function. Its function is not so much to record the past or to speak of origins as to speak of right, to speak of power's right. Basically, the story is a lesson in public right. And it is because it is a lesson in public right that there is no mention of Rome. But Rome is also present in a displaced form, like a double outline or a twin: Rome is there, but it is there in a way that an image is there in a mirror" (*SMBD* 116).

Chapter 2: The Historical Sources of the Myth of Western Civilization

Since this work is intended for a somewhat broader audience, the following section is primarily illustrative in intent. It is generally aimed at those readers whose acquaintance with Roman history is relatively casual (and even this, given the near-ubiquity of Rome in popular media of recent years, I would confidently expect to be at a sufficiently useful level; here the broad outlines will be considerably more important than names and dates). With this in mind, what follows is not necessarily the best introduction either to Roman history or to gladiators; instead, the emphasis rests upon navigating those ancient sources which have formed the bedrock of the study of gladiature's origin and the nature of its pleasure, as well as highlighting enough of the broader contours of Roman history to illustrate the central themes which have subsequently obsessed some of the best and most influential historians of the modern period. At the same time, for those who are well-versed in Roman history, and particularly the sub-field of the practice of gladiature, some material is here gathered together and re-presented to demonstrate the bases upon which a large quantity of evidence has been reduced to a smaller collection of relevant material; the available evidence has been selected for representations of the various themes that this dissertation explores within the discourse of civilization, particularly representations of group difference, group conflict, and attitudes to violence. This is not at all a comprehensive survey of ancient source materials for gladiature[2]: instead, it is a preliminary, grounding assay into an Foucauldian 'reading' of Roman gladiature as a historiographic problem, and as such the sources examined here have been

---

[2] *Comprehensive surveys of source materials are readily available: Mahoney 2001, Futrell 2006.*

chosen based upon how well they demonstrate and/or exemplify several core themes.

Foucault spoke of a great 'theme and theory of social war' as the discursive structure which lies at the heart of historico-political discourse and the closely related construct of civilization: "A binary structure runs through society. (...) There are two groups, two categories of individuals, or two armies, and they are opposed to each other" (*SMBD* 51). It was his claim that historical writing since the end of the eighteenth century can be read as a textual corpus that is dominated by the basic theme of social war, as a thread that runs through successive periods of historical thought and remains essentially constant even as that theme shifts over time into slightly altered forms. Thus the theme of social war is embedded within its own historicity which, in Foucault's analysis, has oscillated between sub-discourses of race and class as the primary identifiers of the 'two armies':

> "The war that is going on beneath order and peace, the war that undermines our society and divides it in a binary mode is, basically, a race war. [...] And then you find a second transcription based upon the great theme and theory of social war, which emerges in the very first years of the nineteenth century, and which tends to erase every trace of racial conflict in order to define itself as class struggle" (*SMBD* 59-60).

This 'discourse of the two races' figures the subtext of the relation between civilization and the barbarian in the historico-political discourse of modernity, and is particularly evident in what might be called 'civilization's historiography' – the historical writing of the west as it produces its own 'history of right', in which political dominance, relations of hegemonic force, and a civilized self-image are constructed through legitimizing historical narratives. (Foucault used the term 'races' as a base term for the discursive structure of categorical groups, in the sense that at its most basic level, historico-political discourse inscribes such categories on an essentialist basis; however, formal shifts and local iterations of the discourse of the two races will not necessarily be articulated around the construct of race *per se*.) The key to comprehending historico-political discourse lies in the inscription of power embedded within the recurrent theme of group conflict: power is narrated over and against a constant, ongoing relation of opposition or struggle with the barbarian or the other race, although as will be seen the exact nature of that power dynamic within the narrative is subject to change, contingent upon the wider historical strategy which contextualizes it. However, Foucault further identified a critical component of the theme of social war when he turned his attention to the structure of the relation between the two races:

> " ...the other race is basically not the race that came from elsewhere or that was, for a time, triumphant and dominant, but that it is a race that is permanently, ceaselessly infiltrating the social body, or which is, rather, constantly being re-created in and by the social fabric. In other words, what we see as a polarity, as a binary rift within society, is not a clash between two distinct races. It is the splitting of a single race into a superrace and a subrace. To put it a different way, it is the reappearance, within a single race, of the past of that race. In a word, the obverse and the underside of the race reappears within it" (*SMBD* 61).

When this notion of Foucault's is critically brought to bear upon the historiography of gladiature, what we find is that Foucault's concepts are writ large and literal. To pose it as a problem, we might say that, if the barbarian is 'the past' of the civilized – i.e., if 'the civilized' perceives itself as a temporally defined entity, in a state of having 'civilized beyond' the barbarous (and thus in a state of perpetual war with not only a designated obverse, but with an obverse that is always already its own underside) – then, if we read the historiography of Rome as the (myth-historical) past of modern 'civilization', what we are confronted with is a discourse in which modernity's ongoing inscription of itself as civilized, and as evolved from civilized origins, is troubled by the presence within that historical narrative of the barbarism of gladiature. In other words, even as modernity constantly re-inscribes Roman history as part of the discursive labour of constructing and 'defending' the modern, civilized social body that designates Rome as a significant element of its origin, the labour of re-creating Rome as a suitable narrative of civilization's origin is persistently disrupted by gladiature as an avatar of Rome's own barbarism. As a result, what we find in modern scholarship is a discourse which very strictly polices the boundaries of what it imagines to be the Roman social body, and constantly re-assigns, in varying ways, the violence/pleasure intersection represented by gladiature to a shifting construct of the barbarian.

This chapter is not a new interpretation of the 'historical truth' of gladiature in antiquity, against which all subsequent modern historiography will be compared and found wanting. The most fundamental starting point of this dissertation is the acceptance that the great phantom of historical writing – a definitive account of 'what really went on' – is sometimes pursued with less certainty and positivism than at other times, and in the case of Roman gladiature in particular, modern historiography has never been able to maintain a consensus for very long. Constructing another new or revised image of what really went on in antiquity is not at all the objective here. A quick visit to antiquity in the form of surviving texts is the most responsible way to introduce the story of gladiature in the Roman world, but it should be very clear that it is precisely as a story, or rather as a myth-history, that the subject of gladiature and its relation to Roman civilization will be approached. To that end, the present section surveys the ancient written evidence for their expression of the themes of that story, which evoke the central themes that structure Foucault's discourse of the two races: social dichotomy, social 'war', and narratives of origin.

This is not to suggest that the textual sources which survive from antiquity should be treated as an example of, or even as equivalent to, the historico-political discourse of post-Enlightenment modernity; however, even a brief survey of the ancient textual evidence for gladiature reveals that the modern discourse of 'civilization', marked by its preoccupations such as dichotomous opposition(s), violence, and origin, has found much to make a meal of in the ancient texts. The materials gathered below exemplify the fragments of antiquity's utterances that connect gladiature to the socio-political identity of the Roman crowd, along with those that have been used by modern scholars as positive evidence for the various hypotheses of gladiature's context of origin. What we will see, over the full course of this dissertation, is that Foucauldian themes of dichotomy, conflict, and origin, which are very easily extrapolated and interpreted from the recurrent motifs and language of the ancient sources, come to be exploited and re-deployed by modern scholarship in terms of historico-political discourse's closely related sub-discourses of 'race war' and 'class war'.

With this in mind, it becomes possible to return to Elias' concept of 'decivilizing' with a newly critical perspective. As discussed in the previous chapter, Elias' language betrayed his fundamentally dichotomous model, which applied 'civilizing' as a label for democratization of social as well as political structures, and opposed that construct to decivilizing, which correlated politically to centralized government or tyranny, and socially to the spectre of breakdown. If we take Elias as a guidebook to civilization auto-narrative, decivilizing appears as a specific theme whose form encapsulates civilization's perception of its more or less self-conscious perpetual war with the barbarian, in a sense with inherently temporal connotations: at a fundamental level, the discursive construct of civilization is deeply haunted by the spectre of the barbarian not only beyond its borders, but also of the barbarian which emerges from civilization's own historical past; these are even two dimensions of the same construct. If historico-political discourse is organized upon the premise that the 'permanent social war' must be and must remain permanent, to prevent the ever-present threat of barbarism's infiltration into the social body, then 'decivilizing', taken as one trope within civilization's account of itself, also invokes the presence of the barbarian concealed within civilization's history, as a state of disorder from which civilization has emerged and into which civilization may revert; moreover, the fear inspired by the possibility of a breakdown of society and a 'descent into barbarism' reproduces within a temporal dimension the same discourse that

Foucault identified as operating on the planes of race and class. What will also be seen in the ancient sources below is that much of the textual material which survived into modernity reverberates with the modern trope of decivilizing, in multiple ways, always subject to multiple competing interpretations.

The Roman 'crowd' and the class war: metaphor of power, political fantasy, and the theme of degeneration

Elias had his own opinion on the pleasure of gladiature, its relationship to the figuration between what he would have called the established and outsider groups of Roman society, and how the perceived gulf of feeling between antiquity and modernity on this point should be understood in terms of his notions of the civilizing process and consequent long-term shifts to the socio-psychological *habitus*:

> "We watch football, not gladiatorial contests. As compared with antiquity, our identification with other people, our sharing in their suffering and death, has increased. To watch hungry lions and tigers devouring living people piece by piece, or gladiators trying by ruse and deceit to wound and murder each other, is scarcely a diversion that we would anticipate with the same relish as the Roman senators decked in purple, or the Roman people. No feeling of identity, it seems, united those spectators with these other people who, below in the bloody arena, were fighting for their lives. As we know, the gladiators greeted the caesar as they marched in with the words '*Morituri te salutant* (Those about to die salute you)'.[3] Some of the caesars doubtless believed themselves actually immortal, like the gods. At all events, it would have been more appropriate had the gladiators shouted: '*Morituri moriturum salutant* (Those about to die salute him who will die)'. But in a society where it would have been possible to say that, there

---

[3] *Also pace those modern classical historians who object to the historicity, veracity, and/or representativeness of this image of the 'gladiators' salute', on grounds that it is anecdotal, only attested once in ancient source materials, and referred to prisoners of war under Claudius rather than professional gladiators. If the value of this passage of Elias invites rejection on grounds of historical inaccuracy, it should certainly be accepted as an example of the uses to which the familiar image of gladiature can be and has been put in the modern historical imagination.*

probably would have been no gladiators or caesars" (*The Loneliness of the Dying* 2-3).

Elias' approach to *habitus*, and its essential relation to social and historical changes in the context of the civilizing process as he saw it, are not the focus of this discussion; the intent here is not upon how humanity has 'actually' changed over time in terms of its attitude to and experience of violence, but to examine one area of historical writing to delineate how that attitude (regardless of its 'actuality' beyond the purely discursive realm of the historical imaginary) has been articulated through gladiatorial historiography, how that articulation has shifted over time (producing multiple, entirely different historical accounts), and how those shifts reveal the underpinning of western modernity's image of itself as 'civilized', as this is revealed through classical historiography as myth-history, and through gladiatorial historiography as a specific extremity or limit-violence defined by the intersection of that violence with pleasure rather than abhorrence. To this end, the value of examining Elias' thoughts about gladiature lies in recognizing that his central claim - that the abhorrence of violence separates modernity from antiquity – expresses a conviction that is crucial to 'civilization's' construction of itself as such. The west in modernity identifies Rome as a dominant figure in the construction of its own ancestry: the foundational impact of Roman antiquity on the political, philosophical, and aesthetic infrastructure of the western world since the Renaissance can scarcely be overstated. However, on the point of gladiature, Rome contradicts its designated role as civilization's myth-historical ancestor and actually takes on a key characteristic of the barbarian through the pleasure it takes in violence. Thus the historiography of gladiature configures Roman antiquity not only as the ancestor, but also as the spectral 'other race' of modern civilization's own conceived past.

More importantly, Elias' passage hits upon the linked idea that the perceived relative 'uncivility' of Rome in its attitudes to violence - though here discussed by Elias as a question of social bonds, the capacity within the *habitus* to 'identify with' fellow humans – can be most clearly *thematically* expressed through reference to the power structures of Roman society, emblematized by the juxtaposition of the gladiator and the emperor. A dichotomized discourse of power, one which heavily emphasizes polar extremes of high and low, lies just beneath the surface veneer of a moralized discourse of social attitudes. For Elias, of course, the polarity between gladiator and emperor is emblematic of the correlation of decivilization with tyranny: the emperor's arbitrary power over the life and death of the gladiator illustrates the extreme limits of tyrannical authority. However, the conceptual or metaphorical limits defined by the emperor/gladiator relation contain a wide field of political discourse, in which space the classical scholarship of modernity has repeatedly re-inscribed its own historical narratives: that space between the social poles is occupied by the arena crowd, and all of its associated questions of mass versus elite domination, the (il/legitmate) relation of power to violence, the discursive formation which structures the political problem of violence/power in terms of a moral problem of violence/pleasure, and the ultimate referral of all such questions to the summary construct of civilization.

The key is to grasp the dense, strong link between three dimensions of the Roman crowd in its tenacious connotations within historical writing both ancient and modern: its (to modernity, allegedly abhorrent) pleasure in gladiatorial

violence, its essential distinction from the 'not-crowd' of its social superiors, and

the recurrent theme (initially suggested by ancient authors, and decisively picked

up and circulated by many modern scholars) of the crowd's degeneration over the

course of Roman history. Connolly describes the image of the Roman crowd in

modernity as a "political fantasy":

> "Part of the moral impact of the image of the decadent imperial
> mob intent on bread and circuses is that it is a deformed version of
> the republican crowd which, if it is not consistently virtuous in
> fact, is associated with the virtue of strong civic participation. This
> is one of Gibbon's iconic images of imperial decline: from the
> habit of "public courage", the Roman crowds eventually
> "demanded only bread and public shows; and were supplied with
> both by the liberal hand of Augustus" [cf. Juvenal below]. From
> the intertwined development of European humanism and
> republicanism in early modernity, to the appropriation of Roman
> symbols, names, and institutions during the American War of
> Independence and the French Revolution, the vision of Rome as an
> ideal balance between popular and aristocratic government has
> helped shape the landscape of modern politics. [...] What the
> Roman republic offered was a model system of checks and
> balances [cf. Polybius[iii]], exempla of martial and domestic virtue,
> and a vision of unity bound by cultural sameness" ("Crowd
> Politics" 81, my insertions of ancient authors).

As Connolly describes, the discourse of Rome – its authors, its poetry, its

history, its architecture, and its public art – was inextricably embedded in much

public discourse from the sixteenth century onwards. Rome was an argot within

the language of political elites across the European nations and America, with the

villainous example of the Empire presenting a useful foil to the virtuous Republic

(at least until the image of Empire underwent certain amendments during the

height of the colonial period, whereupon it served as both a provisional model and

a cautionary tale). It is also correct, however, that the image of the Roman crowd has been of a dual nature, evenly divided between its representation in Polybius' republican "model system of checks and balances" and the far more derogatory image framed even more memorably by Juvenal's imperial 'bread and circuses'. Well into the twentieth century, Polybius' and Juvenal's respective crowds have been easily mapped over the historiographic divide between republic and empire, such that the "decadent imperial mob", as Connolly states, was inscribed by scholars as a corrupted, degraded image of the original republican citizen body.

To Connolly's analysis I would add that the amphitheatre crowd at gladiatorial spectacles (as a specific 'crowd', distinct from, for instance, the circus) is the very apex of this idea. If modernity's image of the Roman crowd draws its meaning from the tensions of mass power versus elite domination in the political imaginary, then the arena crowd represents the limit of this complex image, a concatenation of nightmares about what lies on the other side of the line separating democracy from demagoguery. The infamous Roman practice of 'voting' on the outcome of a combat, delivering a mass verdict (periodically of life or death)[iv] to which the presiding authority at the event was bound by convention to submit, can hardly be overlooked as a perverted echo of the republican electorate, which was steadily disenfranchised in the early imperial period. The result is a tautological image which is seen to reinforce the more powerful socio-political position of the Roman elite: the withdrawal of the republican franchise and its substitution with arena spectacle 'reveals' the appetite for violence among the *populus Romanus*, which in turn justifies the withdrawal of the franchise.

The abhorrence of violence within the self-image or auto-narrative of civilization, then, is more than a matter of either morality or manners: a short, straight line can be drawn between an appetite for violence, even in spectacle form, and an essential incapacity to participate in the government of state. The former is the single most potent proof imaginable of the latter, as the irrational cathexis of violence and pleasure excludes the possibility of the rational exercise of 'civilized' power. The grotesque concatenation of both of these elements, particularly considering the degraded form of the republican franchise which in the amphitheatre allowed a 'vote' expressive only of the crowd's pleasure in violence, was used as the basis for a powerful discourse of elite dominance in ancient Rome, and has since the Enlightenment been co-opted repeatedly in historical writing, to represent contemporary attitudes at a broad level wherein modern figurations have attempted to articulate the construct of civilization through continual re-interpretation of its myth-history.

As an articulation of a 'discourse of two races', modern historiography has repeatedly interpreted ancient sources on the arena crowd to construct an argument for the exclusion of 'the crowd' from the body politic, in the guise of excluding the crowd from the social body on the ostensible basis of a moral argument. Much of what was written about gladiature in antiquity – and this is particularly true of those texts which have formed the stable core of modernity's ever-shifting understanding of gladiature - was already steeped in the language of class-based politics of distinction. For evidence of the enjoyment of gladiature among the *populus*, we have only the massive size of the imperial amphitheatres, their number, their distribution, and the duration of the practice over something like seven hundred years as testimony. In contrast, articulate written expressions of distaste, ambivalence, and condemnation emanating from Rome's socio-political elite are numerous, and this is without incorporating martyrologies and other Christian texts. The Roman elite undoubtedly was engaged in its own ongoing process of identity construction; modern scholarship has repeatedly turned to the remaining fragments of ancient texts to support the construction of modernity's own shifting discourse of civilization, and in its own processes of defining the limits of both the social and of the 'nation'.

In looking briefly at a sample of the relevant ancient texts, it only makes sense to begin with the most (in)famous ancient text of them all: Juvenal's pithy 'bread and circuses' line from Satire 10 which, in light of the aphoristic breeziness with which it is often tossed around (such as immediately above, where it is quoted in a quote from Gibbon quoted by Connolly), is here reproduced with some textual context:

> "What about Remus' plebeian crowd? It follows fortune, as always, and hates those whom fortune condemns. (...) For a long time now, since we've been buying their votes for nothing, they've stopped caring. The Roman people which once dispensed power, consulships, legions, everything, now sits on its hands and anxiously waits for just two things: bread and circuses" (*Satire* 10. 72-81).[v]

The first point to be made is that Juvenal's quip is not technically a reference to gladiature; however, it does encapsulate a great deal of the relevant imagery of the crowd. From an Eliasian standpoint, the essence of Juvenal's lines is its evocation of decivilizing: the plebeians, as an outsider group, have descended from an original myth-historical (i.e. Remus') crowd to its current position of degradation, and as such they are the primary sign of a general social decline. The chasm between these two images of the crowd hinges upon the fitness of either to participate in affairs of state, and the critical shift refers to what modern historiography inscribes as the transition from republic to empire, the period of greatest interest to the current discussion. Moreover, Juvenal's description of their descent from a position of relative power to a position of inefficacy forms a terse and complex case study. Though Juvenal takes a characteristic swipe at his own class in his reference to 'buying votes for nothing', the self-reflexive critique is blunted by the comment that the plebeian crowd "follows fortune, as always"; though the patrician group can be accused here of collusion in the process of social decline, nevertheless the plebeian class are essentially too irrational for meaningful political participation, and always have been. Thus the relatively unequal distribution of power between the two groups is naturalized through the invocation of an immutable and wholly external property. (Part of the richness of such source material, however, arises from the various uses to which it has subsequently been put; in the following chapters we will encounter both scholars who echoed Juvenal's tone and obvious implications wholeheartedly, and those for whom the understanding of spectacle as 'vote-buying' was the corruption to be most strongly condemned.)

Juvenal's slur about vote-buying additionally refers to the (in his day, relatively recent) late-republican power struggle within the patrician class itself, between the *optimates* and *populares* factions and their competing political agendas, a struggle rendered exponentially more complicated by contemporary factors of social mobility and economic shifts. Much more will be said on this in later chapters. For the moment, suffice to say that the identity of 'the plebeian crowd' was not simply that of a group who had ceded, rightly or not, its former political power; rather, the full implication of Juvenal's passage rests upon the perception that the political power of the plebeian outsiders actually persisted in the imperial period, as a potentially dangerous tool of popular politics – available, in most cases, to any member of the Roman elite with the resources to 'buy' the plebs with food doles and spectacles, including gladiators. This political aspect of the crowd was very much in play during the last decades of the Republic, and the perception of the crowd as a perpetual source of (one or both of) social chaos and political force persisted for centuries, both in Roman writing and in modern scholarship on the subject.

This constellation of ideas surrounding the crowd's appetite for spectacle, its legitimate position within political structure, and the bounds of propriety found other, less satirical, outlets of expression. In Fronto's *Elements of History*, for example, Juvenal's excoriation of bread and circuses is actually rehabilitated into a representation of the Roman elite's own praxis of power:

> "In the art of peace, however, hardly anyone stands before Trajan
> in the eyes of the people, if anyone has ever equalled him. Is it not
> this popularity that inflames Trajan's detractors? It appears to
> come from a deep knowledge of the art of governing. The emperor
> was not careless even about actors or other people concerned with
> the stage, the circus, or the arena, since he knew there are two
> things that especially grip the Roman people: the price of grain and
> the spectacles. A government recommends itself by what it does in
> trivial matters no less than in grave ones: to neglect the serious
> ones brings larger punishment, but to neglect the lesser brings

greater ill will. The food-dole provokes less acrimony than the spectacles, since the dole only placates certain specific individuals while the spectacles are for everyone" (*Principia Historiae* 17).[vi]

Fronto's text, which recalls certain epigrams of Martial and Pliny's *Panegyricus*, revisits Juvenal's thoughts roughly a half-century later, when the popular politics of the late Republic had passed from living memory and the structure of imperial government, not least the office of the emperor, was far more firmly entrenched. Bread and circuses are here seen as integral to imperial statecraft, and suggestively as the key to an emperor's popularity in the context of the "art of peace". There is no place in Fronto's reading for the suspicion that Juvenal cast upon 'popularity' as a legitimate force within politics, nor does there remain any discernable memory of the affective political role of the popular assemblies during the Republic. Since the people are available to be bought – and for a 'trivial matter' like shows – then to do just that shows merely a deep and laudable knowledge of the art of governing. Moreover, the "acrimony" of the crowd, its ill will, is represented as a simple truism, not subject to critique or lament as with Juvenal; instead, it exists merely as an object of rational calculation on the part of the governing authority, a perennial but cheap tax on power. Such a rationalization of gladiature and its political entanglements not only coexisted in antiquity with the utterly different moralization seen in Juvenal, but will appear again in the modern period.

In addition, the moralizing response to the cathexis of violence and pleasure represented by the crowd was not always directly implicated in antiquity with discourses of political power; occasionally, that cathexis was examined in isolation from explicitly political considerations, as in Seneca's letter connecting

the debasement of the crowd – and its intrinsically debasing effect upon the stray

member of the established group who wanders into its midst – with not only its

pleasure in violence, but its precise pleasure in particular manifestations of

violence:

> "You ask yourself what you should especially avoid. The crowd.
> You cannot yet trust yourself to be safe in a crowd. I'll admit a
> weakness of my own: I never bring back the same morals as I
> brought out. [...] Being with a lot of people is harmful. There is no
> one who will not recommend some vice to us, or press it upon us,
> or smear us with vice without our knowledge. And the more people
> we are with, the greater the danger. And nothing is so damaging to
> good morals as to hang around at some spectacle. There, through
> pleasure, vices sneak in more easily. [...] I become more greedy,
> more desirous of honour, more dissolute, even more unfeeling and
> cruel, because I have been among people. By chance I happened to
> be at the spectacle at noontime, expecting some witty
> entertainment and relaxation, to rest men's eyes from the gore. It
> was the opposite. Whatever fighting there was before was
> comparative mercy. Now there was pure murder, no more fooling
> around. They have nothing to shield them, and with the whole
> body exposed to the blow, no one ever misses. Many people prefer
> this to the ordinary pairs and the fighting people ask for. Why
> wouldn't they? No helmet or shield pushes the sword away. Where
> is the defense? Where is the skill? These things are just to delay
> death. In the morning men are thrown to lions and bears; at
> noontime, to the audience" (*Epistle* 7.1-5).[vii]

A great deal of ink has been spilled over this passage from Seneca, and

rightly so: these lines have been scrutinized as an expression of an ideal Stoic

philosophical subjectivity, grouped with numerous other texts (especially St.

Augustine) that expound upon ancient thought concerning crowd psychology,

and, by scholars of gladiature, carefully picked over to examine the distinction

between 'gladiature proper' and public execution in the arena (which is what is actually being described here), not least in terms of ancient attitudes to violence and spectacle.

The particular value of Epistle 7 to this illustration lies in the fact that Seneca presents a qualification of the abhorrence of violence through his comments upon pleasure; he articulates, very clearly, the conviction that there is a 'right way' and a 'wrong way' to take pleasure in gladiatorial spectacle, and that the boundary between legitimate and illegitimate pleasure itself defines a crucial distinction between the civilised and the 'other race' of the crowd. In essence, Seneca asserts that gladiature proper represents a legitimate source of pleasure (i.e., is comparatively civilized) provided that it is enjoyed on a 'civilized' basis such as the appreciation of fighting skill; conversely, the 'mock combats' of public executions are an uncivilized pleasure, the pleasure of the crowd, derived from "gore" and "pure murder" and bearing the latent capacity to corrupt the refined morals of even philosophers of the senatorial class. There is a clear expression here of an idea that repeatedly returns throughout the later historiography of gladiature, and is in fact especially salient in the most recent scholarship: the idea that to take pleasure in 'pure murder' is uncivilized, but that to take pleasure in gladiature for any possible reason *other than the ultimate death of the combatants* is acceptable, even laudable.[4]

Seneca's point was reprised even more explicitly, and without the overt buttress of Stoic moral philosophy, some decades later in one of the letters of

---

[4] It is worthwhile to bear this passage of Seneca in mind when examining post- Cold War historiography of Chapter Six, wherein this essential idea echoes loudly in recent academic claims that gladiature was a straightforwardly non-lethal 'sport'.

Pliny the Younger. The subject of Pliny's quip was the circus rather than the arena, but the essential point was the same:

> "When I think about people like that [ie. the plebs attending a spectacle], who so insatiably long for something empty, cold, and impermanent, I take a certain pleasure in never having been taken by this pleasure (*Epistulae* 9.6)". [viii]

Gladiatorial origin

Such discourses surrounding the crowd, construed as consumer of violence/ subject of pleasure – given that the crowd is identified with the 'unnatural' or with 'decline' by the ancient sources themselves, to say nothing of what meals modern scholarship has since made of Juvenal and Seneca – are intimately associated with a second question: where and how that 'decline' originated. Put simply, if the crowd was once noble, and gladiature was the sign (easily conflated with the cause) of the crowd's degradation, where did gladiature come from? What were the characteristics of gladiature's invention, and under what conditions, or by what agency, was such social decline allowed to infect and erode the once-noble Roman *populus*?

Historiographically, the notion of gladiature's origin is in some ways a categorically different construct than that of the crowd, and requires a somewhat altered framework of discussion. For instance, the image of the origin of gladiature is, firstly, characterized by ancient evidence which is far more fragmentary and circumstantial in nature, and secondly is not a construct which enjoys the same sort of organic life in modernity as does the image of the Roman crowd; origin has always been a considerably more esoteric, exclusively academic problem of gladiatorial historiography. Moreover, it is a more modern problem overall – far more clearly a figure of historico-political discourse, with its emphasis upon narratives of origin; there is little surviving evidence of any kind to suggest that the Romans or any other group in antiquity gave much direct thought to gladiatorial origin, or at least not in quite the same terms that modern scholars have used to conceptualize it. Ancient written evidence pertaining to gladiature's origin refer to origin, variously, in terms of its social, its cultural, and less frequently its historical context of emergence; what has survived is a small, tantalizing jumble of clues which offer a number of incomplete possible answers, and what has characterized the modern approach to the problem since the Enlightenment has been characterized by a clear imperative to extract a single, coherent image of origin from a field of multiple competing images.

Surviving ancient sources offer a number of options for social context. While modern historiography has always tended to accept a pervasive connection between 'original' gladiators and funerary rituals (an image which has been suggestively traced back as far as the Greek heroic tradition, such as the funeral of Patroclus described in the *Iliad*)[ix], more secular contexts of origin, such as entertainment at banquets, are also apparent in written sources. The choices of historical or more purely chronological origins are equally varied and often nebulous, ranging anywhere from as early as the Trojan War to as late as the third century B.C. depending upon the prevailing modern definition and identification of 'gladiature' proper. The designated culture of origin (the dimension which will here be focused upon) is the third element which dominates the first two, and which, though only vaguely attested in ancient sources, has in modern writing been marked by a series of successive hypotheses which have been shaped far more deeply by contemporary thinking about violence, civilization, and the myth-history of the west than by anything inherent in the sources themselves.

It was approximately in the middle of the eighteenth century that scholars of classical antiquity began to isolate and define the origins of gladiatorial combat as a question in need of an answer. To map briefly the course of their inquiry over the ensuing three centuries, the pursuit of gladiatorial origins has seen a broad shift in consensus three times. Following the gradual emergence of the question, the period from the middle of the nineteenth century into the early twentieth was the heyday of the so-called 'Etruscan hypothesis', which claimed that gladiature was an innovation of the Etruscan people who had ruled Rome as a monarchy until the violent founding of the republic at the end of the sixth century B.C. The first half of the twentieth century saw the gradual development of the 'Osco-Samnite' or 'Campanian hypothesis', which overtook conventional opinion in the middle of the century and which still holds sway among many; this propounds an image of original gladiature which locates it among the hills of southern Italy, a creation of the Samnite people who were the last to fall to the Roman conquest of the tribes of Italy in the middle Republic. Finally, in the last fifteen years the prevailing Osco-Samnite hypothesis has been confronted by a group of scholars who state that gladiature should be considered an originally Roman practice, marshalling new evidence for the claim and reinterpreting or dismissing old material. The question of origin, however, has lately foundered; the Etruscan hypothesis is still frequently cited alongside the Osco-Samnite, the emergence of the Roman hypothesis seems to have evoked silence rather than debate, and the origin of gladiature appears overall to have been quietly consigned to the unknown, despite the manifest fact that gladiature and the Roman amphitheatre are presently more widespread in popular culture (and, arguably, in academic culture) than ever before.

As discussed above, Foucault claimed that within the articulation of the dichotomous discourse of two races, the specific language of 'race war' was elided from the beginning of the nineteenth century, to be obscured by the discursive refiguring of 'class war'; however, this shift came late to the historiography of gladiature. Clearly recognizable racialized thought has played a major role throughout the long historiography of gladiatorial origin, from the eighteenth century's space of exception carved around the Greeks, through the nineteenth century's embrace of the Etruscan hypothesis of origin on the basis of the 'Asiatic' extraction of the Etruscans themselves, and indeed throughout the twentieth century, including both the positivist language of the prewar debate between the Etruscan and South Italian camps and the postwar intellectual romanticism which marked the ascendance of the Osco-Samnite hypothesis. Such constructs have always been an extremely significant element of gladiatorial historiography, and they will all be examined in detail as they are encountered. Nevertheless, the full importance of the discursive functioning of 'cultural' contexts of gladiature's origin exceeds the obvious critique invoked by, say, the anti-Semitic characterization of the Etruscans found in Rosenberg's *The Myth of the Twentieth Century*, or the problematic sketch in Salmon's *Samnium and the*

Samnites of that group as something akin to an unspoiled warrior/shepherd race emanating from a prehistoric, edenic southern Europe. Taken as a whole, the series of cultural contexts of origin can also be seen as a steady index of increasing proximity between the fixed established group - the Romans – and the various outsider groups that appear over time within the historiographic narrative of origin. Gradually, the gulf of difference – defined in shifting terms which can be tracked over time - between the Romans and the non-Roman originators of gladiature diminishes, until the most recent scholarship has come to suggest that gladiature originated at Rome itself (or, to put it another way, gladiature has been redefined to refer more or less exclusively to the Roman practice, and to be functionally and essentially dissociated from what have previously been regarded as its precursors).

What I would like to suggest is that the construct of gladiatorial origin has been shaped by an indelible association with, and an imperative to respond to, shifts in the prevailing image of *later* gladiature – that the function and the force of the rhetoric of origin, as a site persistently located outside the boundaries of the civilized, is to provide post-hoc rationalization(s) for the Roman practice of gladiature in later centuries. Thus the concept of 'origin' in the historical debate over gladiators is actually doubled. While scholarship consciously has pursued the illumination of a historical site of the *ur*-origin – the absolute first moment in which gladiature appeared in any imaginable context – what drives this pursuit is a set of imperatives derived from the 'secondary origin' of the emergence of gladiature at Rome itself. The dominant historiographic problem which organizes the scholarship of gladiatorial origin is not simply a desire to account for how gladiature came to be, but to account for how gladiature came to be *at Rome*: the continuously shifting *ur*-origin of gladiature thus constructs a rationalization of the barbarian, which exists in dynamic interplay with the construct of civilization in turn. This 'doubling' of origin, then, must be considered not only as a function but also as a strategy, to the extent that the pursuit of an *ur*-origin obscures or elides the 'originality', in a sense, of gladiature's echo at Rome.

With this necessary exteriority in mind, it is important to point out in brief that each of the successive origin hypotheses offers an image of original gladiature that is distinctive in more than its cultural context. The pretext of funerary ritual remains common to all three constructs of origin, but similarity effectively begins and ends with this point. Without going too deeply into detail, the form of the historiographic discourse surrounding gladiatorial origins – its attachment to a concept of *ur*-origin, the consistent doubling of origin, and the peculiar nature of the boundary embedded within the secondary origin which the entire discourse is concerned to police – splits that discourse along several interconnected planes, the fault lines between which are the productive sites of difference between hypotheses and which reveal the outline of what is being negotiated and transformed. Any one 'culture of origin' is itself a constructed entity which has shifted in the specifics of its representation since the eighteenth century; this is of course as true of the image of Rome as of the Etruscans or the Samnites, and must be taken into account when dealing with hypotheses of origin. However, the local meaning ascribed to original gladiature within any one construct of its context, as a spectre of its corresponding account of later gladiature, stands out as the primary fractal factor of the larger discourse. The content of 'original meaning' in any one instance should be read as a symptom of the socio-political relation understood to exist between 'Rome' and the culture of gladiatorial origin at the time of the transmission of gladiature as a cultural practice; put another way, the capacity of any hypothesis of gladiatorial origin to rationalize gladiature at Rome is determined in part by the larger context of relation imagined to have existed between the originating culture and Rome – and this remains valid when the originating culture is Rome itself. Further, the form of the relation structures the interpretation of the means or mechanism of transmission, which in turn exists in a feedback circuit with the larger or overriding interpretation of gladiature within Roman culture after this imagined moment or stage of transmission.

Funerary origin: piety

There is no (surviving) aetiology, whether mythical or more securely historical, for the origin of gladiature among the Roman texts; they themselves do not appear to have had an entirely clear or consensual image of gladiature's roots although, as will be seen, the notion was indeed referenced in antiquity. However, modern historiography identifies a working proxy for the original Roman gladiatorial combat: a surviving summary of one of the lost books of Livy, which attests to the 'earliest known' appearance of gladiators in the Roman sphere. This incident is dated quite precisely (if perhaps not perfectly reliably) to the year 264 BC, it was held in the cattle markets of urban Rome, and it took place in the course of the funerary celebrations/ observances for a patrician statesman. It was referred to as a *munus* (a term variously interpreted to mean duty, obligation, and/or gift); by Livy's day, gladiatorial combats were commonly termed *munera*, and use of the word continued for centuries (see Etienne 1965).

Information survives from four different textual sources, all postdating the alleged event by between two and six hundred years. A brief summary of Book 16 of Livy's Augustan-era history states that in 264 B.C. (some two centuries before Livy's lifetime) one Decius Brutus Pera, in honour of his dead father, was 'the first' to offer gladiators.[x] Valerius Maximus, writing slightly later than Livy, adds the details that Decius organized the event together with his brother Marcus, and that it was staged in the Forum Boarium, Rome's public cattle market on the banks of the Tiber.[xi] A fourth-century poem, the *Griphus* of Ausonius, further specifies that there were six gladiators, armed in the style of Thracians, who fought in three successive pairs.[xii] The fourth source reflects on the use of the word *munus* to signify the offering of gladiators, and speculates that the implied 'obligation' is to 'send captives' to the deceased.[xiii] The 264 B.C. combat is thus an historical event which seems to appear fully formed within the sphere of what is defined as Roman, and considerable academic labour has been invested in the attempt to account for its seemingly uncanny advent, dividing what came after with such provoking clarity from the mystery of what went before.

Firstly, there is the question of what meaning gladiature may have held in relation to a funerary context. Modern historiography of gladiature has exerted uneven emphasis upon the relative significance of the Brutus funeral as the context of the 'original' combat, from multiple angles. Though the perspective is out of vogue at the moment, earlier interpretations of gladiature frequently leaned heavily upon the assumption that a combat undertaken in the course of funerary rites must be understood as a solemnly ritualized affair; this view has always tended to align with notions of the earliest Roman gladiature (and sometimes all gladiature, throughout Roman history) as a rather straightforward form of human sacrifice, though directed not at a deity, but at the deceased.

A significant part of the value of the sacrificial interpretation of earliest gladiature derives from its influence upon the corresponding interpretations of gladiature's 'original pleasure' as this relates to the perceived meaning of the practice. Scholarship which has emphasized the solemnity of funerary ritual as the dominant element of gladiature's original context thereby circumvents the problem of the crowd's pleasure in violence, by effectively banishing such pleasure from the image of origin: the 'original' meaning of gladiature resided first and foremost in religious piety, and if this did not absolve the Roman crowd of its eventual guilt in the later centuries of massive arena spectacles, nonetheless the funerary interpretation has often provided a basis for explaining the entry of gladiature into the Roman world from outside its borders. Such piety has been variously explained as irrational, atavistic, innocent and numerous other nuances, but none of these explicitly connect violence to pleasure.

More specifically, the interpretation of gladiature as a form of human sacrifice (over and above any more general funerary character) - the feeding of human blood to the shades of the noble dead - has been invoked in different and occasionally contradictory ways. Historians well into the nineteenth century viewed sacrificial gladiature as a barbarism which Rome failed, for various reasons, to civilize beyond; in contrast, for a considerably lengthy period in the twentieth century, sacrificial gladiature acquired a reassuringly anthropological cast of rationality, and the survival of such 'primitive' behaviour both invoked a new series of explanations and correspondingly spawned a new set of interpretive connotations regarding the character of Rome as a civilization.

The two[xiv] most important written sources for gladiature as human sacrifice are Servius' fourth century AD commentary on the *Aeneid*, and a second text which, though considerably earlier, is a vitriolic attack upon all forms of public spectacle in Roman society written by a major figure of the early Christian church: Tertullian's 2nd century AD *De Spectaculis*. The categorical differences between the two texts are numerous, but the most important distinction between them lies in the fact that each represents an entirely different interpretation of gladiature's complex association with violence and civilization: where Servius suggested that gladiature's shift from sacrifice to spectacle can be interpreted as a move towards moral refinement – i.e., funerary gladiature 'civilized' over time – Tertullian, in contrast, makes the opposite claim, and insists that gladiature was marked as a 'decivilizing' impetus almost from its inception.

The main contribution of Servius, besides offering a confirming echo of Tertullian, is the term *bustuarii*, implying (although centuries after the event) that the initial connection of funerary sacrifice and something resembling gladiatorial combat was formalized in contemporary language: "...it was the custom to kill captives at the graves of powerful men; because this, in later days, seemed cruel,

it was decided to have gladiators fight before the grave, gladiators who were

called 'bustuarii' for the tombs (*busti*) (*Ad Aeneas* X.519)".[xv] Servius, then,

indicates that gladiature was a 'civility' – a morally refined response to the

perceived cruelty of human sacrifice. Tertullian, conversely, provides exactly the

opposite interpretation:

> "The ancients thought that by this sort of spectacle [ie. gladiature]
> they rendered a service to the dead, after they had tempered it with
> a more cultured form of cruelty. For of old, in the belief that the
> souls of the dead are propitiated with human blood, they used at
> funerals to sacrifice captives or slaves of poor quality whom they
> bought. Afterwards it seemed good to obscure their impiety by
> making it a pleasure. So after the persons procured had been
> trained in such arms as they then had and as best they might – their
> training was to learn to be killed! – they then did them to death on
> the appointed funeral day at the tombs. So they found comfort for
> death in murder. This is the origin of the *munus*. (...) What was
> offered to appease the dead was counted as a funeral rite (*De
> Spectaculis* 12)."[xvi]

Regardless of the choice that might be made between the two texts, when

read in conjunction, Servius and Tertullian associated gladiature with a notion of

civilizing process even at the ur-origin stage of the funeral, irrespective of cultural

context or of discourses of social class. Moreover, the contradiction apparent

between them maintained the existence of ambiguity within the ancient sources

themselves, widening the scope for modern interpretive debate.

Funerary origin: politics

Whether or not sincere funerary piety, with its subtext of relative moral

sensitivity, is accepted by modern historians as the legitimate and/or actual pretext

of the 264 BC event, the funeral as a genetic image of origin also persistently implicates the general theme of dichotomy in socio-political relations between the patrician and plebeian groups as inscribed by antiquity's literate class. A key element of the problem is touched upon by the various interpretations of the word *munus* and the uses to which it has been put by modern scholars. Multiple ancient sources refer to gladiatorial combat, at least in its republican iteration, as a *munus*, a word variously translated as 'duty', 'obligation', or 'gift' (and eventually applied as a term which signified a gladiatorial spectacle). Interpretive variations of the word *munus* have generally encapsulated the multiple versions of the patrician/plebeian figuration that have circulated since the Enlightenment: whether the definitive relation between the two groups was one of tradition, of compulsion, or of generosity, and in which direction the impetus of power flowed from one to the other.

Some scholars apparently restrict the significance of *munus* to gladiature's contested religious/funerary connotations – to put it simply, the 'duty' in question was to the dead in whose honour a gladiatorial combat was staged, and further the 'gift' (as the material dimension of the duty performed) was blood, which Tertullian and others suggested was a desirable sacrifice. However, other historians have interpreted the term *munus* as a duty of the patrician class to the populace – a specific form of that obligatory largesse with which the Roman world abounded, and one which over the past three centuries has been spun as both a burden and a privilege, depending upon the wider image of patrician/plebeian figuration being propounded.

Other, usually more recent, scholars have no time for human sacrifice at any point in Roman history. From this perspective, the key significance of the funeral was barely even funerary: instead the point of the funeral rests upon its 'private' character (ie. controlled by private initiative and funds rather than formally sponsored by the Republican state), thus drawing a connection between gladiature's eventually intense and complex relationship to political performance and its earliest, simplest appearance in the cattle market. This leans heavily upon a perceived continuity between the mid-republican Brutus funeral and an attested series of similar events which studded the middle and late Republic until the Augustan principate: we know, from the collation of numerous sources, that gladiature re-appeared in urban Rome as a feature of several significant public funerals of powerful patrician figures, and that the scale of the staged combats apparently increased over time, from the three pairs of the Brutus funeral to the sixty pairs of the funeral of Publius Licinius Crassus, *pontifex maximus*, some eighty years later.[xvii] The significance of this slow-burning socio-historical phenomenon is typically retrojected through reference to its culmination at the very end of the republic: the greatest and last of the private funerary gladiatorial events, which was staged by Julius Caesar himself in 46 B.C., upon a seemingly flimsy pretext (the 'funeral', contrary to all orthodoxy, was a woman's; granted, she was Caesar's own daughter, but on the other hand she had been dead for eight years). The Julia funeral is frequently interpreted as one element of Caesar's elaborate and long-running program of electioneering, propaganda, and popular politics, in a career whose conditions of possibility arguably had been laid down over the course of many long-term shifts and developments in Roman social politics since the middle Republic – when gladiature ostensibly made its first appearance.

In this historiographic perspective, then, the contextualization of gladiature is bounded by Roman social history alone, without reference to other, earlier cultures. The original Brutus funeral is treated simply as the proto-form of the Julia funeral over two centuries later, and 'original Roman' gladiature as essentially no different from what it became by the end of the Republic. It is a comparatively ahistorical approach, which essentially claims that gladiature's 'uncanny advent' in the middle of the third century BC simply formed the foundation of all successive developments, and carried nothing forward from any earlier period. This abandonment of the trope of the *ur*-origin of course tends to align with the 'Roman hypothesis' of gladiatorial origin. Here, gladiature (or something like it) may well have been practiced in earlier times by non-Roman groups; it may have been practiced in the context of funerals; its earliest Roman funerary iteration may even have had a specific ritual meaning for spectators. All of this, however, is treated as quite beside the implied point, which is that if gladiature performed essentially the same function throughout the Republic, and that function can be seen by the end of the Republic to be dependent upon the crowd's pleasure in violence, then gladiature was equally dependent upon the violence/pleasure cathexis even at its point of origin. Underneath lies the further implication that gladiature did not develop over time – i.e. did not 'civilize' - at least once it was within the Roman sphere; there may have been an original moment of 'conversion' from an earlier non-Roman form, but the Roman relation to gladiature is seen as static.

The Etruscan hypothesis

The only surviving statement from antiquity which specifically addresses the subject of the origin of gladiators is a single fragment from Hermippos' lost work *On Lawgivers*, paraphrased by Athenaeus in the third-century AD *Deipnosophistae*. According to Athenaeus, Hermippos claimed that gladiators were invented by the Mantineans, a people from Arcadian Greece whose territory was the site of the largest land battle in the Peloponnesian War some seven centuries earlier.[xviii] The quotation is more or less a non-sequitur: it appears in the context of a brief discussion about gladiature, which does not otherwise mention gladiature's origin, and which breaks off after the citation from Hermippos. There is no real evidence to suggest that antiquity – whether the Romans, or anyone else – was much concerned with the origin of gladiature in any strictly aetiological sense.

The *Deipnosophistae* is also one of the sources cited in support of the Etruscan hypothesis. Much as he cites Hermippos, Athenaeus also relates a passage by the historian Nicholas of Damascus, who mentions in passing that "the Romans staged spectacles of fighting gladiators ... at their festivals and in their theatres, borrowing the custom from the Etruscans (IV.153)". Numerous other ancient sources are usually marshalled to corroborate Nicholas of Damascus' suggestion. An isolated fragment attributed to a lost work of Suetonius, the *De Regibus*, mentions gladiators in conjunction with an Etruscan king of Rome, one of the sixth-century B.C. Tarquins: "Earlier Tarquinius Priscus exhibited to the Romans two pairs of gladiators which he had matched together for a period of twenty-seven years."[xix] The uncertain nature of the fragment and its odd content perhaps contribute to the reason why it has never been ascribed much weight, but it is included in the corpus. Further, Isidore of Seville's seventh-century A.D. etymology claimed that *lanista*, a term for a trader in and trainer of gladiator slaves, was an Etruscan word.[xx] Although neither of the above pair of quotations specifically refers to Roman 'borrowing' of gladiature from Etruria, the Suetonius passage at least gestures towards a possible incident connecting gladiators with an Etruscan king, and Isidore's claim indicates the retention of an associated Etruscan term in the Latin language of subsequent periods, together adding to the general image of an organic connection, whether actual or imagined, between Etruscans and the trade in gladiators.

Support for the Etruscan hypothesis has not been derived exclusively from written sources: a small corpus of visual evidence has also exerted a strong influence over the notion of an Etruscan gladiatorial origin. The association between original gladiature and funerary ritual created the conditions of possibility for gladiatorial interpretations of certain tomb paintings surviving from antiquity. Tomb paintings that have been taken as evidence for early, non-Roman gladiature will be discussed in greater detail in subsequent chapters; at this point, there are only a few statements which need to be made. One is that different groups of such paintings have been cited in support of both the Etruscan and Osco-Samnite hypotheses, each image of origin having its own body of visual evidence. A second statement is that each hypothesis of origin has held a different relationship to the visual evidence it cites, for although the relevant surviving works of ancient authors have been available to modern scholars since the beginning of the period of the present study, the 'appearance' of tomb paintings has depended upon the history of archaeological excavation and study. Thus the Etruscan hypothesis of gladiatorial origin had already been fully fleshed out on the sole basis of written evidence, before the heavily decorated tombs of Tarquinia and Cerveteri were documented (and interpreted as consistent with the existing notion of original gladiature) across the later nineteenth century; in contrast, it could be argued that the paintings of the region around Paestum were instrumental to the emergence of the Osco-Samnite hypothesis beginning in the early twentieth century. Moreover, the latest hypothesis of Roman origin largely disregards the visual material counted by the other two hypotheses as evidence, via the implied redefinition of 'gladiature proper' as the Roman version of a practice whose 'tribal' iterations were at best only indirectly or analogically related.

The South Italian (Osco-Samnite / Campanian) hypothesis

The presence and interpretation of tomb paintings does contribute something to the Osco-Samnite hypothesis of origin, whose literary evidence is of a rather different character than that which is collected for the Etruscans. Numerous painted tombs of southern Italy have been securely attributed to Osco-Samnite and Campanian peoples of the region, and (perhaps less securely) interpreted as bearing representations of gladiature (to be discussed in greater detail in later chapters). The fact that gladiature thus appears in a funerary context of representation has thus served as the basis for the assumption that 'original' gladiature among the Osco-Samnites was, therefore, funerary gladiature, more or less of a kind with earliest Roman gladiature and even with the image of Etruscan gladiature; indeed, at least one influential scholar floated the theory that gladiature was a "creation of a composite population, Oscan, Samnite, Etruscan" (Ville 1981, my translation). As has been stated, the validity of a funerary context for original Osco-Samnite gladiature, or original Osco-Samnite gladiature at all, is not under debate here. Rather, the interesting point that arises is the fact that the funerary interpretation for the Osco-Samnite hypothesis is not at all reflected in surviving written sources; whether or not the south Italian tribes practiced gladiature at their funerals, the Romans left no written evidence to indicate that they held this belief. Instead, surviving Roman writings strongly associate Osco-Samnite gladiature with entertainment at banquets; at the same time, the collected references to banquet gladiature are generally embedded in various accounts of military history, wherein banquet gladiature is cited as part of a broader characterization of Samnite and Campanians peoples in the context of Rome's official versions of her armed conflicts with these groups.

Three ancient authors, two writing in Latin and one in Greek, reiterate very similar images of a form and context of gladiature which was in no way funerary, and which subsequently inflected an entirely distinct image of origin, associated with a grouping of ideas and connotations fundamentally different from the ideas which clustered around the Etruscan hypothesis at an earlier period of modern historiography. The foremost of these sources is Livy, who is also the

accepted authority on the earliest recorded appearance of gladiature in Rome

itself. Livy's A.U.C. 9.40.17 is a passage describing in brief the aftermath of the

first Samnite War:[5]

> "The war in Samnium ... was attended with equal danger and an
> equally glorious conclusion. The [Samnite] enemy, besides their
> other warlike preparation, had made their battle-line to glitter
> with new and splendid arms. There were two corps: the shields of
> the one were inlaid with gold, and the other with silver ... The
> Romans had already learned of these splendid accoutrements, but
> their generals had taught them that a soldier should be rough to
> look on. Not adorned with gold and silver but putting his trust in
> iron and in courage ... The [Roman] dictator, as decreed by the
> senate, celebrated a triumph, in which by far the finest show was
> afforded by the captured armour. So the Romans made use of the
> splendid armour of their enemies to do honour to the gods; while
> the Campanians, in consequence of their pride and in hatred of
> the Samnites, equipped after this fashion the gladiators who
> furnished them entertainment at their feasts, and bestowed on
> them the name of Samnites."

In addition to imparting some preliminary sense of the complexities of the

cultural and political geography of southern Italy during the early and middle

Republic (for example, the Campanians, though politically at odds with the

Samnites, were ethnically and linguistically quite closely related to their

opponents), Livy's passage also provides an immediate sense of the basis upon

which Rome's image of Campanians/Osco-Samnites was constructed. The long

---

[5]The 'first' Samnite war refers to the first of three wars in the fourth and third centuries BC, which
essentially pitted Rome against Samnium, though the array of allies on either side was an ever-
shifting cast of characters. Although the hypothesis of gladiatorial origin occasionally lumps the
Campanians in with the Samnites, the first Samnite War saw these two groups fighting on
opposing sides. Dench's summary of Livy's account of the first Samnite war "finds Romans and
Samnites competing in 343 for influence between the Middle Liris and Volturnus Valleys. The
Samnites apparently attacked the Sidicini, who sought aid amongst the Campani. When the
Samnites shifted their focus towards Tifata, above Capua, the Campanians were accepted by
Rome into a relationship of deditio; thus, traditionally, Romans and Samnites first found
themselves at war" (1995, p.15).

republican history of bitter and protracted warfare between Rome and Samnium left a deep impress upon the Roman historical self-image, and by the time of Livy's writing at the very beginning of the Empire, the shared negative discourse surrounding these southern peoples had been refined through lengthy circulation and consensus. It is an intrinsically perplexed image: though defined primarily and essentially as warriors, sufficiently "dangerous" as opponents to render a victory over them "glorious", the Samnites' very identity as warriors is also represented as their downfall, since their 'warlike' nature is here represented as corrupted by wealth, in contrast to victorious Rome's more Spartan "iron and courage". The complex network of connections between wealth, luxury, effeteness, weaknesses both military and moral, and the long-maintained official discourse of Roman hegemony and identity cannot possibly be explored here in any detail; however, the point comes through quite clearly that the Samnites are to be seen as a once-noble and strong enemy who have come down in the world, brought low by the corrupting effects of riches, and worthy only to be first stripped of arms by the Romans, and then humiliated by the Campanians, who reincarnate them as banquet gladiators.

Strabo (5.4.13) retraces the same narrative:

"As for the Campanii, it was their lot, because of the fertility of their country, to enjoy in equal degree both evil things and good. For they were so extravagant that they would invite gladiators, in pairs, to dinner, regulating the number by the importance of the diners;and when, on their instant submission to Hannibal, they received his army into winter-quarters, the soldiers became so effeminate because of the pleasures afforded them that Hannibal said that, although victor, he was in danger of falling into the hands of his foes, because the soldiers he had got back were not his men, but only women. But when the Romans got the mastery, they brought them to their sense by many severe lessons..."

Strabo's text makes explicit that which was only hinted at by Livy: that the great crime of the resistant southern tribes, in Roman eyes, was their alliance with Hannibal.

Finally, Silius Italicus (*Pun.* 11.28-54):

"It might be lawful for Celts, lawful for the tribes of the Boii, to renew impious warfare; but who could believe that Capua [an Oscan-speaking centre in Campania] would take the same mad decision as the tribe of Senones, and that a city of Trojan origin would ally herself with a barbarous ruler of Numidians – who could believe this now, when times have changed so greatly? But luxury, and sloth fed by riotous debauchery, and utter shamelessness in sinning, and scandalous respect for wealth and wealth alone – such vices preyed upon an indolent and listless people and a city freed from the restraints of law. Their savage cruelty also bore them to their doom. And they had the means to pamper their vices. No people of Italy possessed gold or silver in more abundance – so favoured were they then by Fortune; their garments, even those worn by men, were dyed with Assyrian purple; their princely banquets began at noon, and the rising sun found them at their revels; and their way of life was defiled by every stain. Moreover, the senators oppressed the people, the masses welcomed the unpopularity of the senate, and civil discord made the parties clash. Meanwhile the old men, more corrupt themselves, outdid the headstrong follies of the young. Men notorious for humble birth and obscure origin asserted their claims, expecting and demanding to hold office before others, and to rule the sinking state. Then too, it was their ancient custom to enliven their banquets with bloodshed, and to combine with their feasting the horrid sight of armed men fighting; often the combatants fell dead above the very cups of the revellers, and the tables were stained with streams of blood." [xxi]

Such imagery has been deployed in the construction of varying historical narratives. It was well understood, from almost the moment that the Osco-Samnite hypothesis was initially suggested, that the image, constructed by officially patronized historians of early imperial Rome, of the greatest threat to Rome's hegemony and its main rival among the cities of peninsular Italy under the Republic, was to be handled with scepticism (see, for example, Couissin on this point). However, as will be seen in later chapters below, these passages, read in combination with the perception of certain tomb paintings as representations of gladiature and other historical details (primarily the concentration of all of the oldest amphitheatre architecture in southern Italy, and additional written evidence to suggest that Capua in particular was a hotbed of gladiature by the end of the Republic), came to be interpreted as sufficient evidence for a south Italian, whether Osco-Samnite or Campanian, origin of gladiature.

Origin as historiographic trope

Having looked at the main contents of the primary sources, it becomes clear that part of the attempt to understand the dominance of the Etruscan hypothesis in the nineteenth century rests partly upon the contemporary historical understanding of Etruria's relation to Rome; in that image, Etruria was inscribed as an enervated Eastern monarchy eventually overthrown, after centuries of oppressive rule, by a nascent western republic which swiftly conquered its erstwhile corrupt masters. Similarly, part of the twentieth century popularity of the Osco-Samnite hypothesis is linked to the contemporary image of Samnium as a wild, unspoilt mountain fastness of warrior-primitive hill-people, more neo-romantic than classically barbaric, who violently resisted Roman imperialist aggression for generations until they were at last tragically ground under the heel of the great war-machine. Each of these is a sketch of a particular power relation in which Rome's image as a civilization changes as much as does the image assigned to its primary barbarian; each of these narratives is associated with a particular strategy of the shifting subject of historico-political discourse; and each of these, as will be seen, is associated in the historiographic archive with a particular image of original gladiature, which bore a certain meaning in its original context, and whose subsequent transmission into and practice within its particular Rome is therefore rationalized according to quite different and exceedingly complex discursive frameworks regarding power, violence, legitimacy, and morality – which, in their turn, are most clearly read through the associated imagery of the crowd, its specific pleasure in violence, and the quality and location (within both Roman and modern society) of abhorrence.

Therefore, the significance of the historiography of gladiature lies in the fact that it manifests, with unusual clarity, modernity's self-image as 'civilized', and the shifting terms of the discourse within which that self-image is constructed and expressed – and, further, that it does so in the context of the attempt, carried across three centuries, to inscribe and rationalize a highly specific image of decivilizing, signified by gladiature as the cathexis of violence and pleasure. The wider background of civilization's self-image, in which 'civilizations' are characterized and understood to have existed in particular relation to one another – more specifically, how the centrally important civilization of Rome had its borders (and thus its essence) defined by a complex and shifting image of the barbarian – additionally become, when gladiature is added into the mix, historico-political narratives which attempt to account for the fear of decivilizing within the construct of civilization. Gladiatorial historiography's position within this wider

narrative-of-civilizations endeavour is to account for civilization's opposite.

Narratives of civilization and the State

> "...the great problem in public right will be the problem of ... "the
> other succession", or in other words: What happens when one State
> succeeds another? What happens – and what becomes of public right
> and the power of kings – when States do not succeed one another as
> [a result of] a sort of continuity that nothing interrupts, but because
> they are born, go through a phase of might, then fall into decadence,
> and finally vanish completely?" (*SMBD* 119).

Post-Enlightenment classical historiography was deeply impressed by the

stamp left upon it by Gibbon, with *The History of the Decline and Fall of the*

Roman Empire (1776); Gibbon of course owed a conceptual debt to Montesquieu,

but in any case, it was the eighteenth century in Europe that saw the birth of the

'fall of Rome' as a major, even definitive trope of the writing of classical history,

as the "spectacle of a great civilization collapsing into oblivion seemed in some

way to offer instruction for those who feared the loss of their own civilization"

(Bowersock 29). However, even at this early date, Rome's fall inhabited a

curiously ambivalent position: Gibbon kept the reference in his title despite the

fact that he ultimately claimed that Rome, via Byzantium, did not 'fall' until

1453, and that the main purpose of his work was to connect the ancient and

modern history of 'the world' (cf. Bowersock) into a continuous whole. The fall

of Rome has functioned perhaps as less a spectacle than as a spectre, a

historiographic trope expressive from the first of both anxiety and affinity: the

first and largest of the 'western' imperial projects, and therefore of crucial and

exemplary significance to modernity for both its success and its failure.

All of that, however, refers to empire. What this dissertation focuses upon, in contrast, is an earlier and somewhat less traditionally central moment in Roman history: the change – sometimes revolution, or rupture, but also at times inscribed as a more gradual shift, an evolution, or even simply the giving of new names to entities which had long since become fundamentally different – between republic and empire, generally attributed in its inception to Julius Caesar and certainly considered more or less complete midway through the lengthy reign of his successor Augustus.

The story of how a republic became an empire has always been a much less tidy tale. While the 'fall of empire' as Gibbon set it down had a fairly clear basic plot broadly hinted at by his history's very title, going back several centuries earlier in Roman history and navigating the road that led from the Republic to the Empire has, in contrast, always been troubled by the imperative to make a decision from the outset about the *directionality* of the narrative – in the arc of 'born, go through a phase of might, fall into decadence, and finally vanish completely', the Republic has been cast, at different times and points of writing, into each and all of these phases. It is possible - while reflecting upon Elias and the civilizing process as an explicit formulation of this sort of thinking – to typify that initial 'decision' as an *a priori* choice between narratives of civilizing and of decivilizing. The shift from Republic to Empire at Rome is possibly the greatest historiographic example of Foucault's 'succession' between two States; in the ongoing labour to resolve the problem of 'what happens', modern historiography has inscribed and re-inscribed the republican-imperial transition in every conceivable way, and at the core of every version is an engagement with the imperative to situate the historical narrative somewhere within a directional, teleological structure that connects the history of the State with the state of civilization.

Was the Republic a Golden Age of ancient, enlightened representative government, with a working (if uneven) system of checks and balances between governing offices, which descended through political corruption, systemic economic inequality, and old-fashioned moral turpitude into the benighted tyranny of decadent Empire? Or was that golden Republic perhaps brought down not by the competitive avarice of those in power, but was instead taken hostage and polluted by the combined degenerative influences of the sprawling, demanding urban lower classes as these ranks were swelled by an influx of foreign opportunists from beyond Rome's ancient borders? Perhaps, in contrast, the Republic was simply a brief preface or slow overture to the real business of Empire; dating the shift to the Augustan age splits the roughly one thousand years of Roman political history into two approximately equal halves, but all the same, Rome's ambitions for imperial expansion were arguably in evidence several centuries before that convenient midpoint, whether or not one accepts (Livy's) claims that the extension of Roman power in the mid-Republic was an ad hoc and often unwilling response to a long series of local factors. Or perhaps, the Empire was simply a logical outgrowth of the way the Republic gathered and fostered men of talent; amidst such a concentration of wealth, brilliance, and political acumen, perhaps it is unsurprising that one would eventually emerge supreme, take up the reins of government into his hands alone, and lead the stumbling Republic into a new age of power and rightful dominion. Or, again, perhaps there was no great substantive difference between the Republic and the Empire at all: the role of emperor had its predecessors in the consul and the triumphator, the citizen army was bound to give way to a professional soldiery as the state expanded, and most significantly, the ascension and dominion of the Roman world was perhaps inevitable – and desirable - given the light of civilization that shone within its eventually massive borders.

All of these versions of the story will be visited in the course of what follows, and there have undoubtedly been more versions told over the past three centuries than are canvassed here. It is more important to realize that, within this broad story of Roman civilization with all of its possible versions, there has always existed a much smaller, far more narrowly defined story of the history of gladiature, and that the story of gladiature - its origin and appearance in Roman culture, its growth over time to massive proportions, its content, its meaning and significance, and ultimately its decline and disappearance – relates to the larger story of Roman civilization in a specific way. In part this is due to the fact that, according to the best of our knowledge, gladiature seems to have appeared in Rome right in the middle of the Republic, just when the body politic was poised between the system of 'checks and balances' described by Polybius and the degenerate mob of Juvenal; the latter may be the imperial corrosion of a republican citizenry contrastively imagined as a political ideal, but the troubling suggestion of all available historical evidence is that it was that subsequently idealized body politic of the mid-Republic which first took up gladiature and began to expand and develop the practice. To put it succinctly, gladiature aligns all too easily with the beginning of one of the strongest narratives of decivilizing ever applied to Rome; scholars of Roman history will immediately recognize that the identification of the middle Republic as the period when the 'rot first set in' was one of the best-attested stories that the Romans subsequently told themselves. Conversely, there also exist versions of Rome's narrative which invert that structure, and which tell the story of the long shift from Republic to Empire as a tale of a wide, unbroken spread of a great civilization across an otherwise backward and benighted world; some articulations of this version are silent on the troubling detail of gladiature (these will not be covered below), but other accounts of this nature actually place gladiature at the heart of the story, and construct an image of civilization that depends upon gladiature as its primary mechanism.

Chapter 3: *Luxus*, *Munus*, Spirit

The origin of the nation: gladiature and the Enlightenment

The primary discursive underpinning which most clearly shaped the

eighteenth-century historiography of ancient gladiature was the emergence of the

nation, constructed at an intersection of race and class, as the true or legitimate

seat of civilization. This 'nation', in Foucault's terms, is the speaking subject

associated with historico-political discourse, as by the end of the eighteenth

century:

> "History is no longer the State talking about itself; it is something
> else talking about itself, and the something else that speaks in
> history and takes itself as the object of its own historical narrative
> is a sort of new entity known as the nation. 'Nation' is, of course,
> to be understood in the broad sense of the term. (...) [I]t is the
> notion of a nation that generates or gives rise to notions like
> nationality, race, and class. In the eighteenth century, this notion
> still has to be understood in a very broad sense. [...] [T]his vague,
> fluid, shifting notion of the nation, this idea of a nation which does
> not stop at the frontiers but which, on the contrary, is a sort of mass
> of individuals who move from one frontier to another, through
> States, beneath States, and at an infra-State level, persists long into
> the nineteenth century ..." (*SMBD* 142).

The 'broad sense' of nation to be found within eighteenth century classical

historiography was represented from the outset in terms of oppositions and

exclusions, as class- and race-based groups were categorized and ordered into an

image of the ancient world which grappled with the discursive development of the

linked constructs of both nation and civilization, through a historiography that

was beginning the labour of separating the barbarous from the civilized. The idea

of the nation, its relation(s) to the State, and the association between the

nation/State complex and the construct of civilization was expressed and refined during this period through the contemporary notion of 'spirit', a term which

initially was used to identify and distinguish whole cultural groups of antiquity –

Greeks, Romans, Etruscans, and others – into categories whose basis gestured

toward constructs of race. As will be seen, 'spirit' was inextricably associated

with the tendency of historico-political discourse to read 'civilization' as a quality

that was signified by attitude(s) to violence, and especially the violence/pleasure

cathexis signalled by gladiature; consequently, gladiature played a (perhaps)

surprisingly important role in the ordering of antiquity, and the sorting of ancient

peoples into categories of civilized and barbarous. However, over the course of

the century, the idea of 'spirit' as the essential identity of a group came to be used

in support of the gradual splitting of previously monadic 'racial' groups into

entities internally divided by distinctions of class – and thus partook of the

hardening of the discursive distinction between the 'nation', which came to be

aligned explicitly with civilization (and, implicitly, with the nobility), and the

'State', which both contained and was exceeded by the nation.

It was during the eighteenth century that the origin of gladiature

began to take shape as an academic question that provoked attention, and that

exerted meaningful influence upon the interpretation of gladiature as a

phenomenon of the ancient world. Prior to this period, the question of gladiature's

origin - indeed, any questions about gladiature at all – were scarce.[xxii]

The genesis of gladiatorial origin in modern historiography was initially

articulated as a site of exclusions rather than identification: the prologue to the

first version of an origin story, as it were, was focused as much upon asserting which ancient groups abhorred gladiature as upon discussing which groups may have practiced it, and the locus of origin was defined from the outset by an observable impetus to construct firm boundaries around it. Within the framework of such thinking, the various cultures of antiquity potentially implicated with early gladiature were ordered according to a proscriptive discourse of abhorrence of violence, which was increasingly identified as a primary sign of 'civilization' as that construct was being produced and elaborated within the language of classical historiography. The main players were the Greeks, the Etruscans, and the Romans; each group was perceived as having its own individual relation to gladiature, distinguished from each other along an imagined continuum defined by the poles of abhorrence and pleasure, and appearing as more or less 'civilized' on this basis.

The articulation of a contemporary attitude of abhorrence for the violence/pleasure cathexis represented by gladiature was the focus of the earliest modern responses in classical scholarship. Abhorrence was constructed in terms which approached ancient civilizations as whole cultural entities, wherein notions related to race and class were subsumed within a comparatively totalizing perspective on culture that, by the end of the century, began visibly to disaggregate. The rhetoric of abhorrence was articulated primarily through reference to ancient Greece, which was held up as an exemplary, highly refined civilization that, among other things, vehemently rejected the practice of gladiature. The increasingly vertical ordering of ancient cultures on terms which included the abhorrence of gladiature gestured, in turn, toward an emergent notion of cultural evolution through historical time, as the defense of essential Greek civility was conflicted by the *Iliad*'s description of the funeral of Patroclus, and its evidence that very ancient Greeks practiced a form of funerary proto-gladiature. The association between the valorous Greeks and gladiature's origin invoked a conceptual separation between funerary gladiature, perceived as comparatively legitimate due to the presumed absence of 'mere' pleasure, and the later spectacular gladiature of Rome: thus there was no separation in the eighteenth century between the moral debate over violence and pleasure, the historical debate over gladiature's origin, and the discursive labour of refinement of the construct of civilization over and against the linked figure of the barbarian – an oppositional construct which would, in the following century, come to be strongly identified with the Etruscans.

What we see in the historiography of gladiature across the eighteenth century is the gradual destabilization of the 'universal table of knowledge' which Foucault considered as the structural foundation of the Enlightenment episteme, and as partly coextensive with juridico-philosophical discourse. As discussed in the Introduction, Foucault distinguished juridico-philosophical from historico-political discourse on the basis of how each formation narrates the 'history of right' – in other words, the voice and language in which the subject of governing power constitutes its own subjectivity as such, and thereby inscribes the space of its own authority. His central metaphor to describe the narration of the history of right within the juridico-political discourse of the eighteenth century was an ordered, taxonomic table: "During the Classical age [i.e., the eighteenth century], the constant, fundamental relation of knowledge ... to a universal mathesis

justified the project ... of a finally unified corpus of learning (...) [which]

expressed, on the visible surface of events or texts, the profound unity that the

Classical age had established by positing the analysis of identities and differences,

and the universal possibility of tabulated order" (*The Order of Things* (*OT*) 247).

The 'universal science of order' represented by the tabular organization of

knowledge tended to posit and to frame ancient peoples as hermetic wholes,

sufficient unto themselves; each occupied a 'cell' in the table of knowledge, and

all were ordered according to a horizontal mathesis which expressed the profound

totalizing unity of the contemporary episteme. The juridico-philosophical history

of right within this discourse was aligned with a speaking historical subject which

occupied the position of a universal, totalizing or neutral subject; the auto-

representation of sovereignty, or the narration of the history of right, associated

with juridico-philosophical discourse and the deeper epistemic structures of the

mathesis represented the sovereign's right to power as a politically neutral right,

stemming from essential and universal order rather than from histories of conflict

or relations of force (*SMBD* 48-54). It is within this context that the period's

scrupulous and totalizing "permanent grid of distinctions" (*OT* 251) between

ancient peoples, and the language in which such thought was expressed, should

best be read.

However, what we see over the course of the eighteenth century is both

the gradual break-up of the mathesis, in an epistemic shift which re-ordered the

formerly horizontal organization of knowledge according to an "obscure verticality ... that [was] to define the law of resemblances, prescribe all adjacencies and discontinuities, provide the foundation for perceptible arrangements, and displace all the great horizontal deployments of the *taxinomia* towards the somewhat accessory region of consequences" (*OT* 251). The beginnings of a particular myth-historical approach to antiquity was a direct result of this shift towards historico-political discourse. Foucault himself dated the transition to the end of the sixteenth century (*SMBD* 49) – exactly the moment when Justus Lipsius brought up the problem of gladiatorial origin (see endnote xxii) – but in terms of gladiature, the eighteenth century marks the appearance of a growing corpus of historical texts which express a concern to penetrate the 'consequences' of the intersection of violence and pleasure. As will be explored below, the vertically ordered region of consequences at play in the historiography of gladiature was defined by the articulation of the construct of civilization, which within this specific discourse was closely identified with the abhorrence of violence.

The elaboration of 'civilization' as a construct gradually destabilized and deconstructed the mathetic perspective from within. At least within classical historiography, the construct of civilization was from its inception associated with an ordering structure which did not perfectly reflect the mathesis of universal tabulation, but instead already expressed the seeds of 'perpetual war' in the sense that the rudiments of a vertical hierarchy pointed to what would become oppositional relations of conflict written into the historical image of antiquity. Moreover, this nascent structure of hierarchy and the trope of conflict which we find embedded in the earliest articulations of the construct of civilization are represented in terms of the (il)legitimacy of violence and the attitude of abhorrence; the principle criterion of distinction in the ordering of the civilizations of antiquity, and thus of civilization itself, appears in classical historiography in the form of a debate surrounding gladiatorial violence as an object of pleasure.

In turn, this learned conversation about the violence/pleasure cathexis of gladiature was couched within a framework which anticipated both of Foucault's key sub-discourses of 'race war' and 'class war', signalling the inauguration of the dynamic, shifting relation between these two terms within historico-political discourse. During this early period the salient discursive dimension pointed towards race, as scholarship attempted to structure the cells of the universal table according to constructs of different cultural groups of antiquity. The particular idiom in which such differences were expressed spoke in terms of the 'spirit of a people' –of the Etruscans, the Romans and, crucially, of the Greeks. One of the most important indexical signifiers of a nation's 'spirit' was the degree of abhorrence or pleasure with which a group responded to the spectacle of gladiature: an abhorrence of violence, such as that ascribed to the Greeks, signified civilization, just as the Romans' pleasure in gladiature signified its relative absence. In this way, eighteenth-century classical historiography held the beginnings of a close discursive connection between a particular proscriptive moral attitude toward a certain kind of violence, and the definition of a 'nation' as a distinct group or 'race'. Further, as the century progressed, scholars of antiquity came with increasing clarity to identify that desirable attitude as an attribute of specific sectors of ancient society, further specifying the idea of the 'nation' (and its coextension with what were coming to be determined as the boundaries of civilization) along lines of class; as referred in the Introduction, the "nobility is one nation, as distinct from many other nations that circulate within the State and come into conflict with one another. It is this notion, this concept of the nation, that will give rise to the famous revolutionary problem of the nation ... It will also give rise to the notion of race. And, finally, it will give rise to the notion of class" (*SMBD* 134).

Over the course of the century, armed with the fantastical example of Greek abhorrence for non-funerary (illegitimate) gladiature, historiographic scholarship turned with increasing specificity to the problem of the absence of such abhorrence within Roman culture, and how it was to be accounted for. By the time of the violent social upheavals of the French Revolution, eighteenth-century scholars began increasingly to isolate the lower classes of Rome, within the Roman cultural whole, as the primary subjects of the violence/pleasure cathect, and thus elaborated the foundations of a discourse of class war alongside a value-laden hierarchical arrangement of ancient 'races', wherein gladiature functioned as one of only a very few diagnostic signs of 'spirit'. Therefore, we find a newly historicist subject articulating a history of right that refers back to antiquity in order to entrench and legitimize its self and its power – this speaking subject was "the nobility that introduced into the great Statist organization of historical discourse this disruptive principle [of] the nation as subject-object of the new history" (*SMBD* 143). Seen in this light, it is perhaps unsurprising that the period's historiography of Rome, particularly as scholarship aligned the construct of civilization more or less exclusively with an image of the Roman nobility, concurrently elided the socially inferior with the racially different in the construction of the barbarian.

Historical nostalgia and the fear of decivilizing

Eighteenth-century philosophy of history in Europe and America was directly and inextricably bound up with what survived of the ancient history of Rome. The writings of the ancient authors were widely read, and in particular texts from the late Republic and the Augustan period were drawn upon to provide an intelligible idiom for contemporary political and social philosophy; such texts, spanning the period of upheaval in the Roman world during the violent transition from republican to imperial government, were closely studied in both the growing empires and the fledgling republics of the early modern period for both their exemplary and cautionary qualities. Roman historical writing between the end of the Republic and the beginning of the Empire is a corpus deeply marked by cynicism and nostalgia for the earliest centuries of the Republic; Roman historians of this period "hated and feared the trends of their own time, and in their writing had contrasted the present with a better past, which they endowed with qualities absent from their own, corrupt era. The earlier age had been full of virtue: simplicity, integrity, a love of justice and liberty; the present was venal, cynical, and oppressive" (Bailyn 25). The prescriptive criticisms of Cicero, Sallust, Tacitus and Seneca, along with the scathing satires of Juvenal, Martial and Petronius, were scrutinized by modern scholars as much for the injustices and corruptions they catalogued as for the virtues they defended. Philosophical rationalism treated antiquity very seriously as a series of case studies in governing structures, and the "history of antiquity ... became a kind of laboratory in which autopsies of the dead republics would lead to a science of social sickness and health matching the science of the natural world" (Wood 53).

At the same time, the ancients' own expressions of nostalgia and sense of historical decline reverberated strongly with much eighteenth century thought. The nostalgic turn arguably would not reach its full flowering until the Romantic period, but nonetheless, the Enlightenment saw its own share of measuring itself against the past and finding the present wanting. Eighteenth century desire for antiquity was, in certain ways, even more intent upon classical Greece than upon republican Rome; the philhellenism that would flourish in the following century was founded in the middle of the century by Winckelmann, whose 1764 *Geschichte der Kunst des Alterthums* was the groundbreaking and inaugural text of what would formally become the discipline of art history. Winckelmann's study of Greek art became a major point of reference for the classical revival of the late eighteenth century (Potts 15), and codified many elements of the model response to antiquity that would dominate successive periods of historiography. Central among such elements was the perspective that the aesthetic significance of Greece set "an example that continually [criticized] modernity as being inadequate" (Ferris 24). Within this historical perspective, Greece was constructed as a fantasy of socio-political figuration, one which was unified, cohesive and free of internal conflict "according to an aesthetic through which every aspect of a nation [could] be conceived of as part of a total cultural representation. (...) [T]he significance of Hellenism [did] not lie in its occurrence as a historical phenomenon, but rather in its establishment of a concept of culture that went by the name of Greece" (Ferris 16). Eighteenth century classical historiography, therefore, was deeply bound up with the development of concepts of the State as a political order, of the nation as a social order, and of civilization as a master trope which emerged from the space of overlap between the State and the nation.

Winckelmann studied Greek aesthetics through a historical perspective which saw the State as a spontaneous, organic expression of its culture or the 'spirit of a people': in essence, the State and the nation were regarded as coextensive, in a manner that would not remain true in the next century. The historical exemplar of Greece was the vehicle for the development of such a conception of history, and eighteenth century thought about antiquity repeatedly represented classical Greece as the avatar of the entire approach to historical thought. The spirit of 'the Greek people' in antiquity - set down by Winckelmann as calm, stately, spontaneous, and joyous – was considered the beating heart of their noble, ordered democratic city-states, and perceived as having enjoyed a simplicity and health that modern states could aspire to, but scarcely hope to attain. Winckelmann's Greeks, then, were governed by an aristocracy purged of contemporary moral corruptions and political complications, and the classical Greek state was an imaginary world in which this ideal of essential social cohesion was directly materialized and expressed by all of its people according to the monolithic spirit of the entire nation. Within this fantasy of state figuration, all Greeks - a 'nation' essentially undifferentiated in terms of either race or class - were 'civilized'.

The widespread invocation of Greek antiquity on these terms in the eighteenth century created an immediate conflict with the emergent history of gladiature, especially in response to the ancient record's hints that gladiature, in its earliest form of funerary human sacrifice as this connection was described by Servius, may have been practiced upon Greek soil. Indeed, it could be argued that the emergence during this period of the discourse of the origin of gladiature – its hardening into a question that required an answer – arose in the wake of an observable desire to 'write out' gladiature from the prevailing conception of ancient Greek culture and the image of its society. Enlightenment philhellenism was focused upon an image of the ancient Greek city-states as idealized polities governed by a calm, self-possessed aristocracy wherein any social conflict was ultimately transcended by a pure unity of national spirit; Winckelmann in particular saw to the codification of this perspective. The ancient Greeks of the eighteenth century were imagined to have universally abhorred gladiature, and to have rejected the practice wholesale by the time of the Roman Republic. This idealized image of an entire civilization reacting with horror to gladiatorial violence, however, was inscribed within the pre-existing construct of ancient Greece as a fantasy of socio-political formation, wherein the essential unity of 'spirit', exemplified and safeguarded by the aristocracy, effectively exceeded the possibility of any power struggle or divergence of political interests between groups within the imagined Greek polity; yet, at the same time, gladiature was gradually coming to be identified quite precisely as a site of power conflicts between social classes. The response to this inadmissible contradiction was an equivocation which can be found already present in Winckelmann's work: though the Greeks were regarded as a civilized whole, the cultured and peaceful spirit of civility which defined them came to be specified as the special precinct of an idealized aristocracy, and the proto-racializing approach to Greece as a 'nation' was thus already mediated by a nascent discourse of class. By the end of the century, the attitude of civilized abhorrence to gladiature in the ancient world began to be restricted to and constitutive of a construct of the *upper* classes only.

The developing image of Greece as a civilized ideal was, of course, inseparable from the linked image of the character of Roman civilization, as the two ancient cultures were invoked in tandem and in tension as a framework within which 'civilization' was articulated in increasingly specific relation to constitutive notions of race, class, and 'nation', as these constructs functioned within eighteenth-century discourse. What arose in the case of Rome, in consequence, was a narrowing of the notion implicit in Winckelmann's construct of Greece; gladiature could not be denied as a historical 'reality' at Rome, as it was denied in Greece, but the notion of the national spirit of the Romans was gradually split into fragments along social fissures of class made manifest by attitudes to gladiatorial violence.

This fragmentation of the Roman whole, however, took place gradually over the course of the century. In the meantime, the tendency to essentialize the national spirit was a perspective not restricted to the historiography of Greece, although the Roman spirit presented an image that was far thornier and more problematic. Roman culture was interpreted in famously negative terms, most canonically in Montesquieu's 1734 *Considerations on the Causes of the Greatness of the Romans and their Decline* and, of course, in Gibbon's 1776-8 *The Decline and Fall of the Roman Empire*; the thematic consonance between the two titles leaves little doubt as to the eighteenth century's perspective on the outcomes of Roman history. Whereas the Greek spirit was codified as an unbroken ideal which declined over centuries in response to external factors, the Roman conquest of Greece not the least of these, the essence of the Roman people contained the seeds of its own self-destruction, whether this inner rot was to be located in the dangerously unchecked strength of its army (Montesquieu), or the enervated lack of resistance to Christianity (Gibbon). Rome as a cultural entity was accorded a greater degree of historicity than Winckelmann allowed the Greeks; it was seen as locked in a spiralling descent from the simpler virtues which strengthened the national spirit of the earliest centuries of the Republic:

"It was not the force of arms which made the ancient republics great or which ultimately destroyed them. It was rather the character and spirit of their people. Frugality, industry, temperance, and simplicity – the rustic traits of the sturdy yeoman – were the stuff that made a society strong. The virile martial qualities – the scorn of ease, the contempt of danger, the love of valour – were what made a nation great. The obsessive term was luxury, both a cause and a symptom of social sickness. This luxury, not mere wealth but that "dull ... animal enjoyment" which left "minds stupefied, and bodies enervated, by wallowing for ever in one continual puddle of voluptuousness", was what corrupted a society ..." (Wood 53).

As scholarly attention to gladiature increased over the course of the eighteenth century, the practice was sorted firmly into the category of luxury, and the worst species of luxury into the bargain. In Roman antiquity itself, *luxus* was repeatedly identified as a social problem, particularly during the late Republic; the period's anti-sumptuary laws were a conservative response to the rapid socioeconomic changes that followed in the wake of Republican expansion and conquest, and were tied to a moral asceticism that struck a chord with eighteenth-century scholars in the midst of contemporary imperialist expansion. From this perspective, gladiature appeared as a mockery of the 'virile martial qualities that made a nation great', and it was considered an emblematic trope of national decay and degeneration. The luxury and voluptuousness into which Rome descended contrasted not only to the rustic valour of the early Republic, but also to the 'noble simplicity and calm grandeur' of the Greek ideal. Rome, then, not only degenerated over time into an inferior version of itself, but the fact of its decline also marked Rome as essentially inferior to Greece in terms of its national spirit. Thus we see the beginnings of decivilizing emerging during this period, shadowing the dawning of the construct of civilization; at the same time, Rome's exemplification of decivilizing was realized through contrast to the civilized 'ideal', framed upon the Greeks, in a conceptual relation of difference which presumed an intercultural plane of conflict that arguably presaged what would become, in the next century, the discourse of race war.

The fantasy of sublime unity, which saw Greece as a socio-political whole emanating from the essentially civilized spirit of which the Greek aristocracy were regarded as the leading example, produced an image of Rome that was marked by a different array of emphases. From a very early period, in contrast to Greece, Roman culture was perceived as relatively conflicted and internally divisive. The internal boundaries between the ranks of Roman society represented much deeper essential differences to eighteenth-century historians, and the national spirit of Rome was a far more fugitive figure of historico-political discourse. However, though *luxus* may have destroyed all that was most noble in the Roman spirit, some Romans were more prepared to resist the seduction of wealth and voluptuous diversions than others: from early on in the eighteenth century, even while the Greek people were represented as despising gladiature from the depths of their essential and immutable civilization, historians began to rescue certain members of Roman society from the image of a contrasting national spirit which was increasingly seen as bloodthirsty and delighted by the suffering of others.

Between the poles of Greece and Rome, an intermediate site was occupied by Etruria. Enlightenment classicists accorded the Etruscans only a limited role in the history of gladiature; they were generally, although not completely, accepted as the culture which had first introduced gladiature to Rome. The forceful consensus around the Etruscans as the original innovators of gladiature, rather than the incidental transmittors, would not emerge until the following century, and would do so under an altered framework of historical discourse. However, during the eighteenth century Etruria was situated as an important mediator between the certainty of Roman gladiature by the middle Republic and the hotly contested hints of Greek gladiature at a much earlier period, as gladiature and its origin were questioned within the broader framework of evaluating the civilizations of antiquity.

Within this broader context, the rhetorical force of an attitude of abhorrence to violence became increasingly significant, and developed in close association with the contemporary condemnation of the pleasure in gladiatorial violence taken by the Roman crowd. This attitude of abhorrence was inscribed through the valued ordering of classical cultures by referring to what were perceived as their own attitudes to gladiature: the gentle Greeks, it was agreed, despised the practice, while the gloomy Etruscans maintained ritual funerary gladiature until the end of their culture's independence from Rome; the Romans themselves eventually secularized it into a form of mass spectacle and entertainment. Scholarly discourse over the course of the century was thus an ongoing attempt to align the range of attitudes toward gladiature with the prevailing images of each culture as a socio-political whole, and to coherently account for the presence and meaning within such structures of a violence whose particular abhorrence was also gradually being refined.

Early approaches to civilization: the exception of the Greeks

In 1730, Scipione Maffei published his magisterial *Compleat History of the Ancient Amphitheatres, more peculiarly regarding the architecture of those buildings, and in particular that of Verona*; his first chapter was devoted to questions *Of the Original of Gladiators at Rome*. The original, he felt, was not Roman; however, the bulk of his argument actually focused upon refuting any floating speculation that the origin of gladiature could have been Greek. In this endeavour he was forced to confront the problem presented by the funeral of Patroclus as described in the *Iliad*, since Achilles' slaughter of Trojan prisoners of war in honour of Patroclus' death resembled all too closely the kind of funerary human sacrifice from which gladiature was presumed to have evolved. This conflict Maffei attempted to resolve by introducing a conceptual distinction between 'very ancient' gladiature, conducted in a context of funerary ritual, and later gladiature as institutionalized mass entertainment. Later gladiatorial spectacle could be securely and exclusively associated with Rome, and Maffei was thus able to detach the abhorrent quality of gladiatorial violence as entertainment from the essential meaning of funerary gladiature in other, earlier contexts. Thus the questioning of the origin of gladiature during this period was far more concerned with inscribing a site of signification than pursuing a fixed point in historical space and time; in fact, gladiature – and especially the relevant attitudes ascribed to the three cultures primarily involved with it – was employed, by Maffei and by others, as an important criterion in establishing the map of boundaries between Greeks, Etruscans, and Romans, in part through invoking what could be interpreted about the 'spirits' of such nations precisely through their abhorrence or enjoyment of gladiatorial violence.

The ultimate origin of gladiature Maffei was content to consign to vagary, provided that it did not touch Greece; following Vitruvius, Maffei claimed that the origins of gladiature were simply 'ancient Italian', "handed down to the Inhabitants of *Italy* by their Fore-fathers" (7, emphasis in the original). However, if the progenitors of gladiature were lost in the mists of ancient Italy, its introduction at Rome was assuredly presaged by the Etruscan form of the practice. Contra Lipsius, for Maffei the important quotation in the *Deipnosophistae* was Nicolas of Damascus' claim that the Romans borrowed the practice of gladiature from the Etruscans, "among whom it was a peculiar and immemorial Institution" (7). He suggestively elided the distinction between mysterious 'ancient Italians' and Etruscans, by citing Etruscan tomb paintings, a collection of which had recently been gathered at Florence, as a primary source for gladiature's antiquity, describing "the Figures upon the sepulchral Monuments of the *Hetrurians*, nothing being oftener seen there than such kinds of Combats, and Men in the Attitudes of killing one another with Knives and Swords, and other various and uncommon Weapons" (7). Maffei is here suggestive rather than explicit, but the association of ideas is clear: the 'peculiar and immemorial' Etruscan relationship to gladiature was demonstrably proven by the national character of baroque violence represented in their funerary art.

Of the Etruscan practice of gladiature or of the Etruscan culture itself, Maffei had no more to say except that the Etruscans, lest anyone think otherwise, "had not their Institutions and Arts from the Grecians" (8). He later went on to introduce his architectural study by demonstrating that the form of the Roman amphitheatre, being elliptical rather than strictly circular, could not usefully be considered to be based upon the classical form of the semi-circular Greek theatre, despite the fact that 'amphitheatre' is a Greek word (21-2); the innovation of the architectural form he ascribed to the Augustan period in valourizing language: "In *Rome* therefore, and not in *Greece*, did the Amphitheatres begin, and may boast of the Glory in having the Founder of the *Roman* Empire for its first Inventor" (23).

However, as has already been pointed out, Maffei was compelled to account for the funeral of Patroclus. He accepted the connection, first suggested by Servius in the fourth century AD, between funerary human sacrifice and gladiature, but Maffei equivocated over several points, and made an altogether jumbled argument that reads as an uncertain attempt to associate the Greeks with a higher degree of humanity in any way possible. The full passage reads as follows:

> "A Motive in Religion paved the way first to the celebrated
> Institution, namely that most ancient Opinion, That the Souls of the
> Deceased, who were in a certain Manner deified by leaving the
> Body, delighted in human Blood; and that the Slaughter of Men,
> by way of Sacrifice in Honour of them, rendered them propitious,
> or at least pleased, and their Wrath appeas'd, as if slain to satisfy
> their Revenge. This occasioned great Cruelty to fall on the
> Prisoners of War: And as to its Antiquity, in one of Homer's most
> considerable Poems, we find that Achilles slew Twelve of the
> young Trojan Nobility at the Pile of Patroclus: But as *Servius*
> observes, the massacring of Men in such a shocking Manner,
> appearing too inhuman, they thought fit to introduce a Practice
> something like it, by way of Combat " (4).

The sense of the passage is generally suggestive and indirect. The funeral

of Patroclus is referred to explicitly only in reference to its antiquity, reinforcing

Maffei's earlier claim that the original context of gladiature must be seen as

unimaginably ancient. The swift turn to the Servian argument, however, seems to

frame the funeral of Patroclus as an example of a practice found shocking and

inhumane, ostensibly here by the ancient Greeks. From this image of origin,

Maffei then marshalled a string of evidence to argue for the essential

incompatibility of Greece with gladiature:

> "Dyillus from Athenaeus writes, that Cassander ... caused four
> soldiers to combat with one another; yet this is thought no proof
> that the Gladiators came originally from Greece to Rome. (...)
> [N]either did the Usage begin in Greece, much less take Footing
> there, by way of Publick Shew. We know very well, that among so
> many Kinds of Exercises at the Olympick Games, there never were
> any gladiatory Combats. [...] We know from Livy, that Perseus the
> last King of Macedon, was the first who instituted Gladiators in
> Greece, whom he made come from Rome thither, more for the
> Terror than Pleasure of that People, who were unaccustomed to
> such kinds of Shews; nor for all that, did that King continue them
> there, nor after him were they established in any Part of *Greece*;
> for if so, we should have had frequent mention thereof in Writers;
> nay, such kinds of Representations would be seen remaining on the
> *Grecian* Monuments of Antiquity" (5-6).

Maffei's representation of the Greek relationship to gladiature and the

practice of funerary human sacrifice purported to be its earliest form, therefore,

actually traced out a basic version of a thoroughly Eliasian motif of 'civilizing' as

a directional process through a brief contrast of two events in ancient Greek

history. Although the funeral of Patroclus was taken as evidence that funerary

human sacrifice, the proto-form of gladiature, had been practiced in the heroic

period in Greece, Greek culture did not in Maffei's view take the crucial step from funerary sacrifice to funerary gladiature. Moreover, when Roman-style gladiature was eventually introduced in Greece, the Greek people recoiled from it in horror and never adopted the practice. Maffei thus inscribed an account of the relation of Greeks to gladiature that would, in fact, persist as scholarly consensus into the twentieth century. While this last claim was amended before the end of the eighteenth century – scholarship came, however grudgingly, to accept that the Greeks did appear to have practiced gladiature at least after the Roman conquest - the conviction that it was at least unpopular with the enlightened Greeks would remain a truism for just under two hundred years after the publication of Maffei's text. The Greeks of the post-classical period, of the period following the birth of democracy and the revolution in aesthetics and philosophy which was so highly valourized in Enlightenment-era Europe and later, are assumed here to have civilized beyond such barbarisms as gladiatorial combat, and even stringently and spontaneously and in a sense naturally resistant to its 'Terror'.

When contrasted to this vehement construction of an ideal of Greek abhorrence of the practice, the path of the development of gladiature among the Romans appears instead as a symptom of Roman decline. Maffei accepted the 264 BC date of the funeral of Iunius Brutus Pera as the first time that "the Solemnity of gladiator Shews" (11) was introduced at Rome, and did not contest the funerary nature of the original practice, both at its non-Roman root and at its first moment of entry into the Roman sphere. However, his description of its eventual development "beyond measure" (10) within Roman culture briefly outlined a significantly different course of events than had taken place in Greece:

> "From the Honours done the Dead, these Things, as *Tertullian*
> says, were immediately applied to the Living also; for as they were
> exceedingly agreeable to the Multitude, those who were advanced
> to certain eminent Stations in the State, began to have them
> celebrated at their own Charge, and that by way of Present or
> Retribution to the People, for having elected them; hence they were
> call'd *Donatives*, or Gifts" (11).

This passage marks the first appearance of the crowd. Maffei's brief

statements here are worth dwelling upon for numerous reasons. Maffei's

interpretation of the Latin word *munus* as referring to a gift or donation sketches

in the structure of a particular relation between the multitude and the ruling class

enacted through the institution of gladiature. Here, the state and its eminent

members are represented as generous and paternalistic, offering gladiatorial

combats to the people freely and without conflict, though without sharing in the

crowd's uncivilized pleasure; translating *munus* as 'gift', and casting the offering

of gladiatorial spectacles as a sort of benevolent reward for electoral support,

represents the relation between social classes at Rome as comparatively

harmonious. It is interesting that Maffei both translated it as gift and interpreted it

as a donative given independently and relatively innocently by the Republican

aristocracy to the crowd. Within fifty years it would appear unthinkable to

perceive gladiature as a site of cohesion between Roman social classes,

particularly during the Republic when the crowd still possessed political power as

an electorate. By the end of the century, the Roman aristocracy's dependence

upon the Republican crowd's votes, and the role played by gladiature and other

spectacles within the political economy, would be written much differently.

Notable also is the manner in which gladiature appears unproblematically as 'exceedingly agreeable to the Multitude' at Rome, in contrast to the terror which it inspired in the socially unified Greeks. The intersection of violence and pleasure was overall considered intelligible, if not rational, under two sets of circumstances: the extremely ancient history of an otherwise eventually 'civilized' society, or among the multitude, as this group is distinct from 'those who were advanced to certain eminent Stations in the State'. The alignment of these two registers begins to construct the image of the barbarian in terms of cultural primitivism, on the one hand, and of social inferiority on the other. It is a superimposition of discourses which will eventually disaggregate into separately defined rationalizations of race and class, between which the structure of critical relation will be seen to shift continuously. At this point, however, the cathexis of violence and pleasure is a totalizing signifier of a lesser civility, and while Maffei accorded the Greeks the capacity to civilize over time, the prevailing theme of Roman culture in eighteenth century historiography was one of decline.

'Spirit' and the nation

Scholarly texts of the later eighteenth century impart the impression that the abhorrence of the violence/pleasure cathexis which had been articulated through recourse to Greece was by this point a truism; historiographic focus shifted to examine more closely that which has been identified as abhorrent, and in a tentative way, to begin to account for the presence and persistence of this specifically abhorrent violence within a great civilization whose decline must urgently be comprehended and avoided in the present. Within this slightly altered perspective, Roman gladiature was increasingly represented as categorically distinct from the funerary ritual practices of deeper antiquity, at the least connected only nominally, and at the most unrelated. The gloomy, inherently violent melancholy of the Etruscan spirit may have accounted for the persistence of gladiature into the third century BC, when the Romans were generally thought to have adopted it, but the increasingly heavy lines being drawn between the various groups of ancient peoples and simultaneously the class divisions of ancient societies slowly produced a re-ordering of the field. This detachment of gladiature from the conditionally 'legitimate' originating context of very ancient funerals developed in tandem with an ever-closer alignment of gladiature with the pleasure of the crowd. Consequently, what we observe during this period is the development of the 'notion of the nation' in the epistemic shift to historico-political discourse, through the idiom of 'spirit'; the nation emerges along the planes of race and class as an effect of the gradual re-ordering of the classical table of knowledge into something more hierarchical, based upon the elaboration of a moral discourse of violence/pleasure which was deployed as an organizing and determinative criterion of 'civilization'.

Scholarly conversation on gladiature's origin was sometimes inconsistent in its particulars; for instance, despite a growing consensus around Etruscans as the antecedents to the Roman adoption of the practice, as late as 1792 Hereford (*The History of Rome, from the Foundation of the city by Romulus, to the death of Marcus Antoninus*) wrote that "the combats of gladiators had been communicated from Greece and Asia to Italy" (vol. II:83). However, writing some thirty years after Maffei, Winckelmann's approach in the *Geschichte der Kunst des*

Alterthums (History of Ancient Art) deepened the perceived network of relations

between Greece, Rome and Etruria in a manner that set the three cultures against

each other on the subject of gladiature. In arguing for the superiority of Greek art,

Winckelmann employed gladiators to construct and defend a fundamental point of

distinction, this time between Greeks and Romans:

> "This [the kindly natures, gentle hearts, and joyous disposition of
> the Greeks] is more easily understood by contrasting the Greeks
> with the Romans. The inhuman, sanguinary games, and the
> agonizing and dying gladiators, in the amphitheatres of the latter,
> even during the period of their greatest refinement, were the most
> gratifying sources of amusement to the whole people. The
> former, on the contrary, abhorred such cruelty [...] The Romans,
> however, finally succeeded in introducing them even at Athens"
> (288-9).

Here again is the claim that the ancient Greeks – and, by extension, all the

many and desirable virtues of their culture as it was constructed during this period

– had no truck with gladiature. Winckelmann's specific insistence upon a Greek

'abhorrence of such cruelty', and the explicit inflection of this abhorrence as a

mark of refinement and gentleness, deliberately connected an abhorrence of

gladiatorial violence with a state of higher civilization. Moreover, the unilateral

contrast between Greek abhorrence and Roman gratification presents a dichotomy

of attitudes to gladiatorial violence which is underscored by the cited Roman

introduction of gladiatorial games at Athens. The image of the despoiling Roman

influence at the foremost city of the classical Greek world gestures toward the

'fear of decivilizing' as an idea already operative within the discursive

development of 'civilization' as a construct.

The ultimate source of decivilizing, however, was already being vaguely located beyond the boundaries of the problematically violent Roman sphere, and discursive conditions were being set that would eventually permit the barbarism of gladiature to be filtered through the developing antithesis to civilization, of which Etruria was the first iteration. The broad contours of the general image of ancient Etruria were sharpened by Winckelmann's summation of the 'Etruscan disposition', with much the same totalizing approach that he took to the Greek spirit; however, Winckelmann's stark assessment of the Etruscan character drew an image very different from the noble simplicity of Greece. Winckelmann read in Etruscan art an essentially 'melancholy' and 'violent' nature, and explicitly based this claim on exactly two Etruscan practices: soothsaying, and "the sanguinary fights at their burials and in their arenas, which were first practiced among them, and afterwards introduced also by the Romans. These combats were an abhorrence to the refined Greeks (...) Hence on Etruscan sepulchral urns are commonly seen representations of bloody fights over the dead. Roman funerary urns, on the contrary, rather have pleasing images, because the greater number were probably executed by Greeks" (226-7). Winckelmann's arguments would contribute significantly to the later nineteenth-century claim, which in turn would persist well into the twentieth, that the ultimate origin of gladiature was to be found in Etruria. More importantly at this point, Winckelmann's statements about gladiature contributed to a refinement of the eighteenth century's 'broad sense of nation', the "vague, fluid, shifting notion of the nation, this idea of a nation which does not stop at the frontiers but which, on the contrary, is a sort of mass of individuals who move from one frontier to another, through States, beneath States, and at an infra-State level ..." (*SMBD* 142). The civilizing spirit of Greece was as important to Winckelmann's perspective as the decivilizing influence of Etruria, and by extension to the development of the idea of the 'nation' as both an essential group identity (i.e. 'Greeks') and as an entity that exceeds and cuts across State political structures (i.e. 'the civilized nobility (of Greeks as well as others)'). Rome, as will be seen below, was situated almost as a crucially contested site between those two poles of Greek and Etruscan influence; by the end of the eighteenth century, the splitting of the Roman cultural whole was more or less complete, and the discourse of the nineteenth century was shaped around the aggressively dichotomous alignment of the Roman aristocracy with the essential civilization enshrined by the Greeks, while the Roman lower classes were elided – sometimes literally – with the foreign barbarian embodied by the Etruscans.

To this end, the moment of gladiature's first appearance within the borders of Roman culture began to attract attention, and a more complex perspective on the significance of gladiature in Rome, and what could be judged thereby about Roman civilization, gradually arose. The attempt to account for the development of gladiature at Rome did not consistently refer the Roman practice of gladiature to the deep antiquity of funerary ritual. Montesquieu's comments on the practice were few and brief, but he did manage in very few words to weave Roman gladiature into his core thesis that the strength of the Roman army and their 'warlike nature' were the primary causes of both their greatness and their eventual downfall: "[The Romans'] chief care was to examine in what way the enemy might be superior to them, and they corrected the defect immediately. They became accustomed to seeing blood and wounds at their gladiatorial exhibitions, which they acquired from the Etruscans" (36). The prevalent trope of Roman gladiature was the theme of decline, and this occasionally eclipsed the relative legitimacy of funerary ritual which had anchored the narrative of Greek abhorrence; the decline of Rome was such a dominant idea that gladiatorial combat gradually became elided with social decay, such that the invocation of an image of an original, less abhorrent form of gladiature was actually periodically dispensed with in favour of an emphasis upon a straightforward correlation between the practice of gladiature and the fall of Rome.

The occasional disconnection of the history of Roman gladiature from the, as it were, prehistory of funerary human sacrifice also took other forms. Oliver Goldsmith, whose *The Roman History, from the foundation of the city of Rome, to the destruction of the western Empire* appeared in print a few years after Winckelmann's study, was among the few scholars who accepted the suggestion in the *De Regibus* fragment attributed to Suetonius that the practice of gladiature in the Roman world dated back to the mythological founding of the city some eight centuries before Christ, and was thus a feature of the monarchic period. Goldsmith's version of the feast that preceded the abduction of the Sabine Women included gladiatorial entertainments (14-5), with no pretext of a funeral. Further, Tarquinius Priscus, the Etruscan king of Rome mentioned in the *De Regibus*, was seen by Goldsmith's readers to build an amphitheatre as a demonstration of the equity and justice of his reign; this was constructed "for the combats of men and beasts, which were afterwards carried to an horrid excess. (...) – How different these from the combats of a later age, in which two thousand gladiators were seen at once expiring, or dead upon the stage!" (35-6).

Gibbon's seminal *The Decline and Fall of the Roman Empire*, published to widespread acclaim on the eve of the French Revolution (1776-1788), made generally little of the amphitheatre in Roman society, referring to the institution and its crowds only glancingly. Gibbon, indeed, preferred to skirt the subject of gladiators; reference to them is unavoidable in his passages on the emperor Commodus, but his handful of additional mentions are perfunctory, and his excursus on the Colosseum in the context of the reign of Carinus focused exclusively upon beast hunts, passing over gladiators in silence. The figure of the Roman crowd, whether inside the amphitheatre or in other spaces, is similarly cast into the background of Gibbon's narrative, with only the barest trace of the decadent, demanding, idle populace that was already developing in the works of contemporaries.

Pollice verso and the political exclusion of the barbarous crowd

By the final decades of the eighteenth century, the character and the position of the Roman crowd came into increasingly sharpened focus, and its attitude to gladiature was the primary site through which the crowd was interpreted and inscribed. In 1783, Adam Ferguson took the trope of decline and applied it specifically to the pre-imperial period in *The Progress and Termination of the Roman Republic*; Ferguson saw the emergence of imperial government at

Rome as a descent into monarchy, and 'the People' as instrumental in the erosion

and collapse of republican governing structure. This central argument focused

very clearly upon an image of Rome that perceived the republican nobility as a

'nation within the State', as discussed above; moreover, this distinction not only

construed the 'nation of the nobility' as the true site of civilization against the

barbarism of the lower classes, but pointed to gladiature as a key signifier of that

posited essential difference. His first mention of gladiature in the first volume

took care to distinguish the pleasure of the crowd in gladiatorial violence from the

original intentions of the mid-Republican aristocracy regarding the earliest known

introduction of gladiature in 264 BC; while gladiatorial combats were "the

favourite entertainments of the People", Ferguson mixed his citations of ancient

authors to co-opt the 'horror' felt by the Greeks at their first encounter with

gladiature and ascribe it to the patricians of the third century:

> "Such exhibitions ... were first introduced in the interval between
> the first and second Punic wars, by a son of the family of Brutus, to
> solemnize the funeral of his father. Though calculated rather to
> move pity and cause horror, than to give pleasure; yet, like all
> other scenes which excite hopes and fears, and keep the mind in
> suspense, they were admired by the multitude, and became
> frequent on all solemn occasions or festivals." (vol. 1:106).

Ferguson further vilified the nature of the crowd's "cruel and barbarous"

pleasure in gladiatorial violence in terms which specifically isolated it from

modernity. The crowd's distasteful and unseemly interest was offensive, and

"must create so much disgust and horror in the recital"; moreover, the crowd's

pleasure was taken as categorically distinct from any modern comparanda, as "the

Romans were more intoxicated than any people in modern Europe now are with the beating of bulls, or the running of horses, probably because they were more deeply affected, and more violently moved" (Ferguson vol. III p.32)

As he traced out the termination of the Republic, Ferguson wove together the tropes of socio-political decline, the idleness that came of wealth, and the barbaric enjoyment of gladiature into a causal model of decivilizing. The benevolent political economy of equal exchange, wherein Maffei saw the Republican aristocracy gifting the multitude with gladiature in return for votes already cast, was by this late point in the century remodelled in favour of a much bleaker image of the Republican state and the figuration which related the crowd to the ruling class. In the middle Republic, treated in the first volume, Maffei's blameless gift of gladiature was transformed by Ferguson into a political investment of the upper class in voting futures, as "the profits of a first appointment were lavished on public shews, fights of gladiators, and baiting of wild beasts, to gain the People in their canvas for further preferments". This sort of political bribery, seen as a species of the general parasitism of the crowd upon the state, "tended, in the highest degree, to corrupt the People, and to render them unworthy of that sovereignty which they actually possessed in the prevalence of the popular faction" (Ferguson vol. 1: 391). At this point, the decline of the crowd was still represented as a historical process, the descent of an originally unified Roman political body into separate factions wherein gladiature operated as an agent of decivilizing; by the following century the crowd would be represented in more fixed and less charitable terms. Moreover, the corruption of gladiature and the distasteful pleasure it evoked was a decivilizing force which struck directly at the value of political franchise, and thus woven intimately into the decline of the

republican system into the monarchic structures of empire. By the Augustan

period, which was still nominally Republican in many of its forms, Ferguson's

narrative represents the degeneration of the crowd as completed, in terms that

echoed Juvenal's bread and circuses:

> "Such had been the arts by which candidates for public favour, in
> the latter times of the republic, maintained in the capital the
> consideration they had gained by their services on the frontiers of
> the empire; and the continuance of these arts had now the more
> effect, that the people, who still had a claim to this species of
> courtship, were become insensible to any other privilege of Roman
> citizens, and were ready to barter a political consequence, which
> they were no longer fit to enjoy, for a succession of sports and
> entertainments that amused their leisure, or for a distribution of
> bread, which, without the usual and hard conditions of industry or
> labour, helped to give them subsistence" (vol. III:353).

The passage highlights several points that both characterize contemporary

discourse and, to a lesser extent, foreshadow certain discursive developments

which would typify scholarly opinion in the following century. Not only is the

notion of 'national spirit' here being tentatively divided along class lines (in an

image which, as the language of class struggle emerges, can be seen increasingly

to locate that spirit in the 'former times of the republic', as an original unity or

monad which declined and fell, as it were, into the sociopolitical changes of the

late republic), but those divisions – the 'nature' of the crowd, seen as increasingly

distinct from the nature of the ruling class – were correspondingly perceived as

historicized phenomena, produced in the context of power relations between the

two broadly defined groups. The crowd *became* insensible to any other privilege

of Roman citizens, no longer fit to enjoy political consequence, as a result of the 'arts' applied against them by candidates for public favour. This move to map a moral language over a political subtext – to elide the distinction between the crowd's pleasure in violence, and its capacity for, or right to, political power – was a key strategy of historico-political discourse which begins to find significant expression at this point. The history of nobility's right that, over the course of the eighteenth century, used Roman historiography as a myth-historical framework of expression is here seen incubating the network of associations that align violence with barbarism and, more importantly, civilization with the abhorrence of violence, and connecting those associations with a deeper set of implications about who had the right to wield power, and how that right could be signified.

Even the encyclopaedic tendencies so characteristic of the eighteenth century gave central and definitive expression to the contemporary abhorrence for gladiature in terms of both the account of its origin and the unseemly pleasure of the lower classes at Rome. Contemporary with Ferguson, the 1788 edition of Lempriere's *Classical Dictionary* returned to the attempt to represent and account for the origins of gladiature. The entry for *Gladiatorii Ludi*, in reference to the pivotal 264 B.C. event of the Brutus brothers, did ascribe to original gladiature a funerary context, and referred to the Servian argument that gladiature evolved as an attempt to soften and refine the perceived cruelty of human sacrifice. However, the posited relative 'humanity' of original gladiature, beyond being divorced from any reference to a specific cultural context, was by this point treated with considerable scepticism; the Servian claim of humanity may have served Maffei well in his defense of the Greeks sixty years earlier, but by Lempriere's time, when the boundary between Greeks and gladiature required less vigilant policing,

the notion that gladiature could be connected to civilized attitudes to violence

could only be expressed in a heavy irony taken straight from Tertullian:

> "It was supposed that the ghosts of the dead were rendered
> propitious by human blood; therefore at funerals, it was usual to
> murder slaves in cool blood. In succeeding ages, it was reckoned
> less cruel to oblige them to kill one another like men, than to
> slaughter them like brutes, therefore the barbarity was covered by
> the specious shew of pleasure, and voluntary combat" (Lempriere
> 313).

Moreover, Ferguson's Juvenalian theme of the degeneration of the

crowd's political authority into a base appetite for pleasure became increasingly

focused on the dramatic image of the *pollice verso*, the 'turning of thumbs'

whereby the crowd in the amphitheatre pronounced popular judgment upon the

fate of an individual gladiator. Lempriere's *Dictionary* invoked the crowd in this

capacity, representing the outcome of all gladiatorial combats as dependent upon

"the leave and approbation of the multitude" (313); Hereford's language, a few

years later, was more stringent and excoriating. In his text, the Romans "were

long accustomed to the habits of slaughter; not only in foreign war and civil

commotion, but in their daily amusements, they exulted in the sufferings of the

human race"; the 'admiration of this savage practice' was such that "if exhausted

with fatigue and faint from wounds, a luckless combatant implored the mercy of

his adversary, too often the theatre resounded with the cries of the frantic

spectators, "Let him receive the sword"; and their sanguinary sentence instantly

was sealed in the blood of the wretched suppliant" (Hereford vol. 2:83-4). The

final stage in the development of the eighteenth century image of the Roman crowd's political corruption was thus the perversion of the popular vote; spoilt by idleness and luxury, insensible to the higher civility of either the exemplary Greeks or the Roman upper classes, the sovereignty which the crowd once possessed and of which it had grown unworthy was fit now only to pronounce sentence upon the fate of gladiators in the arena.

Therefore, what we see throughout the eighteenth century is the emergence of a discourse wherein the crowd is excluded from 'civilization' on the basis of a link being forged between attitude to violence and the 'right' or 'capacity' to exercise legitimate political power. This is argued from two connected perspectives: on the one hand, the increasingly hierarchical ordering of the historical world around the nascent construct of the nation produced an origin story for the cathexis of violence and pleasure, which associates such an 'immoral' attitude with a proto-racializing inscription of the Etruscans as a nation of essentially barbarous character; on the other hand, the 'original barbarity', emanating from outside the Roman social body, is refracted in the lower classes, and eventually specified as not merely a 'melancholy violence of spirit' but as a source of active corruption of political participation, and therefore as grounds for the exclusion of the lower classes from the political state. At the same time, the exigencies of the historicist dimension of discourse that had upset the mathetic perspective - the Gibbonian motif of decline, a master trope of classical scholarship that embodied the epistemic distinction between juridico-philosophical and historico-political discourse – problematized that strategy's representation of itself as an immutable right to power. The abhorrence of violence as a signifier of the civilized necessarily presumed – and, therefore, discursively produced - a violence that *could* threaten civilization. The crowd gradually emerged as an underclass whose relation to the ruling state power in antiquity was inscribed as increasingly politicized on two levels: one, the growing 'awareness' that the ruling class was compelled to court the urban crowd politically during the Republic and was subsequently compelled to keep them amused under the Empire, and two, the repeated return to the image of the *pollice verso* as a grotesque perversion of the franchise. Thus, the 'civilized nation' was bounded on two fronts; moreover, the relation between the civilized and the barbarous was already here inscribed as adversarial, in the sense that a constant threat to civilized order was to be read in the cathexis of violence and pleasure.

Violence, abhorrence, and the discourse of perpetual war

When read as a 'history of right', the early eighteenth-century phase of the historiography of gladiature clearly laid the foundation for the development of this particular discourse into a textual corpus which has historically denied power's association with violence, through the claim that power (which refers to itself as 'civilization') abhors violence. The emergence of the 'nobility' as the speaking subject of historico-political discourse, which "introduced into the great Statist organization of historical discourse this disruptive principle [of] the nation as subject-object" (*SMBD* 143), appeared over the course of the century as the contrasting figure to a construct of the barbarian that was produced through the alignment of the racially different with the socially inferior. Consequently, what we see in the eighteenth-century historiography of Roman gladiature was the opening phase of 'the nobility's' arrogation of the nation to itself via the emergent language of civilization. Viewed another way, the language of civilization was visibly influenced, even during this early period, by the discourse of struggle, conflict, and ultimately war, as 'civilization' appeared in the form of a beleaguered space, which must be defended from barbarians both outside and inside the state. In this particular historico-political discourse, abhorrence of violence was deployed from the beginning as a key sign separating the civilized from the barbaric.

The discourse of perpetual war, then, appeared in its essential form. The simple alliance of civilization with an attitude of abhorrence of violence also simultaneously constructed its own opposite: the identification or constitution of the crowd, through their pleasure in violence, as barbaric – or, rather, the limit-construct of the violence/pleasure cathexis as the ultimate sign of barbarism, which was then deployed as the great signifier of both certain other states and, crucially, of the crowd within the state. The association of the violence/pleasure cathexis with barbarism therefore connoted an incapacity to legitimately participate in politics – in other words, to possess and to exercise power; this further set up the crowd, on these bases, as an increasingly active threat to civilized socio-political order. The eighteenth century's discursive emphasis upon groups as 'whole entities', as essential spirits which were not truly vulnerable to the influences of other groups, meant that decivilizing was not yet the well-articulated anxiety that it would become in the following century; nevertheless, the rising profile of the image of the *pollice verso* foreshadowed the concomitant

rise of decivilizing as a preoccupying theme.

Chapter 4: Imperita Multitudo

Struggle, utopia, and origin

Over the course of the eighteenth century, classical historiography's image

of gladiature came to crystallize around the central problem of violence and its

attendant attitudes on the spectrum of abhorrence to pleasure. This theme, in turn,

was used as a key signifier in the 'ordering of civilizations', especially as the

mathetic framework associated with juridico-philosophical discourse gradually

gave way to a more historico-political approach to history, wherein the re-

ordering of antiquity into something like a hierarchical arrangement of

civilizations was mobilized in no small part by the perceived role of gladiature in

various ancient cultures. The increasing preoccupation with gladiatorial violence

troubled the previously stable (and relatively static) construct of 'national spirit',

which depended upon the apprehension of civilization(s) as indivisible entities:

the previous chapter has traced out the eighteenth century's attempt to reconcile

the tendency to conceive of an ancient people – Greek, Roman, Etruscan, or any

other – as either civilized or not, with the problematic evidence that gladiature

was practiced by any and all of these groups. By the end of the century, the

discursive shifts that emerged to resolve the apparent contradiction were based

upon three central ideas: the introduction of the notion of decline (or

'decivilizing' in Eliasian terms) as a historicized evolution of the formerly static

conception of 'civilization'; the emergence of the concept of the 'nation' as an

entity essentially distinct from the State, with signs of an identification of the

nation with the nobility; and lastly, the advent into historical discourse of the theme of struggle, focused upon the narration of a conflict between a variable,

unstable iteration of Foucault's 'two races', whether of race or of class. Along

these three lines, the historiographic image of gladiature would begin to search for

an external locus of origin (to which the impetus of decivilizing could be traced);

it would lay increasing emphasis of meaning upon both the abhorrence and

pleasure of gladiature's violence, as a critical sign for distinguishing the civilized

from the barbarous and, by eventual extension, the (noble) nation from the State;

it would communicate a growing sense that the drama of struggle should be

staged in the political arena, centred upon the image of the *pollice verso* as an

indication that the barbarity of gladiature perhaps signified a deeper, more

essential barbarism from which the nation, the nobility, the civilized – and the

possession and exercise of political power - should all be excluded.

Nineteenth century classicism would bear the fruit of all of these seeds.

During this period, scholarship on gladiature took the standing preoccupation with

the problem of violence and pleasure and specified the abhorrence it inspired to a

far more conflict-driven narrative of class politics in the late Republic and early

Empire, while scholars at the same time developed a far more fixed and racialized

notion of the cultural context of gladiature's origin. In effect, the nobility's history

of right took up the theme of struggle as its narrative basis: the destabilization of

the once-fixed order of the Enlightenment mathesis, troubled from within by the

directional historicism of Gibbon and his contemporaries, prepared the ground for

a version of the story of Rome which ascribed the great decline to the pernicious

influence of the barbarian, and thus was able to inscribe 'the nation' as locked in a losing struggle to defend itself and the civilization which it embodied. The notion that Elias termed 'decivilizing' functioned within historico-political discourse in its most naked and explicit form during this period, as the shifting construct of civilization was constantly re-inscribed in terms of its relation to the equally mobile construct of barbarism. What had previously been treated as whole entities defined by spirit were increasingly fissured into smaller groups within increasingly complex relations, structured along new lines of race and class. The language of struggle emerged fully, and the nobility's self-representation as the site of civilization was inscribed no longer in splendid and essential distinction from the barbarous, but locked in continuous defensive conflict with barbarism in its many-headed forms – and the semiotic complex of 'decivilizing' signified the threat of a barbarian victory. As this discourse of struggle rose to ascendancy, the emphasis laid upon attitudes to violence was correspondingly increased.

The great theme of classical historiography in the nineteenth century was its inheritance from Gibbon: the 'decline and fall', a trope in the construct of civilization which has been described as "irresistible" to successive classical scholars "because ... the spectacle of a great civilization collapsing into oblivion seemed in some way to offer instruction for those who feared the loss of their own civilization" (Bowersock 29). Post-Gibbon – and, not coincidentally, post-Revolution - the instructive or exemplary properties of Rome took on a new shade for contemporary scholars of history. In the previous century, Rome could be read as a 'historical laboratory of civilization' wherein the many signs of 'decivilizing' – including gladiature, and the cathexis of violence and pleasure that it presumed

– could inductively indicate an essentially decivilized spirit (which 'type' could

then be vigilantly searched out in the fledgling republics, as autopsies lead to a

summative pathology). The nineteenth century, however, construed decivilization

rather differently within the confines of classical historiography: as a signifier of

barbarism (and now, in a certain sense, as a metonym of the barbarian),

decivilization became a mobile element, the sign not simply of barbarism 'beyond

the borders' but of the infiltration of the barbarian into the civilized social body.

Within this altered discourse, the embedding of the notion of 'decline' within the

construct of civilization shifted from a possibility to a preoccupation.

It was a view of history that Foucault described as a "great dream of an

end":

> " In Classical [i.e. eighteenth century] thought, the utopia
> functioned rather as a fantasy of origins: this was because the
> freshness of the world had to provide the ideal unfolding of a table
> in which everything would be present and in its proper place, with
> its adjacencies, its peculiar differences, and its immediate
> equivalences (...) In the nineteenth century, the utopia is
> concerned with the final decline of time rather than with its
> morning: this is because knowledge is no longer constituted in the
> form of a table but in that of a series, of sequential connection, and
> of development: when, with the promised evening, the shadow of
> the denouement comes, the slow erosion or violent eruption of
> History will cause man's anthropological truth to spring forth in its
> stony immobility (...) The great dream of an end to History is the
> utopia of causal systems of thought, just as the dream of the
> world's beginnings was the utopia of the classifying systems of
> thought" (*OT* 262-3).

The advent of 'causal systems of thought' in historiography, such as those

derived from Gibbon, Montesquieu, and others, precipitated an increasingly

strong complex of associations between gladiature, the origin of the practice, and

the pursuit of the 'end' of the contemporary narrative of Roman history. As the 'history of right' subtext of classical historiography came ever more stringently to filter the barbarism of violence, and ever more strictly to prescribe the abhorrence of violence as a moral attitude signifying civilization, the image of the pleasure of gladiatorial violence came to be perceived as a key factor in what was viewed as the decline of Rome. Gibbon himself had not seen it as such.[xxiii] However, for many classical historians across the nineteenth century, gladiature appeared as a crucial element in the course of Roman history, particularly the shift – frequently seen, unsurprisingly, as a 'decline' – from republic to empire. The new imperative to inscribe and rationalize the end of the Republic/origin of the Empire conscripted gladiature from two linked angles. At one level, the active instrumentalization of gladiature as part of the cause of the 'end' of the republican political system meant that gladiature could be read as the 'origin' or root cause of Rome's ultimate decline, as the possibility of decivilizing was now perceived as a continuous threat to any civilization rather than an essential *a priori* characteristic of certain civilizations. On a deeper level, consequently, the linked story of gladiature's *ur*-origin – which was no less than the site of the articulation of the discourse of race struggle alongside and within the discourse of class struggle – was thus invoked as the original sign of the end of Rome. During this period, "European culture is inventing for itself a depth in which what matters is no longer identities, distinctive characters, permanent tables with all their possible paths and routes, but great hidden forces developed on the basis of their primitive and inaccessible nucleus, origin, causality, and history" (*OT* 251). Consequently, classical historiography responded to an imperative to ensure that the barbarian origin of gladiature and the cause or origin of Rome's 'fall' (wherein gladiature

was closely implicated) must support and accord with each other, as two

inseparable images directly linked across sub-divisions of race and class.

Within this structure of origin and end, of causality and root forces, the

language of 'decivilizing' or decline reached its most explicit articulation. Taken

straight as an Eliasian construct, 'decivilizing' may be highly suspect, given the

linear/progressive implications of Elias' wider model of the civilizing process;

Elias' attempt to rehabilitate 'process' in a macro-structural view of social change

by insisting upon the intellectual abandonment of teleology nevertheless

maintained the spectre of teleology in the directionality implied by the

civilizing/decivilizing dichotomy. However, as discussed in the Introduction,

Elias' notion of decivilizing is potentially extremely useful when taken not as a

legitimate critical construct in its own right, but instead as a descriptor of the

idiom wherein the 'nobility', in its self-designation as civilized, speaks of its

correspondingly designated barbarians. Classical historiography as historico-

political discourse had begun to define the figure of the barbarian by the

eighteenth century, but it was in the nineteenth that the civilized and the barbarous

polarized aggressively within the inscription of Roman antiquity, and moreover

that the particular relation of struggle between them clearly emerged. Where the

eighteenth century historiography of gladiature gradually shifted from

descriptions of the essential and immutable distinctions between whole cultural

groups, to the possibility of infiltration between such groups, nineteenth century

scholarship sought to contain the possibility of infiltration by insisting upon the rigidity of hierarchy between differently categorized groups, whether defined culturally by the nascent construct of race, or socially by a newly urgent discourse surrounding class. There emerged a political definition and isolation of the civilized nation (i.e. the nobility, as the speaking subject of history), which correspondingly produced an ordering of all other groups as barbarous along varying race/class lines. Within the boundaries of the State, the emphatic distinction, as Foucault claimed, was that of class; however, the construct of race adhered very closely to the rhetoric of origin, and operated powerfully within class-centric discourse.

This new apprehension of the potential permeability between groups – the new conception of civilization as vulnerable to barbarity as a 'decivilizing force' – entailed that causal systems of historical thought were invariably embedded within the nobility's narration of itself as the speaking subject of history, and by extension within its history of right. 'Decivilizing' was (and, to a different extent, still is) the idiom of expression for the dynamic of 'struggle' which underlies what Foucault termed the discourse of perpetual war: it signified (and signifies) the way in which that struggle was figured within the historical narrative of the nobility, as it articulated its own subjectivity and mythologized the basis of its will to power.

Foucault claimed that by the time the nineteenth century drew to a close, "...race struggle and class struggle became ... the two great schemata that were used to identify the phenomenon of war and the relationship of force within political society" (*SMBD* 19). By the early twentieth century, as will be examined, the 'two great schemata' of race and class struggle were very closely intertwined in the scholarly discourse of gladiature. The scholarship of the nineteenth century presents a study in the earlier oscillation between these two streams of historiographic thought. From the perspective of race struggle, gladiature's ultimate origins - its ur-origin, the initial context of its innovation – became an increasingly pressing point of inquiry. Where the eighteenth century had been content simply to accept gladiature's 'great antiquity', and to specify its origin no further than 'ancient Italy' in the endeavour to bracket out possible Greek forebears, the nineteenth century arrived at a firm, explicit, and specific consensus that gladiature did have a 'racial' origin, and that it was to be found among the Etruscans. The scholarship of gladiature's racial origin, in turn, took place within a wider context of fervid debate over the cultural and geographical origins of the Etruscans themselves (and thus over the terms which underpinned 'race' as a construct), as the interrogation of Etruscans as a 'race' came significantly to impact the meaning attributed to their practice of funerary gladiature, and more crucially the interpretation of how gladiature was transmitted from Etruria to Rome.

At the same time, nineteenth century classical historiography came to deeply integrate gladiature into an account of Roman history which imagined the political decline of the Republic and the associated corruption of the Empire as a phenomenon which was less about the national spirit, and far more attributable to the character of both the Roman 'mob', in accordance with contemporary thought surrounding urban masses, as well as the Roman patrician aristocracy. The pleasure of gladiature, which the Enlightenment had ascribed to Romans *en masse*, was now restricted to the mob and its inherent nature of cruelty and bloodlust; gladiature came to be read as an enticement and a means of controlling political opinion among the voting masses while the franchise yet lasted, and later as a pacifying force against the mob's perceived ever-present capacity to erupt in violence and rioting if not distracted and entertained at the amphitheatre. Within this narrative, the late Republican *populares* of the ruling class (more on this below) were excoriated in contemporary historical writing for exploiting what was seen as the mob's undeserved and directionless political power as a tool, with which the traditional governmental structures of the Republic were destabilized and transformed into a system that replaced oligarchy with autocracy. Once the deed was done, however, the ruling class of the Empire were curiously exempted from similar castigation: within the sociopolitical structure of empire, the disenfranchised mob was represented as a more monolithic and threatening entity, incapable of being meaningfully instrumentalized by even the more corrupt of their social betters, and thus simply a drain upon the imperial state and a constant potential source of violence in its own right, a sprawling underclass from which the upper-class bastion of civilization must be defended.

The parallel discourses of race and class described a network of boundaries that rationalized the presence and practice of gladiature within Roman society, in an overall strategy to exclude the barbarism of gladiature – and all the other, deeper barbarisms that gladiature entailed - from a sphere of civilization that, certainly by the middle of the nineteenth century, was represented solely by the speaking subject of the nobility. The racialization of what was perceived to be the uniquely Etruscan origin of gladiature cast the practice as inherently non-European, in a manner that shifted the 'meaning' of gladiature to a site of essential alienness, and interpreted its transmission and persistence within Roman society as unnatural. This unnaturalness of Roman gladiature was in turn explained through reference to the equally unnatural, uncivilized appetite of the mob for cruelty, bloodshed and violence, informed by a deep contemporary mistrust of 'the masses' inspired not a little by the French Revolution, the movements of 1848, and many other sociopolitical upheavals of the western world over the course of the century. Consequently, gladiature's functional role in the fall of the Republic and the emergence of the Empire gestured toward a cautionary example of imperial social politics which resonated deeply with contemporary European projects of empire. In this period, therefore, the historiography of gladiature mapped out civilization's others as an array of alien groups which threatened the state both from the outside and from below; the pleasure of gladiatorial violence was a sign of a deeper violence against social order, and to express an attitude of abhorrence of violence was in contrast an act in defence of civilization – further, the definitive sign of civilization itself.

Finally, within the idiom of decline or decivilizing as the language of the discourse of perpetual war, the nineteenth century's primary tropes can be thought of as fissure and increasing specification in the separation and ordering of groups. The 'obscure verticality of hidden and inaccessible forces' mobilized the language of 'civilization', and what we see over the course of this period is the withdrawal of civilization from the taxinomia into ever-more constricted definitions of the nation, which coextend not with the state as defined by 'spirit', but with the nobility as identified by abhorrence of violence.

Etruscomania and the roots of civilization

The first half of the nineteenth century was the high period of what has come to be labelled Etruscomania or, more recently, Etruscheria, a cultural phenomenon which had begun in the eighteenth century and which focused upon the practice of amateur excavations of Etruscan tomb fields and necropoleis for the recovery and avid acquisition of grave goods, especially the painted ceramic wares which were frequently found intact *in situ*. The occasionally ecstatic celebration of 'Etruscan' art, particularly painted vases, was during this period largely founded upon misrecognition; it was not until the first decade of the nineteenth century that the Abbé de Lanzi first pointed out that much of the material recovered from Etruscan tombs were actually imported objects of (Athenian) Greek manufacture, an observation which in its turn did not conclusively take hold for another fifty years. Before de Lanzi's findings, however, the desire for 'Etruscan' pottery was strong enough to prompt Wedgewood to found the Etruria factory in Staffordshire, producing inspired reproductions of the vases appearing from opened tombs.

Nineteenth-century Etruscomania constructed and propagated a complex image of the Etruscans as a particular avatar of civilization within the new discourse on the subject. Eighteenth-century notions of 'spirit' did not drop away entirely; Winckelmann's assessment of melancholy persisted, and Mommsen still referred to it nearly a century later.[xxiv] However, the perception of the Etruscans

during this period, within the clearer and more explicit articulation of the notion

of 'hierarchy' as applied to antiquity, placed them at a much higher level of

'civilization' than had previously been the case. On the one hand, the image of

Etruscan civilization was perplexed and inconsistent, characterized by the

coexistence of elements that appeared incompatible: a perceived hyper-religiosity

was now seen to coincide with a high degree of cultural development; their form

of government was tyrannical, but conceded as having been nonetheless

comparatively peaceful. On the other hand, this compelling mix of elements was

subsumed within a broader context of interpretation which specifically saw the

Etruscans as the first great civilization to arise within the geopolitical boundaries

of the West. In a certain sense, therefore, ancient Etruria represented yet another

reach towards origin within contemporary historico-political discourse: to the

nineteenth century, Etruria appeared as a kind of proto-civilization, a prehistoric

miasma from which the 'true' civilizations of antiquity, particularly Rome,

eventually arose, but which was excluded from the construct of civilization proper

on the basis of a few crucial perceived characteristics. Etruscans embodied for

nineteenth-century historians the exact space of 'barbarian civilization' defined by

Foucault – the sense in which the barbarian represents a threat to civilized order in

its manifestation of an alternate order (*SMBD* 196). Quoted in Betham (22), the

commentator on Micali put it best:

> The Quarterly Review for September, 1833, in the Notice of
> Micali's Work on the ancient Italian People, justly observes that
> "Etruria is one of the great, and, as yet, unsolved problems of
> ancient history." "It is clear," adds the judicious critic, "that before

the Romans, there existed in Italy a great nation, in a state of advanced civilization, with public buildings of vast magnitude, and works constructed on scientific principle, and of immense solidity, in order to bring the marshy plains of central and northern Italy into regular cultivation. They were a naval and commercial people, to whom tradition assigned the superiority, at one period, over the navigation of the Mediterranean. Their government seems to have been nearly allied to the oriental theocracies; religion was the dominant principle; and the ruling aristocracy the sacerdotal order. (...) What then was this nation, which – the earliest, as far as history, or even tradition, extends – established in the west an empire resembling those of India, Babylonia, Phoenicia, and Egypt? Was it a purely unmingled race? To what family of the nations did it belong? Did it originate, or receive from some foreign quarter, its remarkable civilization?"

Of the contemporary construct of race, Foucault claimed that the thinking of this period should not be confused with the more explicit and developed language of the twentieth century: "Although this discourse speaks of races, and although the term 'race' appears at a very early stage, it is quite obvious that the word 'race' itself is not pinned to a stable biological meaning. And yet the word is not completely free-floating. Ultimately, it designates a certain historico-political divide" (*SMBD* 77). Within the framework of classical historiography, the construct of race during the nineteenth century was articulated within the circulating language of civilization. 'Civilization' was articulated within an idiom which gestured toward public buildings, scientific principles, commerce – also of advance, of magnitude, of superiority and aristocracy. Even in these early representations, however, a parallel discourse of race was visibly emerging, which referred to the nation as a proto-racial construct; moreover, these broad sub-structural categories of what would become the 'stable biological underpinnings' of race were, within classical historiography, already closely associated with the conceptual separation of east and west, with the notion of 'purity', and with the increasingly pressing question of origin. Race interpolated the framework of the 'hierarchy of civilizations', grounded as it was in the newly historicist rhetoric of origin, in such a way that the barbarian began to connote 'the past' – and by extension, in Foucauldian terms, as the past of the civilized. It was within this context that Etruria, an 'older civilization' than Rome, was able to appear as both a civilization in some contested yet insistent sense, and yet also as barbarous in comparison to Rome.

Etruscan racial origin

This view of Etruria as both an advanced civilization, and yet barbarous, was cemented in both the scholarly and popular historical imagination by George Dennis, who in 1848 wrote the period's most widely read work of Etruscan history, *The Cities and Cemeteries of Etruria*. In his very first paragraph Dennis described the Etruscans as "a nation far advanced in civilization and refinement – that Rome, before her intercourse with Greece, was indebted to Etruria for whatever tended to elevate and humanize her, for her chief lessons in art and science, for the conveniences and enjoyments of peace, and the tactics and appliances of war – for almost everything in short that tended to exalt her as a nation" (1). Dennis' fuller characterization of Etruria, however, was more equivocal in nature, and was intent upon both restricting the possibility of association between Etruria and Rome, and more broadly upon circumscribing Etruscan 'civilization' as belonging ultimately to an alternate order, in an argument based – explicitly and tellingly – upon a doubled construct of barbarism as both primitive and non-western . If Etruria was to be considered to have

exerted a civilizing influence upon Rome in the earlier centuries of the Republic,

this influence was secondary to the greater impact of Greece, which persistently

represented the apex of civilization. Etruria's effect on Rome, as implied by

Dennis' list above, was limited to compartmentalized innovations in technology

and certain luxuries. Indeed, when measured directly against Greece, the national

character of Etruria appeared outright non-European in contrast, much as Micali

had stated earlier:

> "If we measure Etruria by the standard of her own day, we must
> ascribe to her a high degree of civilization – second only to that of
> Greece. It differed indeed, as the civilizations of a country under
> despotic rule will always differ from that of a free people. It
> resided in the mass rather than in the individual; it was the result of
> a set system, not of personal energy and excellence; its tendency
> was stationary rather than progressive; its object was to improve
> the physical condition of the people, and to minister to luxury,
> rather than to advance and elevate the nobler faculties of human
> nature. In all this it assimilated to the civilizations of the East, or of
> the Aztecs and Peruvians" (38).

The most popular and widespread view of the question held that the

Etruscans were originally emigrants from Lydia in Asia Minor; this was argued

on the basis of numerous ancient textual sources.[xxv] Opinion, however, was far

from unanimous. Micali was an isolated advocate of Etruscan autochthony;

Niebuhr, who will be discussed at greater length below, argued that the Etruscans

were originally an alpine tribe who conquered Etruria's original inhabitants, the

Tyrrhene-Pelasgi. Dennis noted Niebuhr's view as well as others, though he

himself was an adherent of the Lydian hypothesis, on the grounds that the

Romans considered the Etruscans to have been immigrants from the east (Tacitus,

Ann. IV 55) and Dennis considered the Romans unlikely to have got it wrong

(17). Niebuhr was further indebted to Schlegel (*Die Etrusken,* 1827), who argued

that the Tyrrhenians and Pelasgians were actually the same people, and further to

Muller, who accepted Schlegel's view that Tyrrhenians and Pelasgians were

eventually Tyrrhene-Pelasgi, but attempted to demonstrate that the Pelasgians

were themselves originally Lydians. Michelet (41) also agreed with this latter

view, although he argued rather that the Pelasgians had split into two groups,

eastern and western, and that the Etruscans derived from the eastern group which

had colonized Lydia and coastal Asia Minor. Pruner-Bey and Lagneau

provisionally concurred with Micali that the majority of the Etruscan population,

at least, was indigenous, but they also emphasized the presence of a 'Semitic

element' within the culture. Pelloutier and Durandi both claimed, on the basis of

perceived linguistic kinship, that the Etruscans were ancestrally Celto-German;

Betham felt the Etruscans were Celt-Iberian – in Dennis' words, Betham

"fraternize[d] them with his pets, the Irish" (Dennis 15). Gobineau, the nineteenth

century's dark doyen of racial degeneracy, conjectured a Slavonian origin. Gray,

along with Buonarotti and several others, was in favour of Egypt. Ellis claimed

the Etruscans were originally Armenian, although Ellis, it must be said, claimed

that many people were originally Armenian.[xxvi] The absurdity of the scope of the

debate was such that Dennis suggested that "a very pretty theory could be set up"

to identify the Etruscans as one of the lost tribes of Israel, and later said of the

human figures painted on the walls of the Tomb of the Triclinium "there is

something Jewish in the female profiles. Mark this, ye seekers of the Ten Tribes!"

(Dennis 329). In the main, however, it was the Lydian theory of origin which held the field, and as will be touched upon again in successive chapters, the perception of ancient Etruscans as an originally and/or essentially non-western group persisted into at least the middle of the twentieth century.

This wider context of debate over Etruscan racial origins, within which the few votes for autochthony on the European continent were overruled by a majority which advocated an eastern origin, exerted a major influence upon the inflected subtext of the Etruscan origins of gladiature and, in turn, upon the interpretation of gladiature within Roman practice. The radical indeterminacy which characterized the question of the 'Etruscan race', on the one hand, pointed to an undercurrent of anxiety surrounding the acceptable conditions of assigning 'civilization' as a designating term; while the celebrated material record of Etruscan culture made it difficult to deny Etruria's high level of cultural development along certain lines, other elements of Etruscan society conflicted with the contemporary construct of what comprised civilization proper. Attempts to definitively connect Etruria to a deeper racial category formed a fascinating discourse in their own right, as classical scholars struggled to reconcile Etruria's problematic defiance of categorization with powerful structures of thought surrounding which ancient groups were to be accepted as conforming with established images of civilization, and which were not.

Further, in terms of gladiature specifically, the general consensus around Etruria's identity as 'Oriental', compounded with the growing agreement that gladiature was originally and thoroughly Etruscan, came to be consistent with a broader rationalization of later Roman gladiature, in terms of how the practice crossed cultural boundaries and then persisted after the conquest of Italy. To a degree, earlier approaches to the classical world were yet maintained; Romantic historiography was in some senses as likely as its Enlightenment forebears to conceive of cultures as whole and distinct entities, and the pattern of separation between groups was still drawn on broadly cultural boundaries that delineated the emergent construct of race, as Foucault commented. However, the heightened development of a system of deeper racial categories – signalling in turn the greater contemporary significance of discourses of origin generally – entailed that gladiature could be, and was, considered an eastern practice: non-European, incompatible with (implicitly western) civilization, and an unnatural, introduced element within Roman society.

Etruscan gladiature and the racial 'origin' of civilization

Within this context, the eighteenth century's suggestive perception of Etruscan gladiature as a form of human sacrifice hardened into the nineteenth century's general consensus. This interpretation was in conformity with the wider perception of Etruscan culture as highly religious and, in some ways, 'death-obsessed', a view which could not have failed to be influenced in part by the fact that a significant proportion of Etruscan material culture known in the period was derived from tombs and necropoleis. However, the rationalization of original gladiature within the Etruscan context of funeral ritual was referred to Etruscan origins at a deeper level; gladiature was contingently acceptable as not necessarily abhorrent within the Etruscan context, but the contemporary abhorrence of gladiature was interpreted through reference to the Etruscans' radically indeterminate, but ultimately barbarian, status in a racial sense.

This fine distinction rested specifically on the delicate point wherein the construct of civilization intersected with the moral discourse surrounding the cathexis of violence and pleasure. 'Civilization', in its liminal manifestation among the Etruscans, raised certain questions which demanded the further specification of that construct: what resolved, as demonstrated by several sources examined below, was the consensus that gladiature as 'religious human sacrifice' was consistent with the restricted designation of civilization conferred upon Etruria because that particular context of gladiature was not predicated upon pleasure. Consequently, the meaning of gladiature for Etruria was debated as a vehicle for a deeper discussion of the terms upon which civilization and barbarism could be constituted and mutually excluded. Some scholars rationalized while others moralized, but all were intent upon essentially the same problem: the abhorrence of violence, as opposed to the pleasure of violence that (non-funerary) gladiature represented, as a sign of civilization which in turn implied power's right. Etruria functioned as an ambivalent, problematic middle ground – half civilized and half barbarous, an Eastern people in western lands, who over time both ruled and were ruled by Rome – wherein civilization's confrontation with the barbarian could be scrutinized.

1841 saw the publication of Elizabeth Caroline Johnstone Gray's *Tour to the Sepulchres of Etruria in 1839*, a personal memoir of Gray's sojourn through central Italy to pore over publically displayed collections of Etruscan artefacts and to excavate tumuli; the text furnished a record of the fashionable practices of

northern European tourism in the Mediterranean during this period, and was

written following an exhibition in Pall Mall of Greek and Etruscan objects in

eleven reconstructed chamber-tombs. Gray was keen to represent Etruscan

practices in a rational light, especially that of human sacrifice. Nowhere in her

lengthy memoir did she in fact mention gladiature by name, although she

arguably alluded to it in a description of the use of scenes on painted vases as a

documentary source for daily life in ancient Etruria: "Thus also are known the

whole of the public games: wrestling, cock-fighting, dice, casting lots, races by

chariots, horse or foot, and I say, Punch. From them also do we learn, that the

Etruscans had human sacrifices" (58-9). Whether or not Gray subscribed to the

perception of gladiature as a form of human sacrifice, human sacrifice among the

Etruscans was to be regarded as a civilized practice:

> "The Etruscans had human sacrifices, as is proved from ... vases,
> and from their sculpture: but only as the Greeks had before them,
> either to avert some great calamity, or to honour some chieftain's
> death. I should think also that they had been very rare, from the
> few ashes which have been found in the very many excavated
> tumuli" (71).

Human sacrifice among the Etruscans was therefore appropriately solemn

and exceptional, and not incompatible in this regard with the Etruscans' high

attainment of civilization. Notably, Gray here evoked Greek parallels; whereas in

the previous century there had been a tendency to dramatically contrast the two

cultures in familiar fashion, the absolute standard of Greece could be used to

buttress rhetorically the perception of an acceptable standard of rationality.

Gray's defense of Etruria encapsulated a view with plenty of contemporary adherents. Although Winckelmann's summary judgment of the Etruscans as 'melancholy' visibly persisted, William Betham's 1842 monograph *Etruria Celtica: Etruscan Literature and Antiquities Investigated; or, the language of that ancient and illustrious people compared and identified with the Ibero-Celtic, and both shown to be Phoenician*, praised Etruscan culture in language that was unequivocal: " The works of Etruscan art demonstrate high civilization, and a progress of the human mind, equal to the most elevated point of any age of Greek or Roman civilization, or even of modern improvement. [...] [I]ndeed all their remains – evince a highly civilized, refined, and glorious people, powerful both by sea and land" (19). Betham saw in the painted tombs "evidence of highly cultivated minds, and ... countenance of character, benevolence, and intelligence which only belongs to an elegant and highly improved state of society, the result of a long and uninterrupted enjoyment of security from the influence of exterior violence or civil convulsion, equal to the most tranquil period of Roman or British greatness; and evince the acquirement of perfection in the arts of civilization" (39).

Voices from within the academy, however, were formulating a slightly different argument. Karl Ottfried Muller's seminal *Die Etrusker* first appeared in 1826 and went into several subsequent editions over the nineteenth century. It was a multi-volume work of great erudition and detail, and in it Muller devoted a little less than two pages to the question of Etruscan gladiature. A century after Maffei, Muller reiterated the image of earliest gladiature as a practice that must have been widespread in ancient Italy; he cited Vitruvius' claim that the rectangular design

of Roman *fora* had arisen as a response to the occasional staging of gladiatorial

combats in forum centres, as evidence in support of the antiquity and ubiquity of

the practice. Muller also continued the paradoxical position of Greek exemplars

for gladiature, to which he alluded in a general fashion but which he also

immediately qualified as exhibitions of virtuosity of weapons use, never involving

a life or death contest. However, Muller's text equivocated somewhat in its

image of original gladiature in Italy, since in the same passage it specified the

practice as "a truly Etruscan game" (*ein echt Tuskisches Spiel*) (vol. IV 1:10).

It is here that Muller's text revealed a critical shift in the scholarly

approach to gladiatorial origin. The assignment of gladiators to Etruscans was

based upon the familiar reference to Nicolas of Damascus as well as to Isidore of

Seville, a seventh-century AD source whose etymological compendium includes

the claim that *lanista*, a word used to designate a trainer of gladiators, was

Etruscan – a language which in the nineteenth century was considered to be

indecipherable, if not entirely lost. Much more significant, however, was Muller's

insistence that the practice of gladiatorial combat within the context of funerary

ritual was specifically an Etruscan innovation. This claim is based upon the prior

assertion that Etruscans had long made a practice of human sacrifice; therefore,

the idea that the blood of vanquished gladiators would satisfy or feed the dead –

an idea transmitted, of course, by Tertullian – would have appeared to the

Etruscans, in Muller's words, as "very appropriate" (*sehr angemessenes*). Thus

the historiography of the nineteenth century began very early on to realign the

Enlightenment's system of boundaries between cultural topoi: gladiature became in no way Greek, but wholly and broadly Italian, although in turn specifically funerary gladiature – gladiature as human sacrifice – was regarded in some essential way an Etruscan practice.

Further, this specification of a funerary context for Etruscan gladiature was rhetorically deployed in two opposing directions. While on the one hand the Greeks were not to be associated with the Etruscans on the common practice of gladiature, on the other hand the funerary nature of Etruscan gladiature was positioned as a legitimization in relation to 'other gladiature' elsewhere in Italy. Muller's description gave equal weight to the evidence for the early practice of gladiature among the Samnites of Campania. The Samnites were introduced to the argument on the strength of those ancient literary sources which refer to a Campanian practice of offering gladiators not as a funerary sacrifice, but as entertainment for guests during banquets (see Chapter One.) However, the image of Samnite banquet-gladiature was not here connected to the question of gladiatorial origin – Muller suggested that the Samnites actually acquired the practice through cultural borrowing from Etruria.[xxvii] Instead, banquet gladiature for entertainment was held up as a negative contrast to the comparatively intelligible or legitimate context of funerary sacrifice. Muller extemporized on this basis that the practice of gladiature among the Samnites was of a more quotidian, less ritualized nature than in Etruria, and attributed the high level of 'acceptance' of gladiatorial combats in Campania to the savagery (*Wild*) of the Samnites and the luxuriousness (*Luxus*) of the region. Among the Etruscans, by contrast, gladiators were exclusively restricted to funerary ritual (*Leichenbegängnissen*).

The relative legitimacy ascribed to the funerary context, diffused in principle and heavily couched in religious ritual, was contrasted to the alternative which was lascivious and pleasure-driven, and significantly represented in its own context of internecine warfare and resistance to Rome. Coextensive with Etruria's relatively high level of civilization, then, the legitimized space which surrounded gladiature was here further specified through the incorporation of an opposing image; the contrast between Etruscan funerary gladiature and Samnite banquet gladiature hinged upon the intersection of gladiatorial violence with pleasure as the key criterion of distinction. In this sense, Muller's distinction between Etruscans and Samnites was not dramatically different from the parallel discursive divide which separated early, 'original' gladiature from later institutionalized gladiature at Rome; the boundary of legitimate violence with regard to pleasure was very much the same. Therefore, what appears in Muller's critically important text - which remained a standard work on ancient Etruria into the following century – was an early, very clear expression of the multiple discourses which delineated the concept of civilization during this period. Civilization arose from a complex discursive dynamic wherein moral constructs arising from attitudes to violence, not unlike earlier notions of 'national spirit', both overlapped with cultural categorizations and ordered those cultural groups into an implicit hierarchy; that hierarchy, in turn, grappled with deeper constructs which, in the labour of separating the barbarous from the civilized, divided the ancient from the modern, the eastern from the western worlds, and the nascent concept of 'the nation' from the manifest presence of the state.

The decivilizing of the Etruscans

A crucial effect of the Etruscan hypothesis of gladiatorial origin was the elaboration and 'hardening' of the discriminating connection between the discourse of civilization as a history of right, and the moral narrative of violence and pleasure as a sign of barbarism (and, conversely, the abhorrence of violence as a sign of civilization). The nineteenth century's initial perspective, that funerary human sacrifice solemnly separated violence from pleasure, meant that the Etruscans could be accepted (at least initially) as both a provisionally or proto-civilized nation and as practitioners of human sacrifice: it was ever more specifically the cathexis of violence and pleasure that disqualified an 'outsider group' from wielding power, legitimately participating in the political sphere, and ultimately holding membership in the (civilized) nation.

Herein we see exactly the expression of Foucault's analysis of nineteenth-century historical discourses of origin: the discourse of origin, as reorganized into historico-political discourse's hierarchical structure (*contra* the universal table of juridico-philosophical discourse), became a narrative of the end of history as much as of its beginning. The mathesis associated with juridico-philosophical discourse had been predicated ultimately upon stasis: the eighteenth century image of the Etruscans freely granted their pleasure in gladiature, and rationalized that pleasure by reference to the 'melancholy' of their essential, immutable national spirit; this melancholy, of which gladiature was held as the signifier, was also regarded as the key to the Etruscans' eventual fall before Rome's superior 'civilization'. Within the discourse of mathesis, however, gladiature itself was not associated with any one ancient civilization more than any other: gladiature was a floating signifier in this sense, simply 'ancient Italian', as Maffei put it, and did not in itself mobilize relations between civilizations. In contrast, the nineteenth century's iteration of historico-political discourse substituted the language of struggle for the language of stasis, and the eventual alignment of gladiature with both the newly-pressing notion of origin and one specific cultural group resulted.

Early attempts to reconcile gladiature with the shifting construct of civilization, which had begun to place greater emphasis on the moralizing discourse surrounding attitudes to violence, saw a conditional acceptance of the Etruscans within the ranks of the civilized provided that their religion separated violence from pleasure in the practice of gladiature as it was perceived. By mid-century, however, contemporary discursive pressure to proclaim the abhorrence of violence pushed the debate over the Etruscan hypothesis into the territory of the barbarian. Consequently, gladiature now came to be seen as a far more comprehensive and insidious signifier of the barbarian: its cathect of violence with pleasure was inherently cruel, its origin was not only resolutely 'non-Roman' but additionally non-European/ 'Oriental', and as a practice it was associated with political and moral corruption and, above all, national degeneracy.

As the nineteenth century wore on, the bloom faded somewhat from the image of ancient Etruria. Etruscomania flourished particularly in the first half of the century; by the middle decades, however, scholarship on ancient Etruria began to take a negative turn, even as Dennis' book reached a large audience. Michelet damned them with faint praise: "The Etruscans had no faith in themselves, and therein they did themselves justice. Their society, inclosed [sic] by the jealous spirit of a sacerdotal aristocracy, could not easily be opened to strangers. The Cyclopean enclosure of the Pelasgic city resisted by its mass, and refused to enlarge itself. (...) It is not either labourers, or warriors, or priests, who will found the city which is to adopt and combine Italy. If, then, we put on one side the foreign nations, the Hellenes on the south and the Celts on the north of the peninsula, we see ... powerless assimilation in the Etruscans, union and unity in Rome" (53).

This last point of Michelet's – the posit of an essential and very particular contrast between the Etruscan and Roman nations, on the level of what the eighteenth century had called 'spirit' and what the nineteenth century was beginning to call 'race', and the extrapolation of this contrast to articulate a particular discourse of the state and, by extension, of civilization – delineated the pathway in classical scholarship by which the debate over Etruscan origins, the origin of gladiature, and the implicit understanding of gladiature as a representation of power and the use of violence as a particular means all coalesced within contemporary historiography. That the idiom of civilization expressed an emerging discourse of race, and that the notion of hierarchy embedded within the ordering of civilizations both past and present promulgated a deeper discursive structure of struggle or conflict, was evident by the middle of the century. What concomitantly arose in the wake of the delicate qualification of

Etruscan 'civilization' – a qualification which had been based upon the provisional legitimization of funerary gladiature due to its separation of violence from pleasure – was a new negative turn: the unstable, uncertain divide between civility and barbarity that the Etruscans had straddled in contemporary perceptions veered away from the cautious image of Etruria as 'civilized', and scholars began instead to declare for barbarism. Interestingly, the new image of Etruscans as barbarians was frequently argued on exactly the same basis which had initially qualified Etruscan gladiature as provisionally civilized: the perceived total permeation of religion throughout Etruscan culture, particularly into the political sphere. Whereas in earlier decades of the nineteenth century, the linking of gladiature to religion had served to legitimate Etruscan gladiature on the moral basis of the separation of violence from pleasure (and, implicitly, the separation of gladiature from the Etruscan political sphere), the latter half of the nineteenth century witnessed an inversion of the same terms, as the new emphasis upon the interpenetration of Etruscan religion with Etruscan statecraft invalidated ancient Etruria's provisional status as 'civilized'. Once again, gladiature was held up as a centrally important signifier within the civility/barbarity debate.

Muller's approach to Etruscan funerary gladiature had emphasized two points – its 'truly Etruscan' nature, and its comparative restraint in practice; however, the next major voice to weigh in on the subject fixed primarily upon the former characteristic. Wilhelm Henzen (1816-1887) was a highly influential figure in the German Archaeological Institute in Rome from 1843 until his death, during which period the Institute expanded from a private association to a state institute. As secretary, he was the principal editor of its *Bullettini* and *Annali* publications. He founded the work which evolved into the *Corpus Inscriptionum Latinarum*, which he compiled and edited with the eventual collaboration of Mommsen and de Rossi. Soon after his arrival in Rome, he published a small study based upon the collection of the Borghese family as it stood at that time, the *Explicatio musivi in villa Burghesiana asservati* (1845). Henzen asserted the existence of funerary combats in ancient Etruria on the basis of representations on "countless grave urns, on which we (…) see men who massacre each other at the altar".[xxviii] The force of Henzen's argument, however, relied upon his constructed claim of a specific 'Etruscan cruelty'.[xxix]

Henzen's pupil, Theodor Mommsen, arose to become arguably the premier scholar of Roman antiquity in the entire nineteenth century. Mommsen published the first edition of his *Römische Geschichte* between 1854 and 1856. His quelling comments on Etruscan history and culture, and in particular on Etruscan art, extended the line of Henzen's perspective *contra* the general thinking from the beginning of the century. As with Winckelmann almost a century earlier, Mommsen's summation of the cruel national character of the Etruscans was argued on the dual basis of their religious practices, in particular human sacrifice, and by extension gladiature. These two terms – the irrationality of Etruscan religion, and the practice of gladiature – were represented by Mommsen as virtually interchangeable. He felt that the Etruscans were characterized by a "gloomy and withal tiresome mysticism ... and that solemn enthroning of pure absurdity which at all times finds its own circle of devotees";

their gods were malignant and mischievous, their worship was cruel, and their

entire religion "presented a veritable hell, in which the poor souls were doomed to

be tortured by mallets and serpents, and to which they were conveyed by the

conductor of the dead, a savage semi-brutal figure of an old man with wings and a

large hammer--a figure which afterwards served in the gladiatorial games at

Rome as a model for the costume of the man who removed the corpses of the

slain from the arena" (190).

Mommsen elaborated the image of Etruria from the third century BC

onward as a failing nation, diagnosing the internal decay from the visible external

decline. The moral rot of the Etruscans was read through contemporary reference

to their "unbounded luxury", as signalled by their superior wine, their

"unchastity" at banquets "such as fall nothing short of the worst Byzantine or

French demoralization ", and - once again – gladiature:

> "Unattested as may be many of the details in these accounts, the
> statement at least appears to be well founded, that the detestable
> amusement of gladiatorial combats – the gangrene of the later
> Rome and of the last epoch of antiquity generally – first came into
> vogue among the Etruscans. At any rate on the whole they leave no
> doubt as to the deep degeneracy of the nation" (Mommsen 348).

Mommsen's lengthy text opened very early on the construction of an

antinomy between the Roman and Etruscan nations. For example, in a

comparative discussion of religious practices, Mommsen invoked religion as an

index of "national character"; the ensuing passage maintains an interesting tension

between the assertion of an essentially inviolate core of Roman culture despite the

strongly malevolent influence of Etruria. Mommsen insisted upon the 'purity' of

the "thoroughly national development" (187) of Roman religion, and disagreed with contemporary claims that the extension of the rights of citizenship in the aftermath of conquest led to an eventual 'denationalization' of the Roman state.

Mommsen maintained very clear distinctions between those elements of entertainment which he considered indigenous and those that had non-Roman origins; moreover, he was similarly definite in distinguishing between those foreign elements which had been deliberately adopted by the state, and those whose incorporation had been of a more insidious nature. The introduction of anything Greek – athletes, boxers, or dramas comic or tragic – were "perhaps of doubtful value, but [they] formed at any rate the best of the acquisitions made at this time" (226). Less acceptable were the perversion of the native sport of "innocent hunts" into animal-baiting, and the "still more revolting gladiatorial games" (227). Mommsen saw gladiature as having "gained admission" from Campania and Etruria despite the severe censure of the state; the initially successful ban of gladiature from public festivals "wanted either the requisite power or the requisite energy" to suppress the inclusion of gladiatorial combats at private funerals, and the low tastes of the multitude thwarted the state's futile efforts to exclude the practice altogether.

When read as a contemporary history of right, what becomes apparent are the strange and particular contemporary resolutions of associated anxieties: the 'Orient' was here constructed as a source of 'civilizations', but the 'alternate order' of such (eastern) barbarians – whose identities arguably overlapped, to a degree, with the barbarians of contemporary projects of western empire – was ultimately corrupt and irrational. Etruscomania, and the judgment of Etruria as civilized or barbarous, represented the structures of a contemporary language of empire which both provisionally included 'eastern barbarians' within the ranks of civilization and simultaneously excluded such groups, whether in their ancient or contemporary forms, as subject to the superiority and dominance of western power. In many ways, in fact, the historical narrative of ancient Etruria – an Asiatic, even suspiciously Semitic people (though ultimately racially indeterminate) who were represented in the nineteenth century as colonists on the European continent, and who *even on western soil* were ultimately subdued by the superior force of Rome – was a narrative which reinforced the 'civilizing mission' of empire: even the 'most civilized', relatively speaking, of the oriental barbarians were naturally subordinate to western dominance.

On the other hand, such an inscription of the 'naturally subordinate' barbarian gave rise to an imperative to account for the fact that gladiature, insofar as it was an essentially non-Roman practice, came to appear within the boundaries of Roman civilization. The question of how it came to be introduced, and by what means it grew to massive proportions like a cancer in the social body, was answered by the reverberating, parallel discourse not of race, but of class struggle – in the nineteenth century's elaborate image of the urban mob, which stood at the heart of an academic discourse which explored structural relationships of class conflict, racial degeneration, and decivilizing.

The discourse of the 'two races'

Foucault saw the historico-political discourse of nineteenth century historical writing as defined by a deeper tension between the linked sub-discourses of race and class struggle. The relatively unanchored definition of 'race' during this period, not yet firmly attached to any biological construct, was nevertheless still a signifier of essential difference between groups, and evocative of conflict or struggle between them; the early discourse of 'race' was always already part of a language for articulating power relations:

> "... two races exist whenever one writes the history of two groups which do not, at least to begin with, have the same language or, in many cases, the same religion. The two groups form a unity and a single polity only as the result of wars, invasions, victories, and defeats, or in other words, acts of violence. The only link between them is the link established by the violence of war. And finally, we can say that two races exist when there are two groups which, although they coexist, have not become mixed because of the differences, dissymmetries, and barriers created by privileges, customs and rights, the distribution of wealth, or the way in which power is exercised" (*SMBD* 77).

'Race', then, invoked a general structure of group conflict that can also be manifested in the particular by class relations: in historico-political discourse, and the historical writing produced within its structure, race and class struggle define the inscription of power relations between 'unmixed' groups, essentially distinct from one another in various possible senses, as relations of violence or struggle. Foucault further claimed that historico-political discourse of the nineteenth century in particular was characterized by a certain flow of tension between race and class as two parallel inscriptions of group struggle: that while 'race war' may be taken as the dominant category, not least given the biological essentialism that it would acquire in the twentieth century, 'class war' was the dominant idiom of historical writing in the nineteenth century:

> "The war that is going on beneath order and peace, the war that undermines our society and divides it in a binary mode is,

basically, a race war. (p.60): And then you find a second
transcription based upon the great theme and theory of social war,
which emerges in the very first years of the nineteenth century, and
which tends to erase every trace of racial conflict in order to define
itself as class struggle" (*SMBD* 59-60).

The historiography of gladiature, as seen in the previous chapter, had

already begun to pick up the discursive threads of the conflict of social class; by

the end of the eighteenth century, the image of the *pollice verso* had taken up a

position at the forefront of the perception of gladiature in the contemporary

historical imagination, and the crowd had already begun to appear as the site

wherein violence and pleasure intersected. Over the course of the nineteenth

century, the social politics of Rome, especially as a prominent factor in the

understanding of the end of the Republic, came increasingly to dominate the

scholarly writing of Roman history.

It is of course not possible to outline an objective account of the events

surrounding the transition from republic to empire, against which the nineteenth

century conversation on the subject can be compared; however, some provisional

version of how the socio-political landscape of Rome shifted between the first

century BC and the first century AD is necessary in order to navigate what

follows, particularly in its ultimate relation to gladiature. While the eighteenth

century's approach to the understanding of gladiature had been couched primarily

in terms of 'whole cultural entities', that century's gradual epistemic

reorganization of what Foucault called the 'universal mathesis' of knowledge

gave way, over the course of the nineteenth century, to a new dominant context

for the interpretation of gladiature: its perceived function within the politics of social class at Rome itself. This statement should not be taken too far: the history of Roman class conflict in the shift from republic to empire was well known in eighteenth-century historical writing; on the other hand, as will be seen, the 'hierarchy of civilizations' that found expression in the eighteenth century was certainly retained in the nineteenth, and increasingly put to use. However, when we focus upon gladiature, as a site of representation of attitude(s) to violence and by extension a sign of 'civilization', what we arguably find in the nineteenth century is a narrowed focus upon Roman class conflict as the relevant historical context for gladiature's interpretation.

Patricians, plebeians, and political change

Taken at its most basic level, the social structure of the republican Roman citizenry was organized around a division between two main groups: the land-holding aristocracy or patricians, and the much larger group of plebeians, who held Roman citizenship and thus possessed voting (and certain other) rights, but who were traditionally excluded from the highest political offices. From many angles, the history of the Republic can be (and has been) told as a history of the lengthy and complex struggle for political power between these two broadly defined groups.

Stepping back, the historiography of the patrician-plebeian relation, as written both in antiquity and in modernity, has been heavily determined by precisely the theme of struggle for power. Beginning with the aptly named Struggle of the Orders, the inaugural contest for power soon after the late sixth-century BC fall of the monarchy and the founding of the Republic, the plebeian class sought to expand its position in the political administration which was traditionally dominated by patrician interests. In the initial period of the Republic, only members of the patrician class were able to stand for political office; however, through more than two centuries of struggle, involving mass plebeian cessations similar to general strikes, the creation of parallel plebeian political bodies and assemblies (particularly the plebeian tribunate), and the eventual ascension of such assemblies to binding legal status, a certain parity of political power was achieved between the two groups.

Throughout the middle centuries of the Republic, the reforms that had been enacted as a result of the Struggle of the Orders remained more or less sufficient, and the political arrangement remained generally stable. Rome's focus during this period largely faced outward, as the political and economic landscape was dominated by wars of conquest, first in peninsular Italy and eventually further afield. This protracted period of relative internal stability and high military activity on the borders, however, precipitated serious economic consequences by the middle of the second century BC. The army's protracted drain of manpower from the yeoman class slowly decimated the livelihood of small-holdings farmers, and the subsequent land grab by the wealthy correlated to, on the one hand, the rise of the *latifundia* system of slave-based plantation agriculture, and the mass migration of the rural dispossessed into urban areas, especially Rome itself. The explosion of an impoverished urban population of citizens who held the vote – augmented further by the extension of citizenship to allied Italian peoples in the outcome of the Social War of 91 BC – was a rich source of political opportunity for those who held and sought power: a large sector of the electorate, with little to lose and everything to gain, was more easily influenced at the polls. At the same time, the army was further swollen by the growing number of plebeians who could make their living in no other way, which contributed in turn to the ongoing shift in the traditional relationship between troops and their general: although consular power had for four centuries been limited to twelve-month terms, the phenomenon of prorogation, which began with Marius' seven terms of consular power at the end of the second century, created the conditions of possibility for the Roman army to begin to attach its loyalty not to the state, but to an individual commander – a loophole most famously exploited by Julius Caesar in the Gallic campaign.

The collision of these three circumstances – the dramatically widening economic gap between social classes and the possibility for individuals to amass staggering personal fortunes, the rapid expansion of the electorate by the movement of impoverished people into the city, and the emergence of a series of extremely politically powerful individuals who, through the offer of land grants and additional financial reward to soldiers, effectively created massive private armies – formed the backdrop of the turn in Roman politics towards populist demagoguery. There arose within the ranks of the governing class a division between *optimates* and *populares* – those who sought to increase the power of the senate, and those who sought to wield power through the popular assemblies and the tribunate. A central strategy of the *populares* faction was largess: from substantial offerings like land grants, cash gifts, and the public corn dole, to more fleeting favours like public entertainments, monies both public and private were funnelled into competition for votes from the people's assemblies. Within this climate, gladiature became a powerful tool for influencing popular opinion; this was potentially true for either faction, but the strong impression imparted by surviving ancient sources – and, more significantly, the strong impression received by classical scholars of the nineteenth century – is that gladiature was a key tool of the populist wing of late republican politics.[xxx]

Some members of the plebeian class thrived in the changing environment. Over time, the laws that gave patricians exclusive rights to Rome's highest offices were repealed or weakened, and a new aristocracy emerged from among the plebeian class: the *novi homines*. Marius himself was a plebeian, as were Pompey and Cicero. The binary separation between patricians and plebeians was far from perfect, and nineteenth century historiography was quite sensitive to this detail. The socio-political role of the 'third tier' formed by the *novi homines* set into high relief the more essentializing substructures of identity distinctions dividing patricians from plebeians in the modern historical imagination, and this intermediary group was in some senses perceived as the corporate version of the shift in late republican political structure which ultimately coalesced around only a handful of Roman figures. By the last century of the Republic, despite the traditional legal constraints against any individual's acquisition of permanent political powers, Roman politics was dominated by a small number of individual leaders – this is the well-trod territory of the triumvirates, of Pompey, Julius Caesar, Mark Antony, and Augustus. Since the Republic was never formally dismantled and the Empire never formally declared, academic opinion has always varied regarding which factor or event, if any, may be considered the primary catalyst in the shift between the two regimes; nevertheless, one of either Julius Caesar or Augustus are generally accepted as the first Emperor of Rome.

The Roman mob of nineteenth century historiography was inscribed with something of a dual nature, politically speaking. It was comprised on the one hand of the late republican mob, whose image was heavily inflected by its perceived swarming of urban Rome, its dangerous possession of political franchise, and the role that was played by a massive economically unproductive voting public in the late Republic's perceived 'descent' into popular politics and demagoguery on the road to the eventual despotism of empire. On the other hand there stood the mob of the Empire itself: still massive, still unemployed, but no longer a voting public; in contrast, the imperial mob was inscribed as a violent, many-headed mass, a drain upon state resources and a direct (though vague) threat to imperial authority, in the sense that their circumstantial idleness and their perceived essential brutishness represented an ever-present potential for some kind of outbreak of destruction and social chaos. The narrative of decline inherited from the eighteenth century was, during this period, very much an account of the rise (or fall, as the case may be) of the republican mob, its further political devolution into the true mob of the Empire, and finally, the mob as one of the circulating theories applied to the notion of the Empire's eventual fall, taken from Gibbon. By the second half of the nineteenth century, the Roman mob was a dominant sign and 'cause' of the perceived fall of Rome; in turn, gladiature, and by extension the entire infrastructure of public spectacle, was repeatedly and explicitly inscribed in

historical scholarship as the metonymic symbol of the mob's definitive inherent

capacity for violence and socio-political decay.

The origin of the mob in nineteenth century classicism

Firstly, and from an early point in the century, historians of this period

inscribed an image of the Roman republican mob that resonated deeply with a

perspective upon contemporary demographic changes, especially the urban

population explosion associated with the industrial revolution. The mob's very

urbanity – its definitive connection with the city of Rome – became a salient

characteristic. Greater attention was paid by scholars to the impact of arable land

distribution in the third and second centuries BC, and the consequent migration of

dispossessed smallholders into the urban centres; it was thought that the mob had

its roots, in part, in the destruction of the yeoman class, which according to

Rome's own ancient propaganda was the backbone of the nation. The force of the

distinction was clearly brought forth by Thomas Arnold in *The History of the*

Later Roman Commonwealth (1845), for whom the corruption of the urban mob

stood in direct contrast to the romantic, nostalgic image of the 'honest yeomen

farmers' - the people, politically legitimate - who populated the pages of Latin

late republican histories of the earlier centuries of the Republic. Arnold's version

of the demographic and socio-political upheavals cast the Roman lower classes as

a specifically city-bound group, comprised of:

> "... that lowest description of populace by which great towns in a
> genial climate are especially infested; where shelter and food and
> clothing being less important, they can more easily live without
> regular employment, as having fewer wants to provide for ...These

men would have all the qualities fitted to make them mischievous: idleness, improvidence, a total absence of all feelings of honest independence, and a great sense of their own importance, both as freemen, while so many who enjoyed far more personal comforts were slaves, and as members of a body whose power was the greatest in the world" (67).

Arnold invited his readers to imagine the Roman plebeians on the basis of contemporary experience, since "we know what the morals of the lower classes in large cities are at this day, when their opportunities of being rightly taught are far greater than could possibly have been enjoyed at Rome" (66). The Roman mob in this aspect was thus an extreme fantasy image of contemporary demographics of urbanization: in contrast to the implication that the contemporary rabble, low in morals though it may have been, was at least held back by a modern state which was to be regarded as comparatively civilized, the mob of Rome was a 'mischievous infestation' without the containment and correction of rational governance.

Race/class struggle and the roots of the nation

Beyond such considerations, throughout the nineteenth century the urban mob was increasingly represented as a group which stood outside the true 'national spirit' of Rome, as the Enlightenment concept of 'spirit' gradually shifted toward what would become a construct of race. The republican conquests had brought Rome into direct contact with other cultures in Italy and abroad, and the expansion of Roman rule allowed colonial and allied peoples to move and migrate more freely than before; in addition, foreign wars exerted considerable impact upon the composition of the slave population under Roman domination, as prisoners of war were frequently enslaved, and victories followed by the establishment of colonies, generally speaking, produced an influx of wealth which raised the living standard for some. These elements of republican social history were focal points of nineteenth century historical writing; the notion that the republican centre of Rome was slowly flooded with foreign groups, whether transported as slaves or freely migrated, was inseparable from the image of the urban mob.

For some historians the urban mob phenomenon, in conjunction with the parallel rise of the plebeian class within the Roman social fabric, represented such a fundamental corruption of 'true' Roman culture that the class division was claimed to overlap with different racial origins. Merivale (*The History of the Romans under the Empire*, 1850) was among the adherents of this theory; he argued that "[t]he patricians and plebeians of Rome represent ... two races of different origin, the former of which has admitted the other, whether on compulsion or by concession, after a fruitless resistance, or by spontaneous arrangement, to a certain prescribed share in the privileges of government and the rights of conquest" (7). The animosity and conflict between the social orders, in the earlier centuries of the republic as in the later, were ascribed to an essential human difference between the social groups, with "a strong undercurrent of hostility between these jealous yokefellows" (7). This idea had influential echoes, such as Fustel de Coulanges in *La Cité Antique* (1864, 361), and can arguably be read as an early instance of the nineteenth century tension between the languages of race and class struggle. Much as Foucault described, class struggle swiftly came to dominate nineteenth century historico-political discourse; however (as will be explored in following chapters), the early germ of conceptual overlap between race and class struggle – the fluidity of the interpretive framework of 'essential human difference' - proved to be persistent, and resurfaced in the twentieth century.

For others, the miscegenated nature of the mob took a more subtle form. The conceptual overlap of race and class, with its subtext of essential difference between patricians and plebeians, was further mobilized in support of an image of the mob that specifically excluded it from the political sphere, and at its furthest extent cast the barbarian mob as a danger to the political order. According to Arnold, the unchecked growth of the Roman urban mob was no cause for particular alarm until the Gracchi sought in the later second century BC to extend Roman citizenship to the Latin tribes, a proposal which held "great attractions for the very lowest class of citizens, as well as for the turbulent and enthusiastic of all classes; for … it was obvious that the indiscriminate admission of all the Italians to the privilege of voting at Rome, would greatly lessen the influence of the richer class of Roman citizens, and by rendering the assembly of the people so immoderately numerous, would in fact reduce it to little better than a mere mob, the ready tool of an eloquent and ambitious leader" (179). This was the sticking point in the conceptualization of the mob: the threat that it posed to the established sociopolitical order, particularly in the late Republic when it still possessed meaningful voting power, was rhetorically contained by constructing the mob as existing essentially outside of that civilized order, and by ascribing its barbarism to a dual origin of both race and class difference. The "worst class of the new citizens" – comprised at least in part of Latins seeking the franchise -

swelled the ranks of the mob, which was already "no better than a needy rabble,

dissolute in morals, and destitute of any sense of national honour" (Arnold 42).

Those who lacked in 'national honour', by implication, could never be admitted

within the ranks of the civilized; at the same time, the intersection of civilization

and the nation was a site occupied exclusively by patricians. It was through such

morally charged language – of which the abhorrence of violence was no small

example – that the contemporary construct of civilization within the nobiliary

history of right obscured the proscription of power through the stringent

distinction of nation from State.

The nation within the State

This increasingly exclusive group comprising the civilized nation,

however, was also undergoing a harrowing of its own in the historical

imagination. The Roman mob did not stand alone in nineteenth century classical

thought as the sole agent of political deterioration and social decay; taken more

broadly, the mob was in fact the instrument of the *populares* faction among the

patricians, which was widely seen during this period as having masterminded the

violence of the late Republic in their own bid for increasingly tyrannical political

power. The rational governance which could contain the mob was not simply

considered to be the birthright of the entire aristocracy; to the contrary, the

historiography of the late Roman republic constructed a narrative wherein a

special-interest group within the ruling class exploited wider social conflict for its

own ends. the growth of the practice at Rome was perceived as a particularly repugnant component of a wider program of electoral bribery, and as the worst species of demagogic tool, since the violent spectacle of gladiature instrumentalized the mob in terms of both its own 'essential' violence and its power as a manifestation of the voting *populus*. The contemporary abhorrence for gladiature pivoted upon this point. The *pollice verso* as a perverse spectre of the franchise now became further associated with a reactionary political discourse which militated against the image of disruptive factions of the ruling establishment, and the potential to harness the chaotic potential of the multiethnic urban masses in the political instability of the late republican period. The greater figuration of Rome as it was inscribed at this time, then, was constructed as a cautionary, even repressive narrative of contemporary socio-political upheaval in the west, in the face of widespread social pressures from below towards extension of the franchise.

This line of thought arguably began with Niebuhr's vastly influential *Römische Geschichte* (1827-8; vol iii posthumously published in 1832). Niebuhr painted the later Republic in broad strokes of dissolution and social decay. He pointed to the success of Rome's wars in Asia, which both impoverished the lower classes and concentrated immense wealth in the hands of the relatively small aristocracy, as the primary causal factor in the social upheaval of the period. The increasing scale of gladiatorial combats, at this time still offered at funerals by individuals in a nominally private capacity, was similarly highlighted as a specific "symptom of corruption" (vol. II 95-6). Much of the argument was familiar from the previous century's discourse on *luxus*, and it was from this perspective that Niebuhr made his few comments on gladiature. By the third volume of his work, however, Niebuhr had reached the moment in the early Empire when the Colosseum was constructed and inaugurated under the Flavian dynasty (vol. I 215); he read the Colosseum's construction as Titus' response to the *imperita multitudo*, which judges more harshly "the sovereign who is not kind, and does not flatter" than the sovereign who neglects other political duties; the construction of the Colosseum was "cruel and disgusting", but was "in accordance with the taste of the Roman populace", although it "makes upon us the impression of something monstrous and revolting". Lest his readers assume that such an edifice could only belong to the Empire, however, Niebuhr underscored that "such prodigality and amusements were not confined to the time of the emperors; they had begun towards the end of the republic" (216).

For his interpretation of the end of the republic, Niebuhr simply looked around himself, and claimed on the basis of contemporary examples that the Empire's eventual despotism of the *imperita multitudo* had its roots in the *populares'* betrayal of the true Roman patrician class – the 'nation' - when the demagogues exploited the electoral mob. In Niebuhr's estimation, "such an aristocracy feels the greatest hatred against those families to which it cannot deny an equal rank, and it usually tried to ally itself with those who are furthest removed from all aristocracy. Such alliances occur very frequently in the south of Europe, where history often shews us the aristocracy leagued with the mob, in order to maintain itself..." (vol I. 385-6). In a later passage he focused his condemnation of demagoguery even more sharply, as in his description of L.

Apuleius Saturninus, a "knave" who worked closely with the plebeian general

Marius, he stated "[i]t would seem that he was a revolutionary spirit, who did not

clearly conceive what would be the result of a revolution, and never thought of

institutions and government, but only of violence and destruction. He was by no

means of vulgar origin: he belonged to one of the noblest plebeian families, *just*

as in the French revolution, men of the highest nobility placed themselves at the

head of the mob" (vol. II 339, emphasis added).

Niebuhr's scathing assessment of the late republican socio-political

figuration was developed and extended by the major classical historians who

followed in his wake. Conflict remained a central element of the nineteenth

century's description of class relations in ancient Rome, whether republican or

imperial, and the major scholars exhibited only the narrowest range of opinions

over the directionality of that conflict, and which group held power over the other.

Niebuhr's image of the disenfranchised mob of the Empire as a vague but

everpresent threat of violence was but the ultimate reduction of the still politically

instrumental, but politically unconscious, mob of the late Republic; the

opportunism of the republican demagogues, conversely, was but the first step on

the slippery slope to the despotic cult of personality that became the Empire,

which within eighty years of its inception was ruled by a plebeian, and within two

hundred was routinely steered by non-Roman rulers from the provinces.

Mommsen echoed Niebuhr's point, although his version of the power

struggle between the patricians and the mob was somewhat different. Mommsen

did lay the original blame for the corrupting force of spectacle in Roman society upon the patricians, and set that initial moment of decline quite far back in the earlier Republic. In his view, the despoiling of Rome's original purity by the demagogic movement rested with Flaminius, the "first Roman demagogue by profession", who instituted the plebeian games in 218 BC; and when "the path was once opened, the evil made rapid progress" (Mommsen 462). Mommsen related the ensuing catalogue of novel and expanded events introduced to the annual calendar over the centuries following Flaminius as a series of irrevocable concessions to the demands of the mob, in their role under the Republic as a significant portion of the voting populace. For Mommsen, the original deviation from the proper asceticism of public festivals was to be pinned to the stresses and exigencies of the Hannibalic war, wherein the burdened Roman government could 'scarcely be blamed' for its incapacity to restrain the opportunism of demagogues. The "sovereign multitude" represented an irresistible force in its collusion with populist demagoguery, and the conservative faction among the patrician class – the nation proper - were betrayed by groups on all sides within the political structure of the state itself.

The mob's pleasure, decivilizing, and nineteenth century anxieties

While Merivale nominally accorded with Arnold that the extension of rights of citizenship to the Latin tribes "dated the decay of the Roman nationality", he actually agreed with Niebuhr that divisions among the patrician class were as significant a factor as the inherent violence of the mob itself in the destabilization of republican governing structures. In his image, from the late Republic onwards, urban Rome "became from henceforth the common resort of all that was neediest and vilest in the suburban population. The forum was occupied by dissolute and reckless mobs, eager to sell themselves to the demagogues of any party, controlling the elections by corruption or violence, obstructing the march of public affairs, rendering law impotent and justice impracticable. Conscious of their strength and services, these hungry mercenaries claimed a subsidy from the faction they kept in power. They quartered themselves on the government, which was compelled to tax, for their maintenance, the industry of the provinces" (*History of the Romans under the Empire* vol. I 15). The *populares* faction among the patricians had "systematically debauched" the urban populace, without any respect for the rule of law:

> "The favour of the people was sought and gained by profuse largesses; the means of seduction allowed by law, such as the covert bribery of shows and festivals, were used openly and boldly; while others which were expressly interdicted, such as the direct proffer of money, were practiced not less lavishly in the polling booths, where the restraint of the ballot was wholly ineffectual. Not infrequently mere violence took the place of bribery: disturbances were purposely created; mobs were formed and drilled, and battles ensued" (*History of the Romans under the Empire* vol. I 42).

In a slightly later work, *The General History of Rome from the foundation of the city to the fall of Augustus*, Merivale suggested that the *populares'* systematic debauchery of the populace had begun with the introduction of gladiature at Rome – the 264 BC funeral of Brutus Pera. Whereas Maffei had inscribed the 264 BC funerary combat as a "Solemnity", and Ferguson some fifty years later had borrowed the notion of an original intent of 'inspiring horror and pity' to exonerate the patricians from responsibility for later developments, Merivale's ruling class was granted no such exception:

"After this commencement [i.e. the Brutus funeral], the practice spread rapidly. From an accompaniment of the funeral rites of such nobles 'matches' became a common public spectacle, produced on the arena of the public theatres, for the enjoyment of the populace on many solemn festive occasions. (...) The usage soon assumed form and system. (...) The shows of human combatants became a recognized portion of the apparatus with which the candidates for public office amused and bribed the populace. At a later period ... when the suffrage of the people ceased to have a political value, few cared to incur the charge of breeding up victims for their amusement. The Romans indulged themselves with the conceit that these cruel spectacles of useless skill and valour helped to train them in sentiments of manly pride and contempt of wounds and death. Throughout all that remains of their literature hardly a whisper is heard of disgust or disapproval of them. The better spirits among them appear, indeed, under the influence of a milder civilisation, to have tacitly withdrawn themselves from the amphitheatre; but no shrewd analyst of human nature can now fail to trace to their influence the hardening of the heart and conscience of the mass of the Roman people" (*General History of Rome* 126).

Michelet weighed in on precisely the same theme of gladiature's implication in late republican political corruption, with some critical extensions to Merivale's above allusion to organized rioting. Private ownership of gladiators increased exponentially in the last century of the Republic; most famously, Julius Caesar owned such a vast quantity of gladiators quartered at the *ludus* in Capua that repressive legislation was enacted to restrict the number of gladiatorial slaves a private individual could possess and – more importantly – could bring within the city walls of Rome. (Possibly the law of Cicero, the *Lex Tullia de ambitu* from 63 BC, which was certainly about forbidding candidates for office to hold gladiatorial games in the two-year period preceding candidacy, but which probably contained the clause mentioned by Suetonius regarding *de numero gladiatorum*). Michelet identified this trend as one of the causes of the Servile War (73-1 BC), arguing that the "barbarous mania for combats of gladiators" had led to the dangerous concentration of slaves who were not "mere slaves, labourers or shepherds, but men exercised expressly in the use of arms, habituated to blood, and devoted beforehand to death"; he made careful note of the fact that such privately owned troops of gladiators (*familiae*) were being used for more purposes than the giving of spectacles, of which the worst was the renting of gladiators "to the factions, who let them loose like furious dogs in the public square, against their enemies and their rivals" (308-9). In Michelet's perspective privately owned gladiatorial troops "constituted for each senator and each knight a little army of assassins" (327). This element of the historical narrative of the fall of the Republic was given greater emphasis as the nineteenth century progressed, and culminated arguably in Froude's 1879 *Caesar: A Sketch*, which made such repetitive reference to 'Milo and his gladiators' that Froude eventually called Milo himself a patrician gladiator (334). Late republican gladiature, then, represented a threat to socio-political order far more insidious than the exploitation of the base appetites of the mob: gladiature allowed the *populares* not simply direct corruption of the malleable electorate, but also a form of direct force, an instrument of physical violence.

Friedlander's *Roman Life and Manners under the Early Empire* (*Romische Sittesgeschichte, 1864-71*) was a text recently described as having formulated the seminal perspective on Roman gladiature (*Roman Amphitheatre from its Origins to the Colosseum* 3); I disagree, but Friedlander's approach to gladiatorial origins would continue to characterize the main thrust of scholarly consensus for at least the rest of the nineteenth century. He conceded gladiature's origin to the

Etruscans without discussion (41) and gestured towards the image of its initial context as a religious practice (1), but his attention was not greatly attracted by such considerations and he neither explained nor explored them. Instead, for Friedlander the significance of his notational representation of gladiatorial origins was simply to establish gladiature as unnatural to Rome ("native to Etruria, but in Latium an innovation", 41) and as a practice that, once introduced into a Roman context, had been perverted by the mob's pleasure in violence. Friedlander's gaze was firmly fixed on a fairly static image of imperial gladiature, with little space allotted to the republican period; his referential image of the amphitheatre, the spectacle and the mob was a pastiche of details marshalled to illustrate his theme, which was the demonstration of gladiatorial spectacle as the public face of a particular type of social and political deterioration. This is where Friedlander earned his position as the epitomizer of nineteenth-century historiography's image of gladiature: by creating a perfect synthesis of the moralizing language of the mob's pleasure in violence with the rationalizing force of economics, which together were held up as a perfect demonstration (and justification) of the urban mob's essential exclusion from the nation as the legitimate seat of political power.

In characterizing the Roman mob, Friedlander rehearsed the trope of *imperita multitudo* that was by now familiar: even under the socio-political conditions of empire, when the masses no longer held the vote, the "omnipotent ruler" was at the mob's mercy. During the early stages of the imperial period, Friedlander painted the emperor and the aristocracy as exercising determinative control over gladiature and public spectacle: "Originally, for the most part, religious celebrations, [spectacles] became, even in the later Republic, the best

means of purchasing popular favour, and, under the Empire, of keeping the

populace contented. [...] The emperors, like Louis XIV, knew how admiration

aids absolute autocracy; like Napoleon, that the imagination of the people must be

excited: splendid festivals were one of their most indispensible and most constant

devices" (1). However, control over the power struggle which gladiature

embodied rapidly slipped the patrician grasp; the emperor "could no longer give

spectacles at his pleasure; they had become an unavoidable necessity. Into the

capital there poured a proletariat, more corrupt and wilder and rougher than in

modern capitals, composed of the dregs of every nation; its predominance was

absolute, and the more dangerous as the mob consisted mostly of idlers. The

Government provided for their maintenance by the great distributions of corn; and

having fed them, had to supply the needs of their leisure" (2).

Here, yet another causal origin was woven into gladiatorial historiography,

as the mob's pleasure, its threatening power and capacity to be politically

instrumentalized, and in a sense its very being was repeatedly associated with the

language of labour and productivity. On the one hand, this thread in scholarly

thought read as an internal update of the trope of *luxus*; on the other hand,

harnessed to the industrial epoch's moralized language of labour, the new sign of

the barbarian was not simply the superifical pleasure of 'luxuries' such as

gladiature, but the lack of economic productivity – the idleness – that the pursuit

of such low pleasures presumed, and the entire power structure represented by the relationship between the patricians who sponsored such entertainments and the mob who consumed them.

It was this struggle between the lowest and highest classes of society – "the mass of beggars, and the world of quality proper" (Mommsen 502) - that, in the opinion of contemporary scholars living through modernity's first great wave of urbanization, shaped the social formation of the entire Roman Republic. The middle republican period saw a massive migration of the agricultural peasantry into the urban centres as a result of the incorporation of smallholdings into large plantations, privately owned and worked by slave rather than free labour; this phenomenon and its attendant outgrowths, specifically the state corn dole and the explosion of the urban poor, visibly exercised classical scholars in the midst of comparable developments of the industrial revolution. Mommsen saw the root of all the Republic's ills in this mass exodus of the dispossessed, as it concentrated a voting public in the city of Rome itself and yet kept them both 'idle', sustained by state support rather than industry, and open in their "beggar's laziness" to political corruption *en masse*; the great demographic shift, with its explicit contemporary parallels, was a powerfully resonant representation of the fear of decivilizing. The pernicious process set in train by the expansion of public festivals in the Hannibalic War culminated in a slow putrefaction of Roman society as it existed in the earliest years of the Republic:

> "The Roman plebeian was fonder of gazing in the theatre than of working; the taverns and brothels were so frequented, that the demagogues found their special account in gaining the possessors of such establishments over to their interests. The gladiatorial games – which revealed, at the same time that they fostered, the worst demoralization of the ancient world – had become so

flourishing that a lucrative business was done in the sale of the programmes for them; and it was at this time that the horrible innovation was adopted by which the decision as to the life or death of the vanquished became dependent, not on the law of duel or on the pleasure of the victor, but on the caprice of the onlooking public" (Mommsen 496).

Gladiature itself was thus represented as a concentrated metonym of the larger image of the mob, inseparable from it, an intense focus of the notion of decivilizing and its inspired anxiety. Across these later texts, gladiature became a mobile site of the nineteenth century form of this anxiety: gladiature did not simply signify the mob, but revealed and fostered it; gladiature was itself a version of the mob, a concatenation of the greatest and most irrational violence. Moreover, in Friedlander's text the amphitheatre and the spectacle of gladiature were represented as possessing a radically totalizing capacity for *creating* the mob phenomenon. This line of thinking somewhat presaged the critical approach to urban mobbing which would reach a much higher level of development by the end of the century with Le Bon's *The Crowd: A Study of the Popular Mind* (1896), a work which would continue to exert deep influence over the orchestration of political theatre in the fascist movements of the first half of the twentieth century; Le Bon was closely read by Mussolini, for example (cf. *Fascist Spectacle* 28). It did not begin even with Friedlander; [xxxi] Arnold had made comments much to the same effect a full generation earlier:

"Above all, the nature of mankind is such, that even the best and most highly educated individuals, when assembled together in a numerous body, are apt to be more swayed by passion and less by principle, than if they were deliberating alone, or in a small society. Much more is this the case, when the inhabitants of a great city are promiscuously crowded together; for then the evil predominates with a fearful ascendancy, and a physical and moral excitement is created, which destroys the exercise of the judgement, and drowns the voice of moderation and self-restraint; leaving the mind open to any unreasonable impression that may be produced, whether of ridicule, of indignation, of compassion, or of pride" (Arnold 68).

The decivilizing force of gladiature was a potential threat even to the civilized group. The patrician aristocracy, in Friedlander's view, were not protected by their social rank from the insidiously polluting effects of "things absolutely exotic, unnatural, nonsensical"; the amphitheatre mob was equally "aristocratic or vulgar" (Friedlander 43), and was rendered so by the "evil moral effects of the games even on the upper classes":

"But the spectacles did not occupy only the masses, for whom they were intended. The impression of these exciting scenes of night fascinated all, infected the intellect of Rome, even the highest and most cultured circles, and especially the women. How the games pervaded every man's thought, the proverbs shows. When they drew breath, they breathed in the passion for the circus, the stage and the arena, 'an original evil begotten in the womb'" (16-7).

The point was later extended even further by Froude, for whom the influence of *luxus*, and the concomitant unbounded pursuit of amusement, led him towards the end of the nineteenth century to describe the patricians in language that had previously been reserved for the mob. The "high society of Rome itself became a society of powerful animals with an enormous appetite for pleasure", and the entire national spirit by the close of the republic was correspondingly degraded below any level which could be considered civilized:

"When natural pleasures had been indulged in to satiety, pleasures which were against nature were imported from the East to stimulate the exhausted appetite. (...) Even the most cultivated patricians were coarse alike in their habits and their amusements. (...) The stage was never more than an artificial taste with [the patrician class]; *their delight was the delight of barbarians*, in spectacles, in athletic exercises, in horse-races and chariot races, in the combats of wild animals in the circus, combats of men with beasts on choice occasions, and, as a rare excitement, in fights between men and men, when select slaves trained as gladiators were matched in pairs to kill each other" (Froude 18-9, emphasis added).

Mapping the nation/State onto antiquity

What we observe, then, is an expression of the way in which the construct of civilization was articulated during this period within the discourse of struggle: civilization was defined by struggle, in a way that had not been true of the eighteenth century with its constructs of immutable national spirit, and in a way that would transform again in the twentieth century as will be explored in the next chapter. For the nineteenth century, barbarity may have been the definitive characteristic of the mob, but 'civilization' was not an immutable, essential property of the aristocracy; the historiography of gladiature, particularly as embedded within the narrative of the fall of the Republic, put forth an image of an aristocratic group which had succumbed to 'decivilizing' through the failure of certain of its members – the *populares* – to resist or to struggle against the influences of barbarism. Contemporary abhorrence of violence was undercut by a current of anxiety regarding the insufficiency of such vigilance against the spectre of decivilizing. Within this context, the 'splitting of the nobility' in the image of the late Republic bespoke a contemporary anxiety regarding the boundaries of the nation and its relation to the State.

Retracing the development of such lines of thought reveals how the abhorrence to violence with respect the gladiature was articulated, and what deeper structures of thought lay underneath. Niebuhr was an early exponent, as seen above, with his knavish aristocratic families and references to the French revolution. For Froude, a contemporary attitude of abhorrence for gladiature was an implicit anodyne to decivilizing forces, which were suggestively represented as processual in an almost Eliasian sense, on three distinct points: gladiature was a threat to western civilization which emerged from the East; its influence degraded the upper classes into a state no better than that of the mob, and thus eroded structures of social hierarchy by dissolving critical differences between class groups; as a final result, it reduced the whole of civilized society to its ultimate opposite of barbarity. This totalized decay was achieved through the intersection of violence and pleasure, which was interwoven during this period with a parallel discourse on the moral value of labour and idleness in the possession of wealth. Froude thus furnished the first clue: new money. Gladiature, and the intersection of violence and pleasure that it represented, signified in the nineteenth century nothing less than the antithesis of civilization, as this was defined as the special precinct of the conservative upper classes; however, gladiature was closely connected in the contemporary historical imagination with the socioeconomic mobility that shaped the late Republic, particularly the rise of the *homines novi* and the promiscuous inclusion of numerous patricians within the ranks of the *populares*. Gladiature provided a narrative context for the articulation of an attitude of abhorrence for violence as a repressive, proscriptive discourse in the nineteenth-century present.

Gladiature's threat to civilization – or, rather, gladiature's value in founding a historical narrative that could function as a disciplinary parable for the nobility – was even inscribed as forceful enough to cast a cloud over Greece.

Mommsen expounded upon the "evil" of gladiature as an irresistible corruption of

even Greek manners, and his version of the gladiatorial spectacle of Antiochus

Epiphanes of Syria represented the 'horror rather than pleasure' of Greek

spectators in the same manner that Friedlander treated 'original loathing' as an

initially spontaneous moral response which became eroded through repeated

exposure; though the Greek public "was more humane and had more sense of art

than the Romans, yet [gladiatorial spectacles] held their ground likewise there,

and gradually came more and more into vogue". Friedlander, in a virtuoso

display, even managed to harness the interdictory language of *luxus* to both the

inveterate corruption of the Orient *and* to the image of noble Greece succumbing

to the baleful influence of gladiature through the failure of their *nouveau riche* to

struggle against it:

> "In Greece, superior civilization at least caused less general
> acceptance of armed combats than elsewhere; yet even there they
> proved irresistible. The first proof of this is when King Antiochus
> Epiphanes gave gladiatorial games for the first time in Syria, and
> perhaps in Greece. The first impression was disgust, but repetition
> changed the feeling into approval; at first he only allowed fights up
> to the point of wounding; later, up to the death of one combatant.
> (...) And the close association of Rome with Greece after the
> conquest rendered easier the introduction of this and other Roman
> customs into Greece, the centre being Caesar's Roman colony of
> Corinth. For Corinth was non-Greek in character, and a wealthy
> port with a large corrupted mob; hence, the games would there be
> popular, and it is the only town in Greece where (before the second
> century) an amphitheatre can be traced; its ruins still exist. [...]
> Plutarch recommends the governors of towns to abolish
> gladiatorial combats, or, at least, to limit and hamper the demand.
> But his complaints of the *uneducated rich*, who did not disdain
> even this mode of corrupting the people and gaining honour, shows
> his counsel to have been a counsel of despair. [...] Gladiatorial
> combats found their way far more easily into Asia Minor with its

mixed half-Asiatic population, and all the East, except Palestine"
(Friedlander 84-5, emphasis added).

The main point brought forth, beyond the perception that the decivilizing
force of gladiature could degrade even the nineteenth century's rhetorical
touchstone of Greece, was that this was achieved first through the influence of the
mob (which, in Friedlander's example of Corinth, was not Greek); secondly
through the 'Asiatics' and all the East, who were summarily dismissed as little
better than a mob in their own right; and thirdly, through the inability of the
nation to uphold its boundaries over and against the State. The decivilized
cathexis of violence and pleasure embodied by gladiature was thus inscribed as a
powerful transgressive force across the boundaries which separated the civilized
from the barbarous. Not only did gladiature have the capacity to unseat the
socially superior and transform them into members of the mob, but its invidious
influence within such rhetoric reduced the Greeks, by this point long since
declared the cradle of western civilization, to a level of behaviour that put them
on the level of the East.

For Friedlander, the distance separating the Roman world and his own was
not great enough for comfort. Of the nineteenth-century historians, he was both
the most explicit in positing analogies between antiquity and modernity with
respect to gladiature, and the most vociferous in his opinions about the attitude
that modernity should adopt. His text gave every appearance of expecting little
better from the mob than the corruption and brutishness he observed within it, and
the bulk of his censure was reserved for the patrician class, which he structured
specifically in terms emphasizing the imperative for contemporary abhorrence: in

his terms the "gulf between the thought and feeling of Rome and modernity is best instanced in the attitude of cultured society towards the amphitheatre. In all Roman literature, there is scarcely one note of the deep horror of to-day at these inhuman delights. Generally the gladiatorial games are passed over with indifference" (76). Friedlander summarized gladiature in brief:

> "In rough warlike times Etruria introduced her sport into Rome; at first it was occasional, but, with the centuries, became usual and frequent. The acquired love of brutality was perpetuated from age to age, an irresistible spirit of the time, which can convert original loathing into pleasure, and pervades every individual" (78).

The cathexis of violence and pleasure has by this point been constructed quite clearly as a process of decline, as the rot and corruption that it represented has been firmly integrated into the dominant 'decline' narrative of Roman (and much other) classical historiography, and has come to be inscribed as a force which originated from outside, was 'introduced', and which accelerated and developed over time to "convert original loathing into pleasure". It is notable that Friedlander maintained the concept of original abhorrence, anchoring his rationalization in an idealist trope of a purer, truer Roman spirit, decivilized over time by the pollution of an Eastern practice which was fed by the opportunistic collusion of the less civic-minded members of the aristocracy and the idle urban mob.

At the same time, however, anxieties surrounding social mobility and the political solidarity of the nobility also held the core elements of another cluster of ideas which would come to dominate discourse in the early decades of the twentieth century. The language of abhorrence and decivilizing within which the nineteenth century spoke of gladiature, even as it tended to castigate the *populares* faction (and suggest that they were not true members of the nation) for seizing power through the use of gladiature as a demagogic instrument, simultaneously created a discursive space wherein the multiplied violences – the doubled barbarism of the mob, its capacity for both direct and political violence, the threat to social order which the mob represented, and gladiature itself, in its status as both effect and cause – became associated with exactly that: instrumentalization. The mob may have been rhetorically contained through its construction as an entity which existed more or less outside of civilized order, but within the imagined relation of nation to State which aligned with such notion of the mob, the discursive disciplining of those unacceptably populist members of the nation who themselves disrupted the civilized order of the late Republic through the instrumentalization of the violence/pleasure cathexis thereby contained the seeds of a potentially different image of the relation between nation and State – or, in other words, a potentially different history of right.

Chapter Five: The Primitive Violence of the Plebs

From struggle to purity

At the turn of the twentieth century, the pendulum swung yet again. The dominance of the discourse of class struggle which had marked the historiography of the latter half of the nineteenth century gave way, from the turn of the century to the end of the world wars, to a renewed emphasis upon race as the leading term of historico-political discourse within classical historiography. In the previous chapter, it was noted that Foucault distinguished nineteenth century from twentieth century notions of race based upon the absence, in the nineteenth century discursive framework, of a 'stable biological meaning' for race as a construct (*SMBD* 77). In the twentieth century, by contrast, a 'counterhistory' began to emerge that "adopt[ed] a bio-medical perspective and crush[ed] the historical dimension":

> "… the theme of the binary society which is divided into two
> races or two groups with different languages, laws, and so on will
> be replaced by that of a society that is, in contrast, biologically
> monist. Its only problem is this: it is threatened by a certain
> number of heterogeneous elements which are not essential to it,
> which do not divide the social body, or the living body of society,
> into two parts, and which are in a sense accidental. Hence the
> idea that foreigners have infiltrated this society, the theme of the
> deviants who are this society's by-products. (…) [T]he State is,
> and must be, the protector of the integrity, the superiority, and the
> purity of the race. The idea of racial purity, with all is monistic,
> Statist, and biological implications: that is what replaces the idea
> of race struggle" (*SMBD* 80-1).

The first decades of the twentieth century were a transitional period in the historiography of gladiature. The deployment of race as a construct with a 'stable biological meaning' coincided with a re-opening of the question of gladiatorial origin in a manner that somewhat evoked the realignment of discursive structures last seen in the eighteenth century: the Etruscan hypothesis did not necessarily come under direct scrutiny as such (that would not take place until the middle of the century), but gladiatorial origin slowly came to be called upon to perform a different function within historico-political discourse. At the same time, the disappearance of the language of struggle had even greater effects in the presently submerged discourse of class. the monist perception of the State was expressed by an entirely new representation of the relation between Roman rulers and Roman ruled, one which fundamentally inverted the power dynamic that had characterized the historiography of the previous century: where the 'struggle of the two races' had been aligned with the image of the lower class as a chaotic mob and a direct threat to the power of the nobility, the emergence of the discourse of racial purity inscribed the power relation between social classes as a highly rational structure of instrumentality, wherein the Roman ruling group controlled the crowd – whose image shifted during this period from 'the mob' to something more like 'the masses' – through a governing strategy that loudly echoed contemporary political developments. Both of these developments – the exploration of different terms for the interpretation of gladiature that arose from the image of its origin, and the instrumentalization of the lower classes by the aristocracy – were linked to the appearance of an entirely new discursive space surrounding violence.

The new historico-political discourse: a case study from the early twentieth century

At the turn of the century, earlier lines of thought were still prevalent; Bury's *History of the Roman Empire from its Foundation to the Death of Marcus Aurelius* (1900), for example, reiterated the familiar dichotomy between civilization and barbarity, firmly tied to the image of gladiature, and even generalized it across all social groups in a tone that still evoked the eighteenth century: "Notwithstanding the advance of [Roman] civilization in other respects, the love of these cruel sports prevailed among all classes and is a mark of barbarism which conspicuously distinguished Rome from Greece" (620).

The shift towards a monist conception of the State within the discourse of civilization, however, was already observably underway in classical historiography. The category of 'class' as an exponent or manifestation of the Foucauldian discourse of struggle began to recede from the forefront of historical narrative with Warde Fowler's 1909 *Social Life at Rome in the Age of Cicero*. As with Bury, much of the structure of Warde Fowler's historical approach again retraced well-worn themes of the previous century: the commitment to the theme of decline, the attempt to diagnose the errors of the late Republic, the perception that the sudden wealth and consequent *luxus* of the mid-republican wars of conquest had spoiled the state at a fundamental level, were still the primary signposts of his narrative. However, his brief portrait of the masses as a socio-political group was quite distinct from the shared image that had dominated earlier scholarly writing. His perspective on the lower classes was tolerant: Warde

Fowler considered it a "melancholy and significant fact that what little we know from literature about this class is derived from the part they occasionally played in riots and revolutionary disorders"; while he never claimed that the ruling class was wrong to have "believed the masses to be degraded and vicious", however, if this were so, it was to be ascribed to the fact that the paternalistic state had "made no effort to redeem them" (27):

> "There was no philanthropist, no devoted inquirer ... to investigate their condition or try to ameliorate it. The statesman, if he troubled himself about them at all, looked on them as a dangerous element of society, only to be considered as human beings at election time; at all other times merely as animals that had to be fed, in order to keep them from becoming an active peril" (26).

What we find in Warde Fowler, then, is an early inscription of a re-imagined power structure between the patrician and plebeian groups of the late Republic, one which is not based upon conflict of the struggle of two 'races' in the Foucauldian sense. The lower class is still clearly imagined as brutish, inveterately violent, and ultimately barbarous; however, whereas nineteenth century historiography had inscribed that group as an urban mob representing a direct threat to the State on the basis of these characteristics, Warde Fowler – and multiple scholars who would follow him – actually dis-empowered the crowd on the basis of precisely these qualities. The degradation, the viciousness, and particularly the disorder of the lower class, once commonly perceived as the basis of the mob's own violent power as a second 'race' locked in struggle with the historical speaking subject of the nobility, was shifting within the historico-political discourse of the early twentieth century to function as the basis of the crowd's exclusion from membership in the nation. Far from representing the 'alternate order of the barbarian', however, the lower class crowd of contemporary scholarship was instead to be re-inscribed as subjected by, and instrumental to, the civilized exercise of state power brought within the structure of legitimate governance. Warde Fowler was an early voice in the substitution of the aggressive, demanding mob so definitive of the perspective of the previous century, whose presence was a constant ill-defined threat to social order and the rational workings of government, for a new image of the crowd in an almost childlike aspect, clamouring for pleasures from the parental state instead of howling with lust for blood. His image was a first step in the process of the mob's 'domestication' into something more like 'the masses' of early twentieth century 'mass politics': where the mob had functioned as an external threat to political order, the masses would come to be represented as a tool to be instrumentalized from within that order.

Gladiature formed only a minor element of Warde Fowler's characterization of late republican socio-political decline, but his comments upon the practice chimed with his overarching image of the structures of late republican power. Again, his argument retraced many familiar lines: late republican gladiatorial combats, "because they were already becoming the favourite amusement of the common people", were increasingly implicated in electioneering during Cicero's lifetime, and as such gladiature was held up by Warde Fowler as symptomatic of the relation between the aristocracy and the crowd just as had been often done in the nineteenth century (303). However, Warde Fowler's text passed entirely over the 'evil' of demagoguery that had been such a characteristic feature of earlier writing; the introduction and rise of the "somewhat loathsome" (303) practice of gladiature was sketched as a gradual progress across the middle Republic, wherein the "stress of the great wars" required that the crowd be consoled by novel additions to the existing calendar of religious festivals; in conjunction with the corn dole, a culture of dependency was created wherein "the people were gradually accustomed to believe that the State was responsible for their enjoyment as well as their food" (299). Responsibility for this process of deterioration, however, lay entirely in the hands of the state which, significantly, was represented by Warde Fowler as a monad, not internally divided into *populares* and *optimates*.

Moreover, the impetus for gladiature was ascribed entirely to the exercise of rational governance, rather than to the previously dominant thinking which had seen gladiature's rise at Rome as a mixture of foreign religion and lower-class moral corruption. Warde Fowler did not address the idea of a non-Roman origin of gladiature; he was not interested in gladiature specifically, and focused instead upon explaining the deterioration of the republican state more generally, including the corn dole and an image of widespread descent into luxury within his analysis. He did sketch a new model of how the games originated at Rome. This model was based strictly on drift, historical accident, and the "evil results" of the originally generous intentions of the state in sponsoring novel spectacles. Warde Fowler was at pains to exonerate the aristocracy, who "drifted into these dangerous shoals in spite of the occasional efforts of intelligent steersmen; and it would indeed have needed a higher political intelligence than was then and there available, to have fully divined the direction of the drift and the dangers ahead of them" (289). The provision of games in conjunction with religious festival, followed by the expansion of the games programme, was intended merely to keep the crowd "cheerful and in good humour" during the stresses of the republican wars of conquest. Nevertheless, despite the lament of the aristocracy's inability to foresee the consequences of their actions, the point was that the governing establishment was portrayed as having taken an active role in bringing gladiature into the boundaries of the Roman state, regardless of the character of its non-Roman origin. The crowd's pleasure in violence, though still a salient trope, was no longer the determinative factor that it had been in the previous century: in the new historical narrative of gladiature, the cathexis of violence and pleasure located among the lower class was secondary to the state's decision to capitalize upon it.

What does remain assured in Warde Fowler's text, as it would remain throughout this portion of the twentieth century, was the conviction that the crowd's pleasures invariably ran to violence: the violence/pleasure cathexis of the lower classes may have been secondary to state power, but it was also anterior to it in imagined historical time. Gladiature as violent spectacle was suggestively equated with the tumultuous (and often physically violent) political struggles played out in the late republican Forum, and the 'degenerating tastes' in the crowd's amusements are mirrored by the corruption and decline of the state apparatus at the hands of the senatorial aristocracy, "as the natural result of luxury and idleness" (306). This degeneration of popular tastes in public entertainment, however, pre-existed the state's (mis-) management. Warde Fowler openly stated that the "last age of the Republic is a transitional one ... the people are not yet thoroughly inured to bloodshed and cruelty ... as they afterwards became when deprived of political excitements, and left with nothing violent to amuse them but displays of the amphitheatre" (313). The clear implication was that the *populus* may have been saved by an intelligent helmsman at the head of the state, but the 'cruelty' from which they failed to be rescued had not been trained into them by the introduction of gladiature into public entertainment – rather, the state had failed to train it out of them.

What this thought implied – and it was an implication which would appear in the work of other scholars of this period – was a particular shift in the old anxiety surrounding what we have been occasionally referring to in this dissertation as 'decivilizing': that persistent trope within historico-political discourse which posits and constructs the relation that 'civilized society', as the speaking subject which constructs its self-image through historical discourse, perceives as existing between itself and the figure of the barbarian. Warde Fowler's work contained an early expression of a new notion, namely that the barbarian (whether conceived of in terms of the presence of the barbarous within the lower social orders of the State, or in the externalized barbarian which dominated scholarly discourse regarding gladiatorial origin) was, on the one hand, well within the scope of control by the ruling class: the 'threat' of decivilizing implied by gladiature, and the cathexis of violence and pleasure represented therein, was receding or re-situating within the historico-political framework of classical historiography. However, despite being seen as ultimately subject to or determined by state control, the threat to social order that gladiature represented was still maintained as grounds for disqualification or exclusion from 'the nation'.

The difference lay in the new relation with the barbarian inscribed within the resituated trope of decivilizing, as this functioned within the broader framework of the historiography of gladiature. The nineteenth century narrative had asserted that 'Rome' – an entity with an essential and inviolable core identity, expressed most clearly by Mommsen – was a state brought low by pressures emanating from one or more *external* conceptions of the barbarian, whose 'externality' was associated with a relatively heightened image of the decivilizing threat posed. In contrast, the historiography of the early twentieth century saw the barbarian as having directly infiltrated the state: the lower classes or the crowd came increasingly to be perceived, more or less literally, as 'non-Roman' in a number of senses. Infiltration of the State, however, was not equated with infiltration of the nation. Thus, once again, in classical historiography we see 'the nation' inscribed as a reserved ruling group or nobility within the social body as well as the political state; what was specific to this period was a re-imagined structure of power relations between the civilized nobility and the new barbarian within the State.

This imagined relation was one of instrumentality: the instrumentalization of the 'new barbarian within the State' to the service of the political ends of the Roman nobility, and specifically the manipulation (with or without consent) of exactly what defined the barbarian as barbarous – in this discourse, the capacity to take pleasure in violence - in order to achieve those ends. In essence, society was defended against the barbarian, in the historical imagination of the early twentieth

century, by using the barbarian against (him)self. Gladiature was no longer taken

by modern scholars as a sign of (political) struggle; if anything, it now functioned

within classical historiography as a sign of state power over the instrumentalized

populus, rather than of the threat that the *populus* represented to the exercise of

state power as in the historical writing of the previous century. The struggle had

been pacified and rationalized. It was within this framework that the discursive

trope of struggle fell into abeyance and the imagined locus of power in

contemporary historical thought reverted entirely to the Roman ruling class,

which became the representation of 'purity' or, rather, part of the language of the

new biology which began to re-define the ruling group as the 'head' of a

biologically monist state/social 'body'.

Race, class, and pleasure

As part of the labour of inscribing the lower classes of the Roman

Republic as 'barbarians within the walls', the early twentieth century witnessed

the renascence, first intimated in the nineteenth century by scholars such as de

Coulanges, Arnold, and Merivale, of the elision of race with class as a central

idiom of the biological construct of race. Warde Fowler had alluded to it when he

spoke of the population of Rome as incorporating "heterogeneous elements" in

the later Republic, and directly associated such demographic change with rioting,

disorder, and gladiatorial shows (Warde Fowler 306; cf. *SMBD* 81 above). Warde

Fowler's comparatively polite language, however, was radically exceeded by

some scholars of his generation. Tenney Frank, whose *A History of Rome*

appeared in 1923, had his own ideas about the causes of the 'moral decline' of
Roman society in the late Republic, and in his view there was no question that the
heterogeneous elements contributing to the internal destabilization of Roman
society were manifest in a "gradual change of race at Rome". Frank described the
socio-political change of the middle and late republican periods as a gradual
replacement of the "old stock of Italy" by "hordes of slaves who bred up a new
race of freedmen and consequently of citizens", slaves who could not, being
"mostly of excitable eastern races, become true citizens of a Roman republic"
(*History of Rome* 242).

Frank's contribution to classical scholarship is notable here as an
extremely clear example of the introduction of the construct and language of
purity, as indicated by Foucault, into historico-political discourse. Frank's notion
of purity, in particular, not only blended categories of race and class, but in fact
leaned heavily upon antiquity. He conceded that "extreme caution is necessary in
attempting to estimate" the influence of racial inheritances upon political
circumstances, and prudently pointed out that "ease of communication has now so
thoroughly mixed peoples of different parts of Europe that 'pure races' hardly
exist from which to draw safe illustrations" (*History of Rome* 566). Therefore, the
illustrative study of antiquity – when the old stock of ancient Italy could be taken
as 'pure', and the influx of conquered and colonised peoples into the emerging
empire could similarly be regarded as a singular event of 'foreign infiltration' –
was a crucial opportunity for Frank, providing an exemplary proof that could not
be duplicated in modernity:

"Race-mixture may produce good results, but it has also been established that in the mixture of two excellent stocks of widely different qualities an unstable fusion often results which perpetuates the poorer qualities of both. Applying this consideration to Rome, if we find that the Latin stock advanced consistently along certain lines so long as it was fairly unmixed, and that it gradually declined from about the time that racial fusion was marked, we may fairly attribute this new trend in some measure to the process of the 'melting-pot'" (*History of Rome* 567).

Antiquity, for Frank, was thus still a 'laboratory of history' in something like the eighteenth-century sense; now, however, the expressions of 'national spirit' for which the annals of classical history were being searched were based upon an emerging biopolitics that not only read 'race' as a biological property, but directly connected it to the construct of civilization, as the infamous decline and fall of Rome could now be seen as an empirical proof of the theory and discourse of race purity.

Moreover, the 'decline' in question was expressed in language which ever more clearly and closely aligned the moral language of civilization and the biological language of 'race' with the political language of state power. The 'racial fusion' that primarily occupied Frank and his adherents (most notably Heaton, whose 1939 *Mob Violence in Ancient Rome* reads as a point-for-point regurgitation) was between "the slow-minded, composed, rationalistic and liberty-loving Roman" and "the versatile, choleric, superstitious, mystical and servile Asian". The former was the race that had built the Republic, and the latter, the slaves and freed descendants of slaves from the campaigns of Roman expansion in the Middle East, were "by temperament incapable of republican government", for "however keen of mind and shrewd of wit they were, their experience as slaves has taught them lessons of individual craftiness rather than of political wisdom" (*History of Rome* 242-3). Thus the categorical elision of race with class defined and defended the borders of the nation, as the seat of legitimate political authority, on multiple fronts at a single stroke, all centred upon the ascendant trope of purity. To an increasing degree, 'purity' was coming to function as the primary construction placed upon the closely related trope of origin in classical scholarship (to be further discussed below).

In his later *Aspects of Social Behaviour in Ancient Rome* (1932), Frank expanded his race theory of the decline of the Republic to encompass gladiature as a signifier and a proof of the alignment between racial purity and political authority. Gladiature was insinuated into his narrative and aligned with the perceived racial admixture of the lower classes, as the "admission of such hordes of slaves that Rome's old population, which had always insisted upon self-determination and individual rights, gave way in time to a docile mass that was willing to trade away self-government for bread and games" (*Aspects of Social Behaviour* 106). Moreover, gladiature was further implicated in an evocation of contemporary totalitarian political movements. The 'docile mass' of the republican citizenry in Frank's text eventually formed the substratum of an empire which, having unwisely opened its borders long since to the flood of crafty Asiatics, was forced to take sinister totalitarian steps in order to maintain control of an empire which would have been better preserved as a small, closed republican state. As the imperial government had assumed the central directive responsibility for such affairs as production, trade, education, public works, charity and amusements such as gladiature, "the primary aims of administration were neglected, the burdens upon the taxpayer passed all bounds, and for self-protection the state was compelled to enchain every citizen and make of him a cog in the universal machine". The second-century reign of the Emperor Hadrian had a clear modern exemplar, as the "committee that rules Russia can alone supply a parallel to this regime in its control over the lives and properties of all citizens of the nation" (*Aspects of Social Behaviour* 105). Here, it was no longer demagoguery and mob rule that threatened the nation and presented itself as the antithesis of civilization; it was Bolshevism.

The withdrawal of the trope of struggle

As the discourse of struggle faded away in classical historiography, it carried in its wake the romantic narrative of the 'fall' of the republic, particularly as this had been thought of as a struggle between a small guard of old republican stalwarts and an equally small group of budding dynastic tyrants. *The Roman Revolution*, Ronald Syme's 1939 study on the social and political developments which presaged the violent transition from republican to imperial government in the later first century B.C., entrenched the emerging scholarly perspective which sought to analyze the period as the result of an internal power shift in the governing party, as the traditional senatorial aristocracy was compelled to admit and eventually cede authority to the rising equestrian/plebeian class. The end of the Republic was no longer to be seen as a fall, but as a revolution – though not a popular one, despite the instrumentalization of populist political tactics, including gladiatorial spectacle. Instead, the revolutionary change in government from the

Republic to the reign of Augustus was reinterpreted as an internal coup within the

ruling class, and the role of the crowd in the reorganization of socio-political

structure was again reduced, ever more clearly, to that of a mere instrument of the

political interests of the emerging power group within the Senate.

Syme's grounding assertion was that it was inaccurate and naïve to view

the Republic as an early democracy which 'fell' to the corrupted self-interest of

individual tyrants, who appeared on the political stage in the first century B.C.

and whose seizure of government represented the triumph of personal interest and

of baser human instincts over the nobler, more evolved social compact embodied

by the Republic. On the contrary, Syme asserted that the traditional governing

system of the Republic as it was founded was itself tyrannical in nature, and, by

implication, the contemporary discursive monism of the State, as this found

expression in classical scholarship, now encompassed not only the internal

solidarity of the ruling class, but the increasingly nominal historicist division

between Republic and Empire:

> "When the patricians expelled the kings from Rome [at the end of
> the sixth century B.C.], they were careful to retain the kingly power,
> vested in a pair of annual magistrates; and though compelled in time
> to admit plebeians to political equality, certain of the great patrician
> houses ... none the less held in turn a dynastic and almost regal
> position. The Senate again being a permanent body, arrogated to
> itself power, and after conceding sovranty [sic] to the assembly of
> the People was able to frustrate its exercise" (10).

The shift in governance from the republican to the early imperial system

was rewritten by Syme as an indictment of Octavian, who in Syme's view seized

intelligently upon existing conditions and exploited them to his fullest advantage.

The political manipulation of the masses was a key to the 'revolutionary' agenda.

In Syme's version of events, the process of the crowd's 'decline' had been

contrived over the course of the middle Republic by the traditional senatorial

aristocracy, as the "politicians of the previous age, whether conservative or

revolutionary, despised so utterly the plebs of Rome that they felt no scruples

when they enhanced its degradation. (...) Debauched by demagogues and largess,

the Roman People was ready for the Empire and the dispensation of bread and

games" (100). The power figuration written here was thus constructed with an

entirely different orientation than had shaped nineteenth-century historiography: if

the Republic could be said to have declined, which condition had traditionally

been read through the character of the mob and the nature of its relation to

instabilities of governance, Syme definitively relocated the impetus for the mob's

position from its previously immutable character of violence to the Senate's

pattern of state administration. Though the urban plebs at the end of the Republic

were still periodically described in the nineteenth-century manner as a mob, this

new crowd – the masses - was one which had been engineered by the state, rather

than as an external barbarian order which posed a threat to the state from beyond

its borders. Syme clearly disagreed with Warde Fowler and Frank over the precise

interpretation of the state's mismanagement of the populace; nevertheless, there

was strong accord over the sense that all real power ultimately resided with the

ruling class, however internally fractious it may have been.

The intensely negative discourse surrounding demagoguery which had

been such a pronounced element of the historiography of the previous century was

effectively replaced by an interpretive focus that pivoted upon the contemporary 'science' of mass politics, which in turn was of course a politics of spectacle, including gladiature. The period of the demagogic *populares* of the later second and first centuries BC, which had earlier been inscribed as a disciplinary narrative against the anomic behaviour of traitorous members within the aristocracy, was now less significant than Octavian's concentration of such deeply-rooted developments into an increasingly institutionalized form of politics that reverberated deeply with contemporary movements in this period of modern history, as twentieth-century totalitarianism exerted an observable impact upon the figure of the tyrant. The old discourse of *luxus* and moral decline which had previously shaped the interpretation of gladiature and the crowd ceded the field to an image of the late Republic which bore a pronounced resemblance to early fascism, wherein the essential bloodlust of the mob as the driving force behind gladiature was replaced by the dominant, centralized authority of the "Republican dynast [who] solicited the favour of the sovran [sic] people by lavish displays at games, shows and triumphs. As a showman, none could compete with Augustus in material resources, skill of organization and sense of the dramatic" (Syme 468).

Syme's text dwelt repeatedly upon the precise nature of the popular vote. In his view, the franchise had not been especially meaningful or effective under the republican system, given the extent to which the public offices decided by the vote were controlled *a priori* by restricted access to the right to stand for office; with this in mind, Augustus' nominal restoration of citizen franchise appeared particularly sinister in its hollowness, though the lower classes were represented as complicit in the superficiality of the observance of democratic forms:

"When Senate and People were ostensibly Sovran, the members of a narrow group contended among themselves for office and for glory: behind the facade of the constitution the political dynasts dealt out offices and commands to their partisans. The dynasts had destroyed the Republic and themselves, down to the last survivor, Caesar's heir. Engrossing all their power and all their patronage, he conveniently revived the Republic to be used as they had used it. To the People Augustus restored freedom of election. Fed by the bounty and flattered by the magnificence of their champion, the plebs of Rome knew how they were expected to use that freedom" (370).

There was an obvious connection, then, between the perceived meaninglessness of the vote and the discursive de-emphasis of the morally charged cathexis of violence with pleasure that had stood behind the image of the *pollice verso* throughout the nineteenth century. In the historical imagination of the early twentieth century, the Roman nobility owned and controlled the popular vote in the final decades of the Republic; the difference perfectly illustrates the extent to which the perceived power of the franchise correlated with the level of urgency in the moralizing language which sought to discredit the capacity of the plebs to exercise it.

The newly reorganized ruling class, for its part, understood perfectly well that "[g]ames and festivals were customary devices for the organization of popular sentiment" (Syme 116), and thus gladiature was incorporated into a contemporary narrative of top-down, hyperconscious political manipulation which formed a complete negation of the account of class conflict, enacted at the site of the amphitheatre, that had dominated scholarship as little as fifty years earlier. The Roman revolution, then, was contained in the fact that Augustus had seized upon the entire "motley and excitable rabble" (Syme 100) as his personal clientele: he "fed them with doles, amused them with games and claimed to be their protector against oppression. Free elections returned – that is to say, a grateful people would unfailingly elect the candidates whom Caesar in his wisdom had chosen, with or without formal commendation" (Syme 322). It is worth pointing out that, where we would likely expect some comment of the *pollice verso* at this point, Syme was completely silent on that subject; though it had gripped the historical imagination of the previous century, the image of the *pollice verso* as a key trope of the interpretation of gladiature was closely tied to the diminished significance of the late republican franchise as a whole. Correspondingly, as the vote was accorded less (or no) real political power in the narrative, the *pollice verso* ceased to invoke the moralized language of abhorrence, which had itself lost its previous force of meaning. The turning of thumbs in the amphitheatre was rendered suddenly irrelevant to the narrative, as the contemporary spectre of decivilizing in the West shifted from the nineteenth-century anxiety over populism to the early twentieth-century anxiety over totalitarianism.

A decade later, Syme's student Ross Taylor repackaged Syme's views in *Party Politics in the Age of Caesar* (1949). Ross Taylor's text opened with an echo of Warde Fowler's lament regarding the heavy senatorial bias in the surviving written source material for the late Republic, and stated that the "failure of our sources here is the more serious because the widening chasm between the upper and lower classes was a major reason for the decay of the political institutions of the republic and for the role played by arms and violence in settling party strife" (2). She duly cited the changing urban demography of Rome in the wake of the wars of conquest, rural dispossession and the competition between free labour and the expanding population of slaves, without a trace of the racialized arguments of Frank (Ross Taylor 5). However, in Ross Taylor's model, the lower classes were otherwise written out almost completely from the narrative of events of the transition between the late Republic and the Empire, which was now inscribed as a political contest between the patrician aristocracy and the *homines novi* (Ross Taylor 22) – itself hardly a new idea, to be sure, but one which had by this point quite lost its once-emphatic rhetoric surrounding the role of the mob, even instrumentally. On the one hand the focus upon a party model of political transformation represented a break away from the 'history of great men' which had been such a pronounced feature of the historiography of ancient Rome; Ross Taylor's account offered a far more corporate account of political events. On the other hand, such a corporate perspective worked to consolidate the notion that the significant and determinative structure of group relations in this period pertained almost exclusively to the various factions of the ruling class.

Ross Taylor's text implied a new insignificance of the lower classes which others stated more openly. Salmon's 1944 *History of the Roman World from 30 BC to AD138*, focusing on the Augustan period and the succeeding century, did not afford gladiature and other spectacles even the limited political force of electoral bribery, representing the practice instead as a true sop to political ignorance as early as Octavian's principate: "Lavish games and doles of grain were a traditional method for diverting public attention from public uncertainties.

By a liberal dose of *panis et circenses* Octavian kept the public from brooding on

recent calamities" (*History of the Roman World from 30 BC* 3). Salmon's image

of the transition from republic to empire, and its aftermath, was conversely intent

not upon the late republican manipulation of the popular vote, but rather upon the

early imperial withdrawal from all but the outward forms of assembly and

election. The lower classes here were not represented as merely complicit in the

popular party's agenda, as in Syme, but as indifferent to it:

> "The Roman plebs does not seem to have bitterly resented its
> exclusion from political activity. From Augustus' time onward, all
> organizations or clubs (*collegia*) of a potentially political nature
> were suppressed. Yet the *cives Romani* acquiesced. For this there
> were several explanations. Even in republican times the political
> participation of the lower orders in politics had been more nominal
> than real. The great noble houses had really controlled the popular
> Assemblies through their dependents (*clientes*). The substitution of
> a Princeps for an oligarchical clique did not make a great deal of
> difference as far as the plebs was concerned. The urban mob could
> not have been conscious of any great loss of political power,
> especially when the Princeps paraded his sensitivity to its moods
> and caprices, and showed concern to keep it fed and amused"
> (*History of the Roman World from 30 BC* 58).

Such inflections found their way even into contemporary academic

accounts of a more traditional bent. For example, Carcopino's 1940 *Daily Life in*

Ancient Rome: The People and the City at the Height of the Empire could not

have been more different from Syme's iconoclastic work: it was a general

historical survey intended largely as an undergraduate text, and its broad focus

was the Empire. However, imperial spectacle was here inscribed as integral to the

mechanics of governing the masses, and Carcopino cited numerous contemporary

European government initiatives to support his point (212):

"The emperors developed skill in canalizing this mass emotion and directing its currents, and often succeeded in transferring to the multitude the responsibility for acts of vengeance which they had already planned but preferred to execute under the appearance of popular duress. Thus the spectacles of Rome, though not forming an integral part of the governmental system of the empire, helped to sustain its structure, and without becoming incorporated in the imperial religion, fanned whatever flame still burned in it. Not was this all: they formed a barrier for autocracy against revolution. In the city there were 150 000 complete idlers supported by the generosity of the public assistance, and perhaps an equal number of workers who from one year's end to the other had no occupation after the hour of noon and yet were deprived of the right to devote their spare time to politics. The shows occupied the time of these people, provided a safety valve for their passions, distorted their instincts, and diverted their activity. A people that yawns is ripe for revolt. The Caesars saw to it that the Roman plebs suffered from neither hunger nor ennui. The spectacles were the great anodyne for their subjects' unemployment, and the sure instrument of their own absolutism. They shrewdly buttressed their power by surrounding the plebs with attentions and expending fabulous sums of money in the process" (210).

Cowell's 1948 *Cicero and the Roman Republic* carried the point even further, and claimed that the "poverty-stricken masses of Rome were and remained politically insignificant, cowed by the sight of a few armed troops. Despite the instinctive support they probably gave to legitimate government, they were ready to cheer any substitute for it clearly able to command them" (278). This eventually total withdrawal of the crowd's agency from the political narrative was the culmination of the replacement, for a discourse of struggle, of a discourse of purity.

Abhorrence, purity, origin

The summary image which emerges from the breadth of the historiography of this period is one in which the imagined structure of socio-political power in late republican Rome, the relation between the ruling class and the crowd and the understanding of each of those groups which arose from and within the context of that relation, had been reversed almost entirely from the imagined structure which had organized the historiography of the previous century. This period inscribed the authority of the ruling class as far more corporate in nature and consolidated in effect (witness 'party politics'); the formerly subversive interests of the *populares* and their demagogic programme were no longer construed as a corrupt, decivilizing erosion of a formerly robust republican state already destabilized by the enervating influence of *luxus* upon an essentially amoral mob, but rather as a party-based precipitation of political consequences already embedded within the Roman constitution. In direct correlation, the crowd was no longer perceived as a violent force of social disruption in its own right, in conformity with the image of the governing authority as possessing such relatively hegemonic control.

A further point that arises from the examination of these sources, albeit obliquely, is the observation that during the first half of the twentieth century, the previously elaborate discourse which surrounded the cathexis of violence and pleasure in the crowd's enjoyment of gladiature had lapsed into almost complete silence. The bloodlust and essential cruelty of the animal nature of the mob, rhetorical motifs which had exerted such strong explanatory force in the nineteenth century, were during this period referred to only occasionally, and then in a perceptibly desultory fashion; Warde Fowler's comments on the innocent pleasures of the crowd are very nearly the last words on the subject, at least within scholarly circles. Directly linked with the new irrelevance of the crowd's pleasure in violence was the similar disappearance of the morally charged and often fulminous expressions of abhorrence. As the historico-political discourse of struggle morphed into a discourse of purity, and the newly monist State, as Foucault described it, came to be perceived as just, gladiature as a means of instrumentalizing the once-chaotic latent power of the lower classes at Rome came to be seen, increasingly, as legitimate, and the moral anxiety which had once driven the language of abhorrence in classical historiography fell briefly silent. As a result, civilization was signified not by a mannerly abhorrence of violence, but by a calculated mastery of its political effects.

In accordance with this shift in the interpretation of Roman power structures surrounding the practice of gladiature, there arose at the same time a renovated interpretation of the violence of gladiature itself, based upon the understanding of gladiature as aligned with a hybrid figure of sport and/or warfare, rather than with religious funerary ritual as had been the case since the Enlightenment. Traces of this new interpretation have already appeared in the sources examined above pertaining to the spectrum of links in classical historiography that connected gladiature to the narrative of political history in describing the transition from Republic to Empire; from Warde Fowler to Cowell, we see a tendency to categorize gladiature with other public 'amusements, games, and shows', without isolating the practice from the theatre or the circus as commonly as was seen in the scholarship of the nineteenth century.

However, a more developed form of the new approach to gladiature, and specifically the problem of its violence as a source of pleasure, appeared during this period in the ongoing investigation into gladiature's origin. Scholarly consensus would not shift definitively just yet – that development did not occur with certainty until the postwar period. Throughout the first half of the century, however, the swing within academia manifested two central characteristics: on the one hand, the interpretation of the Etruscan hypothesis gradually changed its orientation, and on the other it was increasingly challenged by the emergence of a competing hypothesis, which argued that the origin of gladiature was to be sought among a wholly distinct ancient cultural group, the Oscan-speaking Samnites of southern Italy. Within the shift in the image of gladiature's original cultural context were a linked series of deeper shifts in the construction of gladiatorial violence. Classical historiography since the Enlightenment had viewed original gladiature as a form of human sacrifice, which contextualized gladiature as a ritualized, symbolic violence; as discussed in various sections above, the symbolic property of gladiature had generally been located in the sacrifice of human blood to the deceased, and the interpretive discourse surrounding such symbolism had oscillated over a moral point of whether or not gladiature as a symbolic form represented a civilizing or decivilizing change in the imagined historical development of ritual human sacrifice. At the turn of the twentieth century, however, this basic structure in the approach to gladiatorial violence shifted comprehensively, as the assumption of ritual symbolism was displaced by a new *a priori* belief that the violence of gladiature was best understood, first and foremost, as mimetically associated with another violence: in effect, where original gladiature had once been rationalized by reference to the symbolic structures of ancient religious belief, it was now referred to as a mimetic performance related directly to ancient warfare and, to a lesser extent, to sport. These alternative perspective were closely aligned with the Etruscan hypothesis of origin, and the South Italian/Samnite hypothesis, respectively.

The debate surrounding the cultural origin of gladiature, however, was of course accompanied by a concomitant shift in the contextual framework of historico-political discourse, particularly in terms of race:

> "The racism that came into being as a transformation of and an alternative to revolutionary discourse, or the old discourse of race struggle, underwent two further transformations in the twentieth century. At the end of the nineteenth century, we see the appearance of what might be called a State racism, of a biological and centralized racism. And it was this theme that was, if not profoundly modified, at least transformed and utilized in strategies specific to the twentieth century. On the one hand, we have the Nazi transformation, which takes up the theme, established at the end of the nineteenth century, of a State racism that is responsible for the biological protection of the race. This theme is, however, reworked and converted, in a sort of regressive mode, in such a way that it is implanted in and functions within the very prophetic discourse from which the theme of race struggle once emerged. Nazism was thus able to reuse a whole popular, almost medieval, mythology that allowed State racism to function within an ideologico-mythical landscape similar to that of the popular struggle which, at a given moment, could support and make it possible to formulate the theme of a race struggle. It was also accompanied by the theme of ... the empire of the last days which will ensure the millenarian victory of the race ... (*SMBD* 82).

Gladiatorial historiography's articulation of 'the new discourse of race struggle' in the study of cultural origin should be examined as a particular expression of what Foucault above terms the 'regressive mode'. What we find in the classical scholarship of the early twentieth century is a conceptualization of race that appears at times to regress to the language of spirit that marked the eighteenth century. As suggested by Foucault above in *Society Must Be Defended*, and hearkening back to several of his other comments in *The Order of Things* discussed in earlier chapters, the State racism found in the early twentieth century did in some sense invoke both the nineteenth century's discourse of 'series, of sequential connection, and of development' (*OT* 263) as well as the notion of the universal mathesis which had preceded it: in such a regressive mode, the 'ideological mythology' that was possible during this period invoked a 'prophetic discourse' that seemed almost to suggest or imply a new mathesis arising as the (utopian) outcome of race struggle as such. The discourse of race struggle during this period bore a representation of its own imagined historical end which was formulated, arguably, as an (altered) return to that discourse's own historical origin. Nazism, in this sense, was only one exceptionally clear representation of the west's historico-political discourse surrounding the great global clashes of the early twentieth century: despite the risk of absurd reduction, it is nevertheless fair to say that more than one nation was engaged in struggle over socio-political order on an unprecedented scale. What we find in classical historiography – taken, as always, as the constituting 'mythology' held in common by the western nations as such – is the development of a new construct of origin which both invoked the universalizing, essentializing language of the Enlightenment, and at the same time represented an altered relationship between modernity and antiquity.

Both the Etruscan and Samnite hypotheses of origin (as canvassed in Chapter One) could be read in the suggestive evidence provided by surviving ancient sources. What remains, then, is the question of why scholarly consensus changed during this period from one perspective to the other. It is true that new evidence was incorporated at this time; both the Etruscan and South Italian/Samnite hypotheses in the first half of the twentieth century took into account a certain amount of new visual evidence from antiquity, largely in the form of tomb paintings, much of which had not been known or well-studied previously. However, it is fairly clear, from an examination of contemporary scholarship, that the exchange of one image of gladiatorial origin for another was not achieved simply on the basis of 'new evidence'. A broader discursive shift was in play that prefigured the discussion surrounding new research. Hints of this broadly-based change in framework are contained in one of Foucault's comments, already cited in Chapter One above:

> "...the other race is basically not the race that came from elsewhere or that was, for a time, triumphant and dominant, but that it is a race that is permanently, ceaselessly infiltrating the social body ... In other words, what we see as a polarity, as a binary rift within society, is not a clash between two distinct races. It is the splitting of a single race into a superrace and a subrace. To put it a different way, it is the reappearance, within a single race, of the past of that race" (*SMBD* 61).

This new figuration in twentieth century classicism's historico-political discourse – the inscription or conception of the barbarian as emanating from civilization's own past, which differed significantly from the eighteenth or nineteenth century figure(s) of the barbarian as representatives of 'different races' in a more literal sense (according to the ordering construct of race as such) – was the single most significant discursive development of this period of historical writing regarding gladiature. It is this thought that shaped the 'altered relationship between modernity and antiquity' alluded to above: this period's 'regressive mode' of historical thought, which seized upon the existing mythological function of antiquity and re-cast it as something more directly mythical, more directly and 'literally' connected with the modern west, was perhaps not articulated in as developed a language as, say, the contemporary imagined Aryan roots of Nazism; nevertheless, the same basic structures of discourse were manifest in classical historiography. A new construct of primitivism was in play, and as a consequence, the barbarian was not primarily sought or perceived outside the (either social or racial) boundaries of the State; instead, the barbarian was dominantly located as the 'past of the race': still fundamentally excluded from the 'nation' as circumscribed by the nobility as historical speaking subject, of course, but ceaselessly infiltrating the social body from the underside of the State (as seen above in contemporary constructions of republican social power structures) and – on a different level – standing always at the origin of civilization itself. In this sense, the regressive mode of the early twentieth century was a 'regression' of a specific structure, which arguably partook of elements from both eighteenth and nineteenth century thought in conjunction with the new biologism: we see a return to something like the essentialism of the concept of 'spirit' dominant in the eighteenth century, invoked alongside a post-Enlightenment rationality of hierarchical series whose temporal dimension (i.e. the relation between antiquity and modernity) was transformed by the implications of the concept of race purity. To attempt to sum up in language that bears directly on the discussion at hand, the 'new barbarian', rather than a perpetual enemy, was now an ancestor; further, that ancestral barbarian was present for civilization in a doubled manner, as both manifest in the essential nature of the lower classes of society (who represented, as ever, one face of the barbarian) and as some element of the essential nature or 'spirit' of the nation as the locus of civilization. In the face of a 'biological' connection to the past, the nation (qua race) now rested far more heavily and directly upon the construct of 'origin' as the very basis of the history of right, especially in its myth-historical iteration of classical historiography.

This discursive shift, in turn, generated three subsequent effects pertinent to the discussion at hand: one, the new legitimacy surrounding the instrumentalization of violence entailed that this approach to violence was written in to the image of gladiatorial origin, in specific ways that will be addressed below; two, the fundamental alteration in the construct of civilization, especially with respect to violence, naturally produced a corresponding shift in the trope of 'decivilizing' within the language of civilization as this was articulated in the contemporary historiography of Rome; and three – as has already been hinted at above, in the discussion of this period's iteration of the discourse of class struggle – a widespread lapsing into silence of the abhorrence of violence. All of these changes, in turn, produced a new image of the cultural context of gladiatorial origin with an entirely different array of connotations to inscribe the space of violence within the history of right of the modern west.

The mimetic conceptualization of violence which connected gladiatorial origin, in some essential way, to warfare provided the foundation for an entirely new historico-political discourse that inscribed the new legitimacy of the political instrumentalization of violence, specifically in the cathexis of violence and pleasure that marked the lower classes of the State. This correlated with a shift of the 'originating culture' of gladiature from the foreign barbarian represented by the nineteenth century's image of Etruria, to the new barbarian of ancient Samnium, which figure was primarily defined, not by its 'foreignness', but by its primitivism. Samnium functioned as a historicized barbarian representing civilization's prehistory, directly or ancestrally linked by virtue of the emergent discourse of biologism, and whose relationship to civilized society thus reproduced or echoed the relation also occupied by the image of the crowd as simultaneously inside and outside of civilized society, or as 'part of the State but not members of the Nation'. This new mythology for the history of right, as based upon the imperative to inscribe the legitimization of a certain instrumentalization of violence by the nation, consequently wrote for gladiature a new origin, one which was 'racially European' in contrast to nineteenth-century thinking, and which rationalized the violence/pleasure cathexis of gladiature not only as a kind of mythical, regressive origin story for warfare, but also as inherently 'primitive', and thereby staged the political instrumentalization of violence-*cum*-gladiature - a myth-historical proxy for the nobility's political dominance in general - not as abhorrent but, in fact, as civilized. The expressions of all of these shifts would become dramatically clearer and more explicit in decades to follow, but the seeds of many later developments were to be found in the gestures and directions of thought articulated in the first half of the twentieth century.

The Etruscan hypothesis

Even as the Samnite hypothesis of gladiatorial origin began to build momentum, the older Etruscan hypothesis persisted well into the middle of the twentieth century. However, the new conceptualization of violence markedly permeated and reshaped the Etruscan image of original gladiature, as the perception of gladiature as essentially characterized by a mimetic violence evoking warfare or combat (rather than as a sacrificial violence primarily to be understood within the framework of religion) was interwoven with contemporary thinking regarding the Etruscans themselves in a wider sense.

A major new emphasis within the material record from antiquity was visual art, especially tomb paintings which had been excavated sporadically over the second half of the nineteenth century and now were coming to be studied as collections. A series of collected studies of Etruscan tomb painting in the first half of the century (Weege's 1921 *Etruskische Malerei*, Poulsen's 1922 *Etruscan Tomb Paintings: Their Subjects and Significance*, Ducati's 1941 *Pittura etrusca italo-greca e romana* and Pallottino's 1952 *Etruscan Painting* among the major works) culminated in a strong association between the composite image of early Etruscan gladiature and certain images on the walls of the Tarquinian Tomb of the Augurs, which had been excavated in 1877. Specifically, the singular image of a named individual Phersu (variously interpreted as a masked actor or a deity)

holding a large animal (usually interpreted as a dog) on a long leash, while the

animal attacks an unnamed and visibly wounded man who is armed with a club

but blinded by a hood, was repeatedly interpreted as visual evidence of a practice

which was at least uniquely Etruscan and to be considered as associated with the

origins of funerary gladiature. The original excavation notes in *Notizia degli Scavi*

had not suggested this interpretive connection, but the idea circulated widely

during this period and is still periodically under discussion in the present (cf.

Thuillier). Poulsen's interpretation strove to interpret the images in terms of

combat, and to connect them to Roman gladiature according to that essential

characteristic:

> "The explanation of this exciting and brutal contest, to which no
> parallel can be found in Greek art, is evidently that Phersu tries to
> make the dog bite his antagonist to death before the latter can get
> his head out of the sack and hit man and dog with his club. If the
> club-bearer succeeds in freeing himself from the sack and the dog,
> Phersu has only one chance: to run away. [...] But we know of no
> example from Hellas of a fight like that between Phersu,
> accompanied by his blood-hound, and the muffled club-bearer: a
> fight the attraction of which, apart from its sanguinary character,
> evidently depended on the disparity of the weapons, as it did in the
> combat between gladiator and *retiarius*, the man armed with net
> and trident, in the Roman arenas of a later day" (Poulsen 12).

Even thirty years later, Pallottino reiterated Poulsen's interpretation in full,

contributing only the assertion that *Phersu*, as an Etruscan cognate to the Latin

persona, must therefore have been an actor dressed in a mask with a false beard.

(Poulsen's comments will briefly be pertinent again to the discussion in the next

section.) The ascendance of 'mimetic violence' in the interpretation of gladiature

was more or less generalized during this period, and it was applied to Etruria as much as to Samnium; this factor alone was not sufficient to explain the shift of the image of gladiatorial origin from one to the other.

The return of 'national spirit': the Samnites

As hinted at by the passage from Poulsen above, the return of an altered form of the language of 'spirit' was circulating during this period all through scholarly inquiry into gladiatorial origin, regardless of which cultural origin was being weighed; Poulsen's opinion, for example, though attentive to the new emphasis upon combat, was also evidently built around a notion of 'Greek character' that arguably bore echoes of voices from as far back as Winckelmann. The emergence of the Samnite hypothesis of gladiatorial origin was, from its outset, closely wedded to this same language of 'national character' that connoted the deeper discourse of racial purity, and at the same time was framed by scholarship's turn to combat and warfare.

It is a bit disingenuous to speak of 'the emergence of the Samnite hypothesis' as a *fait accomplit* during this period of classical historiography. The most current scholarship on the subject usually attributes the Samnite hypothesis to Ville's posthumously published 1981 monograph, which is inaccurate; on the other hand, what 'emerged' in the first half of the twentieth century was less a hypothesis or definitive claim for a Samnite origin, and more a network of telling associations which tended to draw the Samnites in its wake, and which shed a critical light on later, stronger assertions. The driving discursive force was the strengthening link between gladiature, the interpretation of its violence, and warfare; this both set the stage for a new consensus in the meaning and function of gladiature for Rome, and at the same time veered academic focus away from Etruria and towards Samnium, a cultural group which even in ancient Roman sources was closely associated with warfare or a 'warlike nature', and who inhabited a unique position in Roman history, particularly in their always volatile, often hostile political relationship with republican Rome itself.[xxxii] The fuller history of the mid-republican Samnite wars, the image (largely derived from Livy) of the Samnite people as rustic, aggressive hill-dwellers, will be canvassed in much greater detail in Chapter Six, as that section deals with the postwar period wherein academic research into the Samnites and other southern Italian tribes expanded considerably; for the moment, let it be sufficient to bookmark the thought that, roughly sketched though it may have been during the period of the world wars, the historico-political discourse of gladiature was formulating a new rationality that, in linking gladiatorial violence with war, saw in the Samnites a context of origin that was far better suited.

This new perspective on gladiatorial origin was inaugurated in 1908, with Pais' *Italia Antica*. The Etruscan hypothesis was orthodoxy before the appearance of this text, which did not address gladiatorial origin directly but which did initiate a shift of academic focus to the south, in critical conjunction with an entirely distinct interpretation of the 'meaning' of gladiature that focused on several features. Pais argued that, while there was no reason to doubt Nicholas of Damascus regarding the transmission of gladiature from Etruria to Rome, nevertheless there was literary evidence to suggest that gladiature had appeared in Campania even before the fabled Brutus Pera funeral of 264 B.C.; beyond this,

Pais further suggested that the organization of gladiatorial games at Rome should perhaps be viewed in connection with the 'superior military system of the peoples of southern Italy', with the corollary that gladiature itself should be thought of as a "branch of athletic and warlike training" (324-5).

Pais's text was quickly followed by Weege's 1909 study on the painted tombs of Lucania and Campania in southern Italy, *Oskische Grabmalerei*.[xxxiii] The content and, as Weege claimed, the style of the tomb paintings that he suggested represented gladiatorial combats were quite different from the Etruscan painted tombs of Tarquinia and Cerveteri. The main thrust of Weege's text stemmed more or less directly from the emphasis upon weighing and distinguishing 'Greek' elements and influences from Italian and Roman – and, in sum, identifying the 'racial purity' of the Oscan-speaking peoples through a close reading of their funerary art. Although Weege stated that both Etruscan and south Italian tomb painting between the sixth and third centuries BC derived stylistically from Greek art, he felt that the Etruscan artistic tradition assimilated or 'indigenized' Greek aesthetic influences much more rapidly and comprehensively; by contrast, south Italian painting was slow to develop a distinct regional aesthetic, and remained essentially derivative of Greek art until the Roman conquest of the Italian peninsula was complete. However, Weege's articulation of this position was somewhat equivocal. He laid far greater emphasis on the eventual "triumph of the national mind" that he perceived in the south Italian tombs (131); he claimed that the "entire spirit which comes through the tomb paintings is a national one" (132, my translation).

Moreover, in Weege's assessment, the point at which the southern tombs diverged furthest from Greek art was the repeated motif, common from the fourth century BC onwards, of matched pairs of swordfighters or duellists. Grouping the paintings by subject matter, Weege identified a visual category of *Tod und Begräbnis abspiele* (death and burial games). These included depictions of sports such as racing and boxing, which were referred to ceramic comparanda from both Etruria and Greece. However, even as paired combat imagery was categorized with competitive sports, Weege maintained an exceptional status for duellists in the sense that they had no clear comparanda in the visual art of other cultures; specifically, they were "un-Greek and very national" (*ungriechisch und echt national,* 133). Representations of the duellist motif were marked by three significant elements: they were depicted as organized and formal contests, signified by the presence of a figure Weege interpreted as a referee; the combatants were clearly Samnites, since they were armed in a manner that seemed to fit Livy's much later description of distinct Samnite armature; and they were openly bloody, with combatants frequently shown wounded and occasionally succumbing (133). However, Weege's insistence upon the national character of the visual theme of duellists lacked the moralising implications that had informed much academic labour invested in the separation of Greeks from other groups. Instead, the emphatically 'Samnite' character of the paintings was argued in support of the further claim that the practice represented by the motif of the duellists was by extension to be interpreted as similarly 'national'. In many ways, Weege's entire survey of south Italian tomb painting was organized in service to this point.

Couissin's 1930 article *Guerriers et gladiateurs samnites*[xxxiv] was focused upon a close study of only two Roman lamps; however, in his attempt to argue that pre-conquest Samnite armature could be reconstructed from much later representations of 'Samnite gladiators', Couissin offered considerable support to the fledgling competitive hypothesis of gladiatorial origin. Couissin's most critical contribution to the growing argument was to claim specifically that while Roman sources identified gladiature at Capua in Campania as early as the late fourth century BC, the true origin of the practice was to be attributed to the Samnites, who 'almost certainly' (271) had introduced its funerary form at Capua almost a century earlier. He referred to evidence of painted tombs from Lucania to indicate that Samnites had carried gladiature abroad before. The later existence of gladiators at Capua called 'Samnites', Couissin speculated, should be explained by the fact that although the Samnites at Capua assimilated to Campanian culture, they maintained the term 'Samnites' in the practice of gladiature as a way of maintaining their ancestral cultural identity. Therefore the early class of 'Samnite' gladiators at Rome was to be accounted for by exactly the same process: the movement of Samnites to Rome, who brought with them this purportedly crucial identifying practice.

The new mythos of origin

At the same time, the search for a specific historical and cultural context of gladiature's origin unfolded alongside a parallel discussion, which framed the original meaning of gladiature in more trans-historical terms. Such scholars represented a perspective which addressed the violence/pleasure cathexis directly, and began to rationalize it through the invocation of the primitive. The trans-historical barbarian that sprang up within this discursive space would eventually appear as a 'warrior ancestor' for all the west to hold in common. In the postwar period, the quasi-mystical (or 'regressive') figure of the barbarian as warrior-ancestor would come to be more narrowly defined, and would be attached more closely to the Etruscan/Samnite debate; in the meantime, the barbarian's constitutive definition as such, and particularly the barbarous cathexis of violence and pleasure, were discussed in terms of an image of gladiatorial origin that sought a compromise between the irrationality of religious belief, and the hyper-rational instrumentalization of violence in the form of warfare.

In particular, three scholars – Cumont, Piganiol, and Malten – contributed to the shift in the idea that gladiature could be interpreted as a practice fundamentally defined by combat, rather than by ritual sacrifice. Cumont's *After Life in Roman Paganism* (1922) as yet maintained the inherited consensus that gladiature was in fact a funerary rite, and described funerary gladiature as "barbarous" as had been seen before. However, Cumont signalled a new approach to the extent that he discussed the subject without any reference to Etruria; rather than invoking a specific 'Etruscan cruelty', with that construct's full array of connotations, Cumont instead referred funerary gladiature to Roman 'paganism', without reference to a non-Roman origin at all:

> "Fights of gladiators, whose blood drenched the soil, originally
> formed part of the funeral ceremonies by which the last duty was

paid to the remains of an illustrious personage. It is said that these
sacrifices were intended to provide him who had gone to the other
world with servants and companions, as the offering of a horse
gave him a steed, or else that, in case of violent death, they were
meant to appease the shade of a victim who claimed vengeance"
(Cumont 51).

Such 'paganism' did not signify the traditional boundary between eastern

barbarism and western civilization that had formed the fundamental order of the

nineteenth century discourse of race struggle; Rome was of course still firmly

considered part of the bedrock of the history of the west. Instead, what began to

appear during this period, of which Cumont was only an early harbinger, was a

new master trope, as the eastern-western divide that had dominated the nineteenth

century discourse of race struggle gave way to a twentieth-century framework

organized around the construct of primitivism, and its capacity to both connect

and divide antiquity and modernity. This new determinative order functioned

within the advent of the idea of racial purity, as discussed above; as a broadly

conceived myth-history of the west, classical scholarship articulated historico-

political discourse's contemporary preoccupation with "the integrity, the

superiority, and the purity of the race" (*SMBD* 81) in terms of a broadened

conception of origin that was more intent upon tilling a large field for the ancient

roots of 'the race' before those roots were firmly laid down. This broadening, or

shift away from cultural specification in favour of an attempt to posit cross-

cultural generalities, was a provisional phase that would eventually end in a

renewed narrowing of gladiatorial origin to a specific cultural context; during this

phase, however, the discourse of race purity, within its regression to ideologico-

mythical language, sought a correspondingly mythical origin upon which to base a historical narrative that was now required to construct a space of legitimacy for the nobility's instrumentalization of the masses' pleasure in violence. Rome remained the avatar of the civilized nobility of the present, but within the new historicity – wherein the Enlightenment's laboratory was displaced by a new mythology, and antiquity was regarded as connected to modernity in a far more realist manner arising from the biologism of the construct of race – gladiature and its associated violence were being written into the history of right, crucially contingent upon a 'civilizing' reinvention of that violence.

At the same time, the interwar period's shift toward a mimetic rationality slowly built up interpretive connections between gladiatorial combat and combat's readily available cognate of warfare. Piganiol's *Recherches sur les Jeux Romaines* (1923)[xxxv] was similarly silent on the Etruscans, though equally accepting of funerary sacrifice as an originating context (126), stating that "*munera* celebrated ... in honour of the dead requires no further study. One knows well enough that, under the Republic and the Empire, gladiatorial combats inevitably accompany the funerals of great men. They are also often celebrated in the commemoration of death: it happens that they reveal in this regard ... the true perpetual foundations [of gladiature]" (135). Piganiol's innovative claim, however, was to extend from these 'perpetual foundations' a rather different narrative for the development of gladiature throughout the Roman Republic: significantly, his account circumvented completely the well-rehearsed narrative of the development of gladiature at Rome as affiliated with the rise of the *populares* faction in the late Republic. In contrast, Piganiol was intent upon the argument that gladiature should be seen in terms of the state cult of Saturn (126, 130);

original funerary ritual aside, whatever its precise context, the Roman

development of the practice was to be seen as an eventually official element of the

Saturnalia, and consequently a state-sponsored rite which retained, rather than

losing, its character of human sacrifice. This precise argument regarding the

Saturnalia was not subsequently influential to any great degree; nevertheless, it

expressed two significant and linked ideas. First, it reiterated from a different

angle the perspective already represented in contemporary scholarship on the

republican structures of class power and conflict, in the sense that here again,

gladiature was no longer being viewed as anything but the fully-mastered political

instrument of the State; at the same time, while the Saturnalia argument basically

retraced the traditional interpretation of republican gladiature as a gradual

secularization of an originally religious practice, that religious origin was no

longer referred to any non-Roman group. Second, amidst his characterisation of

gladiature as "odious" and his careful separation of earlier private gladiature from

later publicly-sponsored events, Piganiol's interpretation of the 'crossover event'

that signalled gladiature's conversion from private practice to public spectacle

conferred a particular interpretation upon a line from Ennodius, and expressed a

new approach to the interpretation of the cathexis of violence and pleasure (and

the state instrumentalization thereof) which would gain a great deal of currency

over the next fifty years:

> "One accepts in effect that gladiatorial combats were celebrated in
> Rome for the first time by individuals in 264, and that the State
> adopted this odious ritual only in 105. (...) The only text which
> alludes to the origin of the games of gladiators given by the State, a

passage of Ennodius, says definitely that in 105, for the first time, the consuls gave games of gladiators in the theatre, *inter theatrales caveas*, to awaken the taste for war" (130).[xxxvi]

The notion that gladiature could 'awaken the taste for war', whether or not this was indeed what Ennodius was driving at, was not an entirely new idea. The important point is that such an interpretation had not been found in the mainstream of academic consensus before this period. Piganiol's image was a far cry from Warde Fowler's characterization of gladiature, only fourteen years earlier, as a 'consolation for the stresses of war', and it carried a completely different network of connotations not only in terms of the imagined power structures of late republican Rome, but also in terms of the ongoing shifts in the construct of gladiatorial origin. The notion that gladiature functioned as a wholly legitimate instrumentalization of violence in the political mobilization of the lower classes could not be more clearly expressed, and the alignment of such an interpretation with a Roman context of gladiatorial practice was a profound expression of contemporary classical historiography's function as a myth-historical dimension of the nobility's history of right.

Piganiol explicitly disagreed with the growing discussion surrounding the extent to which gladiature could be viewed as a form of sport, stating that "[s]ince *munera* are a survival of human sacrifices, it is irrelevant who is the loser of the combat: the victorious gladiator does not acquire the almost divine honours to which ... the athlete can aspire; the only relevant matter is the spilling of blood" (135). However, in the same year, there was published an unusual short text which blended human sacrifice, sport, and the 'taste for war': Malten's

Leichenspiel und Totenkult (lit., *Corpse-play and Death-cult*).[xxxvii] Malten was

inclined to agree with the Etruscan hypothesis, although gladiatorial origin, or

even gladiature specifically, was not Malten's object; rather, he contributed to the

'almost medieval mythology' of contemporary historico-political discourse

through an unstructured, quasi-anthropological approach which sought the

apparently mystical roots of gladiature, and constructed a loose, very multi-

cultural typology by which certain practices could be considered under the same

categorical heading.

This unifying category Malten designated the *agon*, a 'fight' or 'contest'

which he used interchangeably with both the German *Kampf* and the deliberately

ambiguous Ψ, a symbol which he used to refer to a posited, imagined ur-*agon*,

carried out at some unknowable moment in human history and forming the

conceptual quasi-mystical origin of a host of Egyptian, Etruscan, Roman and

other funerary rituals. In the various early funerary forms of gladiature, "in the

bloody decision, and in the flowing blood", he perceived "the dark face of this

agon"; he emphasized what he felt to be the physical connection between the

blood of the sacrificed gladiator at a graveside and the corpse of the deceased, and

suggested that this form of funerary *agon* could be considered a truly mimetic re-

enactment of the deceased's death (the deceased being, as Servius had suggested,

a warrior) with the vanquished gladiator substituting for the original victim

(Malten 302).

Malten's second major contribution to scholarship on gladiature emerged

from his inclusion, in his survey of the descendents of original *agon*, of the slaughter of Trojan prisoners at the funeral of Patroclus in the *Iliad* (Malten 305-7). This, as we know, was not an entirely new idea; gladiature as funerary ritual had been discussed in relation to the funeral of Patroclus since at least the eighteenth century. However, Malten's taxonomy completely inverted the formerly adamant insistence upon the fundamental difference between original gladiature and even the most ancient and exceptional practices of the Greeks – the exemplary group which had long been held up as the standard of abhorrence. Malten claimed that a direct line could be traced from a singularity represented in Greek epic to Etruscan and Roman gladiature, in its early funerary context; more specifically, there was at least a strong affinity, if not a path of historical descent, between Achilles' ritual vengeance and the fact that Etruscan/Roman funerary gladiature was an *agon* which culminated in death. An echo of *agon*'s dark face, therefore, was to be found in heroic Greece as well as ancient Etruria, republican and imperial Rome. Further, their commonality of descent was established on the basis of their mimetic relation to warfare (Malten 305).

Taken in sum, this entire angle of scholarship articulated a certain new *mythos* of violence that posited an immeasurably ancient and ultimately civilized history for the nobility's instrumentalization of, and power over, all members of the State. The discourse of racial purity, as its inscription of power as dedicated to the 'protection of the integrity, the superiority, and the purity of the race', meant that not only was classical scholarship writing a legitimate, noble, European, or otherwise civilized origin for gladiature, such scholarship was also, by extension, writing the same sort of origin story for warfare itself, since 'warfare' was taken as the basis for the re-definition of gladiatorial violence via mimesis. The discourse of racial purity re-positioned the violence of gladiature as consistent with civilization, rather than antithetical to it, and consequently supported and rationalized a space of legitimacy around the presence of violence within the workings of state power.

That legitimized space of violence was closely aligned with war. Within this period of historiography, war functioned in a manner inversely related to the function previously carried out by the *pollice verso*: it connoted the true site of authority, the site upon which the 'two races' would contend with one another for power. Where the mob had represented an animalistic, anarchistic force for chaos and disorder, an unchannelled and threatening violence in its own right, the masses – as a legitimate instrument within the apparatus of the State – were (provisionally) associated with warfare, insofar as warfare was, during this period, a dominating construction of politics, power, and order. It was not as an electorate, but as an army, that the State was suborned to the nation; as a result, the figure of the barbarian came to be inscribed as a warrior, as the discursive framework which underpinned the historiography of gladiature shifted toward a rhetoric of origin which imagined 'tribal warfare' as a primitive ancestor of contemporary geopolitics.

Abhorrence and Greece

As a final stroke, before the first half of the twentieth century was over, the barbarian as 'warrior-ancestor' would already begin to take on the signs of civilization, as gladiature's nebulous association with sport (invoked through the influence of the *agon* and its attempt to nudge gladiature away from 'combat' and toward 'contest') would find a grounding within the rhetoric of origin. Malten was not alone in arguing that the scope of the 'new origin' of gladiature – legitimate, civilized, and European or 'western' – included ancient Greece; not many years later, the long-cherished conviction of the Greek abhorrence of the practice was directly and penetratingly re-examined, in Robert's 1940 work *Les Gladiateurs dans l'Orient Grec*.[xxxviii] Robert spoke against prevailing opinion by establishing that, despite the relative scarcity of actual amphitheatres in the Greek world in antiquity, amphitheatrical spectacles were regularly staged by Greeks in theatres adapted to the purpose (35-6). Robert argued that gladiature had been introduced into Greece under Roman influence as a component of imperial cult (24), and that the previously much-vaunted historical references to the republican period – the episode of Antiochus Epiphanes, for example – were exceptional in character and possibly fictional, and did not diminish the demonstrable fact that by the imperial period gladiature throve in Greece (Robert 263-4).

Robert spoke directly to the familiar and long-standing space of exception accorded to Greece, as the exemplary touchstone of the abhorrence of gladiature as a cruel and inhuman practice (Robert 13-5). He referred to three Greek literary sources[xxxix] upon which this perceived Greek aversion to gladiature might be claimed, and summarily dismissed them all as isolated exceptions to the general run of ancient Greek opinion (248-53): "Our documents show that, contrary to the affirmations of modern erudite persons, the Greeks adopted this Roman show and did not baulk at it at all" (24). Robert further attacked the associated claim that the inroads gladiature had made into Greek culture were to be attributed entirely to the lower classes:

> "One reads in many place that, in the Greek east, "gladiatorial combats were left to the little people (Lafaye)", that they "pleased only the lower classes in East", while "the cultivated class did not hide its dislike (Chapot)"; "in Greece it was always only the dregs of the people, that found enjoyment in these cruel pleasures (Friedlander, my translation)". This is an opinion which is, for the most part, *a priori*. "Inferior classes" are not necessarily inhuman and bloodthirsty; "cultivated classes" do not necessarily assign great value to human life, especially to the life of a poor devil. The observation of our similarity allows us to assume that, also with the Greeks, there were in all classes certain individuals whom the amphitheatre disgusted and others than it attracted. But we can, I believe, draw from these texts and monuments some definite facts that [cited scholars] neglected. It is not only the *hoi polloi* who take pleasure in gladiatorial combats" (254).

Further quashed was the concomitant assertion that the lower classes shared blame with the cosmopolitan, racially mixed populations of the larger centres such as Alexandria; this argument went back at least as far as Friedlander, who had claimed that "[g]ladiatorial combats found their way far more easily into Asia Minor with its mixed half-Asiatic population, and all the East" (85). Robert pointed to the evidence of gladiature in cities of indubitably Hellenic character, such as Gortyne, Thasos, Mytilene, Samos, Kos, Halikarnassos and numerous others (24), in his arguments against the prevailing tendency to connect the presence of gladiators to the tastes of 'non-hellenized' populations of Asiatic peoples in the more easterly territories of the former Alexandrian empire. Distinctions of neither race nor class, then, were sufficient to account for and explain away the cathexis of violence and pleasure surrounding Greek gladiature.

Robert's claim that gladiature must be incorporated into the image of Greek civilization within the contemporary historical imagination was contingent upon a very specific reservation: that the Greek perception or construction of gladiature, and therefore the essence of specifically Greek pleasure in gladiatorial violence, defined gladiature as a form of sport. Robert sidestepped the 'mimetic warfare' interpretation and argued that the Greek practice of gladiature was entirely uncorrupted by such parallel historical issues as the governance of the lower classes, mystical ur-*agones,* and a 'taste for war'; instead, the best way to interpret the presence of gladiature in this most civilized of ancient contexts was through the *über*-civilized lens of the Olympics. In his close study of epigraphic data, including inscriptions from surviving tombs of gladiators (much of which had already been collected, though not critically studied, by Friedlander), Robert questioned the strict distinction that had long been maintained between gladiatorial combat and 'athletic sport' proper, at least within the Greek world. He pointed to the 'armature' associated with Greek boxing, for example, and examined textual evidence which showed the close similarities between the terminology applied to both boxing and gladiature, arguing that since Greeks referred to gladiature "in the technical language of athletic combat ", the practice had held among them the status of a sport (although he did question, without resolve, why the terminology of boxing was applied in preference to words borrowed from the far more violent and occasionally lethal pancration; Robert 19-21).

However, Robert did not extend his analysis so far as to suggest that the Greek perception of gladiature as a sport rendered the practice any less abhorrent to modern eyes. Rather, he described gladiature as a 'gangrene' that had been carried into Greek society by Rome (263), disseminated in the context of a 'link' between gladiature and the cult of emperor worship. The infection of Greece was fortuitously contained by the divide between urban and rural spheres, as the cities were the centres of imperial cult and gladiature was thus an inherently urban spectacle, unlike the more widespread practices of traditional Greek athletics; therefore the "greater part of the country did not have the barbarism of the [gladiatorial] shows under its eyes" (Robert 243).

For all its careful circumscriptions and reservations, however, the function of Robert's text within the contemporary shifts of historical discourse was clear enough. Greece was not here dethroned from its traditional position as the avatar of true 'civilization'; rather, the radical effect of Robert's work was to construct an origin story for the legitimate position of gladiature, with all of its conflicting connotations surrounding violence, pleasure, abhorrence, and power, within the boundaries of the civilized State. The incorporation of Greece into the narrative of gladiature was to exert a legitimizing, civilizing effect. The analysis was dependent upon several contingent points, and the ultimate 'civility' of gladiature was a thought that would not reach its full flowering until later in the century. Nevertheless, we see a number of interesting features in the inception of this idea. As in the paragraph above, for example, Robert's work paid a certain amount of passing lip service to the inherited language of abhorrence of violence, in the description of gladiature as a 'gangrene' (note, of course, the medicalized/ biopolitical terminology); further, the rot was to be considered as quarantined within the sites wherein the urban crowd was concentrated, in a construction which reached back again to the nineteenth century's tendency to locate the seat of true civilization among the landed gentry, behind the romantic mask of the rural yeoman class. Nevertheless, the mystical force of Greek civilization within the historical imagination was sufficiently strong to, if not positively resist infection from outside of itself, at least convert or filter the barbarism of gladiature into a relatively civilized form, into a practice defined not by warfare but by sport.

Abhorrence and decivilizing

Before this section concludes, it may be helpful to reiterate that the early decades of the twentieth century in gladiatorial historiography were a time of transition in many ways; the period was characterized by new questions within research rather than by positive statements. The Etruscan hypothesis of origin was not closely interrogated, but scholarly work began to accumulate in support of the Samnite claim; the teeth were drawn from the nineteenth-century mob, but the content of that image was not otherwise much altered. However, as the forms of the historiography of gladiature remained relatively stable, a transformation was taking place in the discursive structure within which those forms were articulated. With the lapse of the discourse of struggle – which is not the same as a lapse in the discourse of perpetual war, only a change in the basis of its rationality – came a shift in the construction and deployment of violence: its locus, its imagined effect, its position, and the language of abhorrence and pleasure which surrounds the problem of violence in relation to gladiature.

As violence was instrumentalized and brought within the 'legitimate' structure of state power (this within the altered terms of membership within the nation *qua* State), gladiature as a specific signifier of violence was gradually decoupled from, or no longer aligned with, the barbarous in the way it had been formerly. Thus the disappearance (however temporary, as it would soon reappear in another form) of the language of abhorrence: the regressive discourse of purity did not require the 'struggle' against barbarism that the language of abhorrence had articulated, and the legitimation of instrumentalized violence entailed that abhorrence no longer functioned as a signifier of the nation over and against the State in the historico-political discourse of gladiature.

The lapse of the language of abhorrence of violence, however, did not correspond to a similar disappearance of the notion of decivilizing. 'Decivilizing' may no longer have been spoken of in the exceptionally clear terms that were encountered in the historiography of the nineteenth century, but the notion of course persisted: within the discursive shift of the early twentieth century, decivilizing was perceived as a question of 'race purity' rather than of socio-political descent or any other collapse of boundaries between upper and lower classes. Civilization was during this period a matter of the purity of the race – and it was this newly biological notion of race that inaugurated the conceptual union of nation with State. In what we have examined above, that unification of two socio-political entities was as yet still emergent; it is not entirely obvious, of course, how the suggestion that the Roman plebeians were of a different 'racial stock' than the patricians, or even how the political instrumentalization of the former class by the latter, can be construed as any basis for a fundamental union of the two. The fuller consequences of such developments become clearer in the postwar period.

In the meanwhile, the emergent 'union' of nation with State connoted a construct of civilization wherein another fundamental shift was underway, one which required that a space be created within its boundaries for a certain type of barbarian, whose face has been glimpsed; it is the past of the civilized, the primitive echo of origin, and its violence is of a mystical, 'pure' variety. Such a reinvention of violence – which would become much more profound in the middle of the century, as western modernity would struggle to come to grips with its postwar legacy by altering the inscription of violence in its own myth-history – would inevitably occasion a concomitant reinvention of gladiature's pleasure.

Chapter 6: *Romanitas et Violentia*

Postwar historico-political discourse: the barbarian democracy

The postwar period of the third quarter of the twentieth century saw a

fundamental shift in the modern historiography of gladiature, a change in

historico-political discourse equalled in scope perhaps only by the inception of the

'problem' of gladiatorial violence in the eighteenth century itself. As Foucault

explained, and as explored above in the Introduction, the emergence of historico-

political discourse as an entire framework, distinct from juridico-philosophical

discourse, is best understood as the emergence of a new language of power, and

thereby as an expression and construction of a particular relation between the

nation and the State; the discourses of struggle, purity, and 'perpetual war' are all

species of nobiliary historicism. However,"... [historico-political] discourse,

which was originally bound up with the nobiliary reaction, became generalized ...

not only in the sense that it became, so to speak, the regular and canonical form of

historical discourse, but to the extent that it became a tactical instrument that

could be used not only by the nobility, but ultimately in various different

strategies" (*SMBD* 189).

The 'different strategy' was the historico-political rise of the bourgeois as

the speaking subject of history. (This is not to suggest that *all* areas of

historiography in the west underwent a sudden *embourgeoisement* following the

close of the second world war; in fact, the case could possibly be argued that, as a

particular myth-history, the central tropes of classical historiography have never shifted in tandem with other areas of historiographic thought among the various

nations who look back to Rome.) Foucault explains:

> "…those who had the least interest in investing their political
> projects in history were of course the people of the bourgeoisie or
> the Third Estate, because going back to a constitution or
> demanding a return to something resembling an equilibrium of
> forces implies in some way that you know where you stand in the
> equilibrium of forces. …the Third Estate or the bourgeoisie could
> scarcely, at least until the middle of the Middle Ages, identify itself
> as a historical subject within the play of relations of force. (…)
> Which is why, whatever has been said to the contrary, the
> bourgeoisie was, in the eighteenth century, certainly the class that
> was most hostile, most resistant to history. In a profound sense, it
> was the aristocracy that was historical. (...) But for a long time, the
> bourgeoisie remained antihistoricist or ... antihistoric" (*SMBD*
> 208).

Classical historiography of the first half of the twentieth century had

already, in some senses, begun to suggest the advent of the bourgeois. On the one

hand, the early twentieth century was largely characterized by what appears in

retrospect as the final phase of the discursive centrality of the nobiliary subject;

certainly the nearly-total dominance of the Roman ruling class in the late

Republic, whether discussed in terms of its social and/or racial 'purity' as a group

or not, was a widespread theme which recognizably echoed earlier phases of

historical discourse. On the other hand, it is also possible to interpret the sort of

systemic hegemony that was such a salient theme of the previous period as a

forerunner of what will be encountered below: the gradual emergence of a

prevailing image of Rome, even Rome of the late Republic, as a profoundly

unified society. The regressive mode of the discourse of purity had realigned the

nineteenth century notion of the relation between the nation and the State, to

create a discursive construct which, though still marked by highly unequal relations of power, was at the same time also defined by a deeply essentialist biopolitics that implied connections across the nation/State divide which had not existed previously, and which reverberated in the tentative exploration of an image of gladiatorial origin that invoked a mystical notion of prehistoric unity across cultural groupings. The historiographic writing of the mid-twentieth century – and, eventually, its final decades as well –would seize upon the trope of profound unity, and reinscribe it in "the reworking – in political and not historical terms – of the famous notion of the 'nation', which the aristocracy had made both the subject and the object of history in the eighteenth century" (*SMBD* 216-7). In the historiography of gladiature specifically, the reworking of the nation can be seen to have progressed in successive stages; the first of these will be explored in this chapter, and is signalled by a new approach to the filtering of barbarism, from what had been a strategy of stringent exclusion of the barbarian from civilization to a new 'economy of barbarism' (*SMBD* 198).

Historico-political discourse avails itself of 'three great models' for the filtering of barbarism. The first we have already encountered, at length; this model is "the most vigorous, the most absolute, and it tries to allow no aspect of the barbarian into history"; in Foucault's illustration, "this position is an attempt to show that the French monarchy [for example] is not descended from some Germanic invasion which brought it to France or which, in some sense, gave birth to it", but wherein the nobility traces its descent – and therefore founds the origin story of its own history of right – from the Roman period of sovereignty, from 'Romanity' (*SMBD* 199). Precisely from where the nobility claims the basis of its power in this first model – Rome literal, or Rome metaphorical - is unimportant;

the point is that this construct of 'civilization' excludes the barbarian completely

from itself, and its nobility's exclusive claim to 'the nation' is defined by

something like autochthony or birthright, by a historical narrative which is free

from invasions or incursions of barbarian influence.

In contrast, what began to appear within classical historiography at the

beginning of the twentieth century, becoming more explicit in the postwar period

explored below, was a 'second model' of filtering barbarism:

> "The goal of this different type of discourse is to dissociate the
> Germanic freedom, or in other words, a barbarian freedom, from
> the exclusive nature of the privileges of the aristocracy. Its goal is
> … to go on laying claim to the freedom the barbarians and Franks
> brought to France by resisting the Roman absolutism of the
> monarchy. The hairy bands from across the Rhine did indeed enter
> Gaul, and they did bring their freedoms with them. These hairy
> bands were not, however, bands of German warriors who made up
> the nucleus of an aristocracy that remained an aristocracy within
> the body of Gallo-Roman society. Those who flooded in were
> certainly warriors, but they were also a whole people in arms. The
> political and social form that was introduced into Gaul was not that
> of an aristocracy but, on the contrary, that of a democracy, the
> widest possible democracy. (…) So, the barbarian democracy …
> who knew no form of aristocracy, and who know only an
> egalitarian people of soldier-citizens" (*SMBD* 202).

This barbarian – a free, hairy, democratic, egalitarian soldier-citizen –

appeared quickly and with uncanny accuracy in the historiography of the postwar

generation, and re-invented the origin of gladiature and its transmission into

Roman society. Much of the relevant historiographic work of this period can be

organized around the delineation of the new barbarian, and the consequences that

this figure implied for the construct of civilization as articulated in the myth-

history of Rome. The 'reworking of the notion of the nation', and of the relation between the nation and the State, is a further stage in the *embourgeoisement* of

gladiatorial historiography that, although intimated in several texts of this period,

will be examined more fully in the next chapter. The focus of the present section

will be the democratic barbarian himself, the impact that a new image of origin

exerted upon the interpretation of gladiature, and the emergence of the notion of

gladiatorial 'violence' as a locus of social cohesion, when it had previously been

seen to divide the social, and even to function as the very plane along which it

was split.

Civilization and the indigenization of Etruria

Pallottino in his *Etruscheria* argued as far back as 1942 for the conceptual

redefinition of the Etruscans as "a nation that flourished in Etruria between the

eighth and the first centuries B.C., possessing its own language and its own

customs" (78) – i.e., not the descendants, in any knowable or meaningful sense, of

some originally 'non-western' group. However, it was not until after the Second

World War that Pallottino's call for a re-framing of the Etruscans reached a wider

audience. Von Vacano (30-2) and Heurgon (7-8) were prepared to consider the

Eastern origins of the Etruscans as, at most, legendary; Hus' 1959 *Les Etrusques*

dismissed the entire question and, following Pallottino, anchored his discussion of

ancient Etruria firmly in the Villanovan period of the eighth century in Italy (37).

The most important development was Ward-Perkins' 1959 article *The Problem of*

Etruscan Origins: Some Thoughts on Historical Method, which critiqued the

long-standing elision between Etruscan language and Etruscan cultural origin, and

spearheaded a swift movement among scholars to agree that "whatever the origins of the Etruscan people or the Etruscan language, the historical Etruscan civilization as we know it took shape on Italian soil; even if the people principally responsible for its formation came from elsewhere, they certainly did not bring the Etruscan culture with them ready-made" (10). By this point, the discussion of Etruscan autochthony was being articulated within a wider, more reflexive conversation about the construct of race and its associated language within classical scholarship, particularly as it pertained to the Etruscans. For example, Ward-Perkins' comments were published in the context of the 1959 CIBA Foundation's symposium on 'Medical Biology and Etruscan Origins'; the results of genetic research at this time were inconclusive, but the advent of the term 'genetical' was eagerly greeted as preferable in referring to those "peculiar physical characteristics which were vulgarly called racial before 'race' became a term of political propaganda" (Cook 1959). Ward-Perkins echoed Cook in a reactionary response to the previous generation of scholars such as Frank, stating that 'race' was a term of convenience rather than real significance, "[w]hatever dictators may like to pretend" (Ward-Perkins 8).

Unlike the swiftness with which Ward-Perkins' arguments gained acceptance, the transfer of gladiature's origin story from Etruria to Samnium took place in gradual stages. In the immediate postwar period, the origin of gladiature that was maintained by the majority of scholars was a composite image, which admitted the existence of both Etruscan and Samnite/Campaniangladiature centuries before the practice was known to have appeared at Rome and refrained from explicitly choosing between the two possibilities. Bloch's 1956 *Le mystére*

Etrusque cited both competing claims of the original source of Roman "borrowing" of gladiature, but further argued that the practice as a whole derived in the last analysis from the funeral games of Etruria, which he described as offerings of blood to the dead in the course of "merciless combats between adversaries, who sought desperately to save their lives" (134). Von Vacano, in the 1957 *Die Etrusker in der Welt der Antike*, claimed that the Romans "learned" gladiature in Campania, but swiftly pointed out that the southern region had been "long governed by Tyrrhenians [Etruscans]"; this passage was sandwiched between a discussion of historical instances of sacrificial execution of war prisoners, committed both by the Etruscans and upon them, and a summary comment that the superstitious character of Etruscan religion had effectively prevented a gradual civilizing away from the "cold-blooded slaughter of human beings to comply with some religious dogma", as had happened relatively early in Greece (122-4). Von Vacano was not alone in keeping life in the traditional referent of Greece as a civilized ideal. *The World of Rome*, the 1960 offering from Grant's one-man publishing house of classical history, summarized his discussion of gladiature with the statement that its "ever-recurrent horrors and brutalities ... were ultimately of Etruscan origin, and could not have happened in classical Greece where – for all its faults – there had always been a certain number of people, including men in high places, who tried to think and live on more reasonable, rational lines" (149). The widespread acceptance of Robert's theories, as we see, was even slower to take hold.

At the same time (and frequently by the same scholars) the yet ongoing 'Greek exception' was also being provisionally extended to Etruria: in essence, as the traditional perceptions of both Greece and Etruria – and, more to the point, the discursive economies of barbarism and civilization which underpinned them - were coming under interrogation, the slow toppling of the Greeks from the apex of civilized nations was paralleled by the fleeting appearance of a space wherein the Etruscans could suddenly appear as relatively civilized in relation to gladiature. Hus, for example (and for all his comments on the inhumanity of the practice imagined behind the Phersu scene), accorded a relatively legitimate status to Etruscan funerary ritual, arguing that "in Tuscany these spectacles did not have the brutal and pointless character they assumed later" (170). Heurgon similarly espoused the Servian argument, and felt that it was impossible to "ignore certain testimonies and certain facts which attribute to the Etruscans the institution of gladiatorial games, which the ancients regarded as progressive because, instead of killing prisoners on the tomb, they were made to fight in front of it, which gave them a chance" (211). Yet Heurgon also qualified the evidence for Etruscan gladiature by directly invoking Greece and the funeral of Patroclus, aligning the still-circulating referent of Greece's assumed exceptionality to the imagined meaning of Etruscan gladiature. Etruscan funerary sacrifice was not to be elided with gladiature; moreover, funerary sacrifice's association with the funeral of Patroclus was to be considered explicit and direct, as the "vision of the funeral of Patroclus never ceased to haunt the imaginations of the Etruscans. (...) It enabled the families of dead persons to enhance their mourning by raising it to the level of a Greek legend, and to console themselves for the mortal condition of humanity through the enchantments of poetry" (210-1). In this relatively early stage of articulation, the bourgeois strategy of historico-political discourse tended frequently to return to the central tropes of gladiatorial historiography which were already familiar, and to re-interpret them accordingly – witness the co-option of both the Servian argument of 'civilizing' implied by the suggestion of funerary gladiature as 'consoling poetry', and the buttressing of that interpretation through a traditional reference to the ultimate rhetorical legitimacy of Greece, despite the work of Robert and Greek gladiature. Bourgeois historico-political discourse thus returned to the earlier forms of the nobiliary reaction, and sought again to re-define for itself a civilized vs. barbaric gladiature on the basis of the cathect of violence and pleasure, in spite of the fact that the scholarship of the interwar period had significantly departed from the moral problem of pleasure. The discursive shift to the bourgeois, however, returned to the old strategy of abhorrence, and began the work of ordering its own set of terms for gladiatorial violence.

Heurgon – who within less than a decade would stand as the primary authority for Ville, the scholar who would serve subsequently as the definitive source for all scholarship of gladiatorial origin into the present – turned briefly to the tomb paintings of southern Italy to illustrate the crucial point of his interpretations surrounding the Etruscan tomb imagery associated with funerary ritual and eschatology.

"Yet it was not in Etruria but in Campania and in Lucania that the gladiatorial games must have come to their full development and taken on their classic form. From the fourth century, in the paintings of Capua and Paestum, we see pairs of gladiators fighting it out, in their aigretted helmets, carrying buckler and lance, covered in wounds and dripping with blood. In southern Italy, the Samnites of the mountains provided abundant material for these games: among the various classes in which the gladiators had to arrange themselves, those called after the 'Samnites' were the most ancient, and the only kind that was known before Sulla added the 'Thracian' and Caesar the 'Gaulish' kinds. *Samnis* was for a long time a generic term [for 'gladiator'], and Campania always remained the centre for their schools and the theatre for their revolts. Nothing like this is known to have existed in Etruria. We search in vain ... for examples of these duels between two gladiators, sword in hand" (211).

The push to civilize Etruscan gladiature was thus articulated through a re-deployment of the language that had long been used to represent Greece: Heurgon's insistence that "nothing like this is known to have existed in Etruria" was an uncannily precise echo of Poulsen's framing, forty years earlier, of the Phersu scenes as having 'no known example from Hellas'. More importantly, it becomes clear, particularly in the face of the indigenization of the Etruscans, that the exchange of one erstwhile barbarian for another in the origin story of gladiature was not based upon a selection between cultural or 'racial' groups, notwithstanding the contemporary anxiety surrounding classical scholarship's engagement with race as a construct. Instead, the core subtext of the entrenchment of the Samnite hypothesis arose from the *embourgeoisement* of the historico-political discourse of civilization as produced within the context of Roman historiography. As the 'Third Estate' was gradually admitted into the position of historical speaking subject within the account of Rome's transition from republic to empire – or, seen from another angle, as the modern myth-historical narrative of civilization that had long been associated with and articulated through the historiographic labour of interpreting that socio-political shift, and gladiature's

role within it, came to be fundamentally reconfigured as a 'bourgeois' myth-

history which pivoted upon the construction of an altered image of 'civilization'

itself, a new imagined power structure shaping the historiographic expression of

the discourse of perpetual war – a new barbarian was required who, through the

provision of a suitable origin story for gladiature, could support the total

reinvention of gladiatorial historiography and thereby defend a re-inscribed

history of right emanating from a bourgeois construct of civilization, insofar as

the historiography of gladiature expresses particular presuppositions about the

State, the nation, and the space of violence which separates and defines those two

things. In the context of Foucault's 'second great model' of filtering barbarism,

classical scholarship was perceptibly shifting its boundaries to construct a

narrative which no longer stringently excluded the barbarian which had once been

the superstitious, irrational, monarchic Etruscan; instead, as will be seen below, in

the course of 'laying claim to barbarian freedom' within an altered construct of

civilization.

The key distinction between the nobiliary and bourgeois discourses of

civilization, which already had been signalled by developments earlier in the

century, was an entirely different approach to the space of violence, and its role in

policing the historico-political boundary between the State and the nation. In

effect, gladiatorial historiography before the twentieth century had been

constructed and deployed to serve a nobiliary history of right in which

gladiature's cathect of violence and pleasure had defined both the fundamental incapacity of the 'second race' to possess and exercise power, while at the same time also defining the nobility's essential 'right' both to possess power and, via the rhetoric of abhorrence *contra* pleasure, ultimately to exercise power legitimately through violent means. This history had hinged upon the presence of a particular type of barbarian, whose total exclusion on all possible counts from the sphere of civilization was an echo of (or was echoed by) the strict separation maintained between the nation, comprised of the nobility, and the wider framework of the State which included the governed. Beginning in the early twentieth century, and taking clear shape here in the postwar period, modernity altered its myth-history to reflect a contemporary shift in the construct of civilization: the bourgeois history of right bespoke a new relation between power and violence, a new structure of the civilized society which must be defended, and a new relation between nation and State wherein attitudes to violence could be read as indicating not the fundamental separation between those two spheres, but their fundamental continuity.

The barbarian democracy: the Samnites

The emergent associations between pre-conquest southern Italian tribes, warfare, and the origin of gladiature which had begun to appear in the previous period continued to gain momentum in the postwar period of classical historiography, especially as this discussion concentrated upon the Samnites who had ruled over the territory of Campania as well as Samnium by the fifth century BC. Salmon's 1967 *Samnium and the Samnites* was a monumental synthesis of much of the information then available. Salmon felt that the Samnite origin of gladiature could not be conclusively proven, but he expressed no doubts over the

growing consensus that it had at least appeared much earlier in Samnium than in

Rome (60). Salmon's monograph had an immediate and groundbreaking effect in

classical scholarship on southern Italy of the Republican period, as the mid-

century war had interrupted what relatively little archaeological research had been

conducted in the region (cf. Ward-Perkins 220-1), and much of the ancient textual

information, upon which Salmon's work relied heavily, was scattered through the

source materials and filtered by Roman perceptions.[xl] He cited all of the

retrojective arguments already familiar from Heurgon – that, by the point in the

late Republic wherein the Romans were practicing gladiature, Campania was the

"headquarters of the profession"; that the earliest known named class of gladiator

at Rome was the 'Samnite', and that the until the first century BC the terms

'Samnite' and 'gladiator' were "synonymous" (60). He also remarked upon the

absence of 'gladiatorial' representations in Etruscan art, in direct contrast to the

scenes represented in the southern tombs paintings studied by Weege, wherein the

"the savage sport is shown in all its gruesome reality":

> "Originally the combats may have taken place only at funerals and
> were probably not fought *jusqu'a la mort* ... But, when the contests
> ceased to be part of a funeral rite, they did not remain thus
> relatively innocuous. A painting found in 1954 shows a gladiator
> who is obviously mortally wounded. How the bloody
> entertainments were provided amongst the Samnites is not
> recorded: perhaps by the upper-class leaders, either privately or
> when holding public office. One way of getting the spectacles may
> have been to match prisoners-of-war in pairs and let them fight to
> the death with the victor saving his life" (60).

Of gladiature among the Samnites before the Roman conquest was

concluded, Salmon had virtually nothing else to say. His major contribution to gladiatorial historiography lay not in his sketch of gladiatorial origin - which, as is immediately apparent, took all of its cues from previous scholarship – but, instead, in his portrait of the Samnites as the new barbarian for the *embourgeoisement* of historico-political discourse, and the radically different set of tropes and connotations that the Samnites provided to contextualize gladiature's origin story in the service of an emergent construct of civilization.

Salmon's sketch of the Samnites, though highly lauded by contemporaries, was distinctive for its unmistakably 'pro-Samnite' perspective; Dench reviewed the work as one of a scholar who "has almost changed into a Samnite himself" (224). The work represented Samnium, particularly in the period of the Samnite Wars with Rome between the early third and late second centuries BC, as a rival power who presented the greatest threat to Roman rule, the "stalwart possessors of a larger territory and of a more determined temperament than any other people in the peninsula. They were numerous and spirited enough to refuse to submit tamely to Rome, and the military and political opposition that they put up against her was of the toughest. It is a commonplace that they, and they alone, were the really redoubtable rivals of Rome for the hegemony of peninsular Italy, and they came within a measurable distance of winning it (...) characteristically displaying greater tenacity and a more resolute will to resist that any of the other insurgents" (Salmon 1).

Salmon's description of the Samnites as an 'anti-Rome' hinged especially upon key distinctions in social and political structure that collectively represented Samnium as a more or less idealized 'barbarian democracy'. First were the obvious differences: the Samnites were rural rather than urban, a "nation of peasants and herdsmen", who "may not even have had their own native word for 'city'", and did not extensively rely upon slavery (Salmon 50-2). This image of simplicity and remoteness was deepened by descriptors such as "simple, crude (...) coarse and unpretentious" (140), "frugal", a life "devoid of luxuries of any kind; its austerity indeed became a by-word [cf. Juvenal *Sat*.3.169]" (77). Correlated with this rustic way of life was, crucially, a comparatively less stratified social structure and a more direct system of governance; the primary unit of government was not the city-state, but the *touto*, an Oscan word with no direct translation but whose closest equivalent in Latin Salmon took to be *populus*, 'the people' (78). While the Samnite state was therefore to be regarded as a democracy, Salmon felt that this was not to be confused with the 'modern sense' of democracy, for in Samnium, "as in the less developed parts of Italy generally, dynastic families with large estates commanded the allegiance of whole regions" (83); overall the governing system was to be imagined as marked by elements of feudalism, consistent with the organization of rural communities rather than city-states (52). However, Salmon also cited Livy's description of Samnites as "openly and loudly critical of their magistrates" (82), and claimed there was "no indication that the Samnite masses were dissatisfied because a comparatively small group thus perpetuated its own power. A clique imposed by the Romans, such as the senate at Capua, was bound to be hated by the commons; but the lower orders may have willingly acquiesced in the rule of families who traditionally had always been their leaders" (84). Thus again, the Samnites were here constructed as the embodiment of the 'widest possible democracy', a 'whole people in arms, an egalitarian people of soldier-citizens' whose particular barbarism was filtered *into* the sphere of the civilized, rather than strictly excluded.

Salmon went even further with what he saw as the full ramifications of Samnium's barbarian democracy and, effectively, created a historical narrative that perfectly expressed what Foucault described as 'laying claim to the anti-aristocratic freedom of the barbarians'. His text contained several suggestions that Samnite social rusticity and political directness was to be considered as evocative of the earliest periods of Roman socio-political structure itself; the above image of Samnium was likened directly to early Rome (84). Further, one of Salmon's major (and more controversial) conclusions was that the reach of Samnite power across southern Italy during the early republican period insulated Roman cultural development from Greek influences emanating from Magna Graecia; thus the Samnites were the "unwitting cause of some of the major developments in Roman history (...) [T]he inevitable consequence of the interruption had been to keep the national character of the Romans true to itself. They developed their own forms of government and civil institutions and they perfected their military organization in the face of the hard challenge of a virile and valiant opponent" (400). In Salmon's construct, Samnium's status as an anti-Rome was thus doubled: not only was it, in one sense, a nostalgic avatar of early Rome before Rome's ascent to dominance – i.e., the past of the first race - but further, Samnium's oppositional relation to Rome was held up as responsible for the purity of the Roman nation. His analysis exposed the discursive structure which constituted the bourgeois inversion of

what had been the nobiliary strategy underlying the history of right: the

'barbarian' now became the historical (and even biological) origin of civilization:

> "The Romans did not admit and may not have realized the
> importance of the Samnites in their development. They felt a
> hostility for them that never abated. The emperor Claudius later
> insisted that the true secret of successful imperialism lay in a
> willingness to accept the defeated. But the Romans of the Republic
> showed a marked reluctance to make the Samnites one with
> themselves. (...) With other Italians they were willing to let
> bygones be bygones; to the Samnites they never really opened their
> ranks. The latter might be an Italic people – indeed they were the
> most Italic of all the peoples in the peninsula – but they were not fit
> for inclusion within the Roman pale" (403-4).

Salmon's image of the perfect barbarian for a bourgeois history of

civilization – a whole people, a democratic soldier-citizenry, a hairy band from

across the border who brought with them a 'freedom' unsullied by class struggle,

and signifying a unity of nation and State (the "most Italic of all the peoples") that

is a critical key to a bourgeois history of right – was the new contextualizing

image for the origin of gladiature. The notion of gladiatorial origin which had

predominated in historico-political discourse, comprised of funerary rite, religious

belief, and human sacrifice, was ceding the field in the historical imagination to a

concept of gladiature as the celebration of armed combat, as a contest of strength

and exercise of military skill, pertaining to an imagined cultural context which

proclaimed such virtues within an agreeably rugged and cohesive structure of

social solidarity and relative political simplicity.

Within the Samnite hypothesis, then, the significant point is the relation

between these two conditions: that the new construct of civilization could invoke a barbarian that was defined on the one hand by characteristics such as democracy, freedom, and social cohesion, and on the other hand by a particular association with warfare that not only underwrote and in a sense constituted those socio-political values, but even thereby created the conditions of possibility for a legitimate space for violence within the image of the barbarian democracy. The new strategy operating within the historico-political discourse surrounding the west's construct of civilization was this re-positioning of violence to a space of legitimacy, and the effect within gladiatorial historiography was the inscription of a new origin story wherein the language of abhorrence need no longer be invoked in response to the cathexis of violence and pleasure.

Filtering the new barbarian

Salmon's characterization of the Samnites as the ideal barbarian was not the full scope of the shift during this period; it must be recalled that he did not, in fact, have a great deal to say about gladiature itself, and about the relation between Samnite and Roman iteration of the practice he was entirely silent. Closing the gap between the Samnite barbarian and the civilization of Rome was also the focus of the contemporary work of Ville, whose work not only reverberated closely with Salmon's, but even reached back to the scholarship of earlier in the century to produce a new summary image of gladiature which was not only unusually explicit in its examination of gladiatorial origin's relation to subsequent developments at Rome, but also picked up on emergent ideas from Malten onwards to sum up the new mythos of postwar civilization contained within a romanticized and purified image of warfare, the mystical distillation of the *agon* that had been produced by the regressive historical discourse of the previous generation, and the powerful suggestion that a legitimate, civilized violence was not only *ipso facto* legitimately pleasurable, but in its furthest logical extension was not, in fact, actually violence at all.

Ville's major contribution to the scholarship of gladiature was the 1981 *La gladiature en Occident: des origins à la mort de Domitien*, a work still widely cited as the definitive word on the south Italian origin of gladiature; the monograph was a posthumous publication of sometimes meandering notes printed after Ville's untimely death, and much of the core of his thinking in fact appeared in his 1969 article "La Guerre et la Munus", in the same year as Salmon's work on Samnium. The article's title was a clear indication of the direction of Ville's thought. Navigating through Ville's texts, particularly the 1981 monograph, is challenging; much of his reasoning was based upon what he termed "thought experiments" (*La gladiature* 18), and while he was diligent in his handling of the limited evidence that was available to him, his imaginative forays into the earliest history of gladiature sought to synthesize widely disparate details into a totalizing account that, like Malten's, stretched from the funeral of Patroclus to the inauguration of the Colosseum. While attempts to connect scenes from the *Iliad* with imperial gladiatorial spectacle were at least two centuries old already, Ville was content with nothing less than a continuous narrative. Consequently, his work constructed an image of gladiature's descent from its relatively legitimate prehistoric foundations to the comparatively debased form it eventually assumed under Rome. This was also, on the surface, an old story; however, Ville's subsequent influence arose from the terms upon which his expanded narrative rested, which, like Salmon, not only gestured toward Rome as an aristocratic debasement of a purer 'civilization' but further fleshed out an analysis wherein the barbarian civility was essentially defined according to a socio-political structure that was constituted by, and most clearly perceived through, the practice of gladiature. Thus was the new historiographic strategy deepened: not only was classical scholarship (to use a Foucauldian framework) bypassing or eliding the Romanity of the nobility to construct an origin story for the civilization of the barbarian democracy, but was in fact pointing directly to gladiatorial violence as a centrally important signifier of the civility of the barbarian.

Key to Ville's work was the re-definition of what could be interpreted as the ritual content of funerary gladiature. Ville took great exception to the long-standing consensus that original gladiature was related in any way to human sacrifice, either by historical connection or analogous reasoning; laicisation was not simply a new term for Tertullian's interpretation of gladiature as the co-option or corruption of a religious practice into a profane one. At least once in the collection of notes from which his 1981 manuscript was compiled, Ville suggested that the connection was perhaps, in fact, imagined; the "historical memory [of human sacrifices], or their psychological phantasm, sometimes haunts the imagination of the Romans, as the sacrifice of Isaac and of Iphigenia haunted the Hebrews and the Greeks. This dark phantasm serves as an AITION[xli] to gladiature: when the first Roman historians sought to imagine an origin of gladiature, they provenanced this cruel game to that cruel rite" (*La gladiature*14, my translation). Instead, Ville firmly followed Malten's earlier claim that original

funerary gladiature was to be constructed not as a form of sacrifice, but as an

agon; the critical distinction – which we have already encountered with Robert

and Heurgon, and which will be discussed in greater detail in the next chapter -

was that gladiature was by definition a game or a sport, and had been since its

origin.

For Ville, the most significant element of the nebulous image of the early

funerary foundations of gladiatorial combat was the suggestion that, as an

exceptional rite restricted to the funerals of high-status males who, in Ville's

view, were most likely to have been warriors who died in combat, funerary

gladiature was intimately connected to warfare, and was likely to have involved

the death of prisoners of war; he referred to the funeral of Patroclus as a

celebrated example of a practice that he, along with Cumont and Malten, felt was

likely to have been a relatively widespread archaic practice ("La Guerre et la

Munus" 10-11).[xlii] This was a key point whose significance cannot be understated:

at a stroke, and with deceptive simplicity, Ville effectively historicized the quasi-

mystical trope of *agon* and, in so doing, co-opted that central trope into a

bourgeois history of right. By positing a direct connection between the erstwhile-

nobiliary construct of *agon* and the image of original gladiature as a practice more

closely and literally associated with warfare than with religion – and, at the same

time, tying that entire network of connections between warfare and gladiature to

the Samnites as an idealized barbarian, among whom 'warfare' was already re-

inscribed as a signifier of civilization, or the 'barbarian democracy' - Ville set up the necessary conditions for the consequent re-inscription of gladiature itself as a signifier of civilization. Agonistic gladiature, as a 'natural', mimetic practice, was not abhorrent; Ville explicitly stated that "peoples still semi-barbarous"- and such noble barbarians included Samnites, Campanians, and mid-republican Romans alike[xliii] - "engage each other in combat for pleasure, without considering it to be immoral or an offense to the public peace" (15). Consequently, the new basis of authority for the origin story of gladiature as an expression of a bourgeois history of right, the *agon*, was positioned to perfectly and completely interpolate and over-write the nobiliary rationalization of human sacrifice, and gladiature's signifying power within historico-political discourse began to align the two great constructs of civilization and violence which had previously been maintained in strict mutual exclusion.

Ville greatly extended the tentative suggestion in Salmon's work that gladiature was to be understood in terms of the gradual transformation of funerary ritual, rather than to consider gladiature as funerary ritual itself, and termed the transformation of funerary rite into gladiatorial spectacle a process of 'laicisation'. This "natural" (*La gladiature* 11) transformation pertained to both the Samnites and to the Romans; Roman gladiature, like Samnite gladiature, was initially funerary, but Ville mounted a complex argument to claim that the detachment from funerary rite was a categorically different event for the Samnites than it was for the Romans. The apparent practice among the Campanians of 'banquet gladiature', already encountered in the discussion of ancient sources, was cited by Ville in support of such naturalness; details such as the fourth-century BC tomb paintings taken as representations of gladiatorial combat, or the

second-century BC flourishing in Campania of gladiatorial infrastructure such as

stone amphitheatres and *ludi* (gladiatorial barracks) further demonstrated that the

laicisation of gladiature happened earlier in southern Italy than in Rome ("La

Guerre" 187, *La gladiature* 23-4). Ultimately, though, what happened at Rome

was considerably different, in Ville's view, and formed the basis of Ville's work

as a central articulation of the *embourgeoisement* of gladiatorial historiography.

Initially, the Roman process of laicisation was straightforward: Ville

upheld the interpretation of gladiature's gradual association with political

manoeuvring in the mid-Republic, wherein the funerary pretext of gladiatorial

combat became increasingly superficial and expedient, motivated by political

goals rather than directly associated with the death (in combat or otherwise) of

high-status individuals. However, a second development followed on the heels of

Rome's detachment of gladiature from funerals, a development which was, Ville

argued, unique to Rome: the professionalization of gladiature (*La gladiature* 16).

Professionalization hinged upon the legal status of Roman gladiators as slaves,

which Ville connected to Rome's wars of conquest across the Italian peninsula

throughout the latter half of the republican period.

For Ville, gladiatorial professionalization represented the real departure

from original *agon*, particularly as that pure *agon* was represented by – as one

might anticipate – the funeral of Patroclus. Ville cited the *Iliad* to assert that the

straightforward pleasure of heroic warriors in the contest of pitched combat, "the

craving to compete and to beat each other" (*La gladiature* 15), beyond all other possible motivations and responses, was a key to the interpretation of the original

agon. The *agon* of the *Iliad* was carried out by aristocratic Greek warriors at the

funeral of a peer, which Ville saw as consistent with the practice in the Greek

world of citizens participating in athletic competitions and contests; laicized

Roman gladiature, in contrast, diverged from the Greek model since the

participants were primarily slaves and, eventually, enslaved prisoners of war (*La

gladiature*17). Laicization, then, was to be considered as decivilizing; Ville had

co-opted the 'Tertullian argument', and deployed it against the nobility of Rome.

The two gladiatures – agonistic and 'laicized' – were represented as expressions

of different socio-political power structures, and the superiority of the barbarian

democracy, with its free competition between citizens, to Romanity with its

coerced slaves, was a cornerstone of Ville's interpretation. The invocation of

Patroclus was not only an additional support to Ville's argument, but the manner

in which Patroclus was referenced was also especially telling: whereas Malten

had used Greece in the traditional manner as a signifier of civilization and, via the

funeral of Patroclus, posited the *agon* as a foundation for multiple possible origin

stories for the 'barbarian civilization', Ville took Malten's primitivist

generalization and incorporated it into biopolitical discourse by using the funeral

of Patroclus not as a detached, floating signifier of 'original agonism', but as a

historical example, with an organic connection to all forms of gladiature that

followed it.

At the same time, Ville's specific deployment of the Tertullian argument

put forth a spectre of decivilizing which inverted the traditional relation between violence and pleasure, long familiar from the nobiliary history of right. Though Ville's argument superficially contained an implicit critique of the dramatically unequal power structures that the Roman amphitheatre embodied, Ville's use of pleasure as a rationalization for gladiatorial violence obscured that critique at the very moment of its articulation: the 'barbarism' of professional/laicised Roman gladiature was located in the absence of 'legitimate pleasure', not in the potential site of conflict or coercion between rulers and ruled. This may seem like hair-splitting, and it could be argued that the point about 'craving to compete', far from eliding Ville's critique of power, was integral to and inseparable from it; however, Ville's arguments opened the discursive space around 'legitimate violence', which was rapidly expanding in gladiatorial historiography, wide enough to also admit the notion of a 'legitimate pleasure in violence'.

Ville alluded to this legitimate violence/pleasure through reference to what it wasn't: the truly problematic aspect of decivilized, laicized Roman gladiature – the new object of abhorrence – lay in the claim that the advent of professional gladiatorial slaves precipitated the transformation of gladiature into a lethal practice, into combat to the death. A significant element of the legitimate position that Ville constructed for original agonistic gladiature, and certainly for the pleasure it involved, arose from his speculative claim that the fundamental rules of the *agon* required a degree of restraint to be exercised in funerary combat – thus, one more contingency of the link being forged between gladiatorial violence and civilization was the radical suggestion that original gladiature – which, recall, had long been regarded as a form of human sacrifice – was in fact not lethal. As will be seen below, the uncoupling of gladiature from death did not trail very far

behind the subsequent transformation, hinted at above, of the relation between

gladiature and violence.

The consequences of this image of original gladiature were many. Salmon

in 1969 had suggested that original gladiature among the Samnites was non-

lethal; conversely, the full (and sometimes inchoate) scope of Ville's thought

considered the image of non-lethal gladiature from several angles, always

maintaining a space for it within his conjectures although that position shifted

between 1969 and 1981. In "La Guerre et la Munus", Ville located the transition

from non-lethal to lethal gladiature within the larger transition from Republic to

Empire in the Roman sphere; during the late Republic, he implied, professional

gladiature, though a departure from original *agon*, was still connected to its

fundamental meaning by association with contemporary wars of conquest, as

indicated by evidence that the standard 'types' of gladiators were named after

conquered groups such as Samnites, Gauls, and Thracians, equipped with the

traditional armaments of those peoples. The suggestion was that during this

period, the pleasure of spectators was primarily intent upon the "quality" of

combat, and the death of gladiators was not the desired objective, as the defeated

gladiator was habitually granted *missio* (i.e., allowed to leave the combat alive).

The Augustan-period reorganization of gladiatorial spectacle, with its erasure of

the old racial types and the development of what Ville termed 'fantasy-types'

equipped with armaments expressly designed for gladiature, represented the final

break with the interpretive context of the original *agon*, and further correlated with an increase in gladiator mortality ("La Guerre" 193). *Agon*, being non-lethal,

posited the standard of civilized acceptability; laicised gladiature was similarly

passable provided that the focus of pleasure was combat rather than death; and

only professionalized imperial gladiature was to be abhorred, as "it appears that

the essence of pleasure in gladiators ... was constituted exclusively by the

spectacle and by combat to the death" ("La Guerre" 193).

The 1981 monograph actually specified Rome's break with original,

civilized *agon* by exploring the figure of the *editor*, the individual who formally

offered gladiatorial combats to the public in the Roman sphere; the kernel of this

idea formed the conclusion to the 1969 article, but Ville took it considerably

further in the later text. By the time of the Flavian dynasty, gladiatorial combats

were fully incorporated into the state programme of public spectacle, and were

associated with the formal duties of the office of quaestor, with the exception of

occasional spectacles offered directly by the emperor. This process of integration,

however, was gradual over the course of the first century AD, and did not begin

before the principate of Augustus. Over the last three centuries of the Republic, in

contrast, gladiatorial combats were technically an exceptional affair of private

initiative (given their funerary context, which remained a nominal pretext even in

Caesar's time), and the individual who offered combats was termed in this

capacity an *editor*.

Ville's later text connected the ultimate disengagement of gladiature from

agon with the emergence of the figure of the *editor*, for a nested series of reasons

that gestured toward the upheavals in the social politics of the later Republic. The political popularity and attention that a patrician *editor* garnered with gladiatorial combat, in Ville's view, directly conflicted with the original religious meaning of agonistic funerary gladiature. This signalled a politically motivated change in the social function of gladiature over the middle Republic, as "burials quickly became pretexts to electoral campaigns. The funeral cortege of a grand personage could not be a narrowly familial ceremony: the entire city was a big family, and each big family was a little of the whole city; the population followed these numerous funerals, attended the funeral games, took part in the banquet. Soon the funerals were nothing more than a pretext and ... a simple means to render [the heir, who was the *editor*] popular" (*La gladiature*15-6). Within this model, Ville pushed back his 1969 interpretation of the crowd; while his earlier image of the crowd's pleasure had been constructed as responsive to the form of gladiature with which it was presented by the increasingly involved state administration in the early Empire, that affective force of change was here delegated entirely to the figure of the private republican *editor*. Ville stated baldly that "[i]t goes without saying that as gladiature changed function and became a pure spectacle, it became also deadlier and the public wanted to see the blood flow" (*La gladiature*16). Death as the locus of the cathexis of violence and pleasure, or rather death as the form of that violence, was categorically distinct from the 'combat for pleasure between semi-barbarous peoples', and connoted a decline from civilization.

However, Ville's main preoccupation with the *editor* sprang from his role in the 'moment of decision' at the climax of a gladiatorial combat, as the judgement of the outcome of a combat was ultimately made on his authority; the public may have wanted to see the blood flow, but the opportunity to satisfy their desire for this pleasure rested entirely in his hands. Referring again to the funeral of Patroclus as the avatar of true *agon*, Ville felt that the non-lethal character of original gladiature was dependent in some sense upon the intervention of spectators in deciding the outcome of a combat; he claimed that the scene of combat between Diomedes and Ajax, which was stopped by the watching Achaeans, demonstrated at least that the author of the *Iliad* had represented the act of intervention as a significant element in the funerary *agon*, and that therefore the conventional restriction of combat to first blood, rather than to death, was consistent with the "dignity of epic" (*La gladiature* 18). He then went on to suggest that the figure of the Roman *editor*, in his capacity as arbiter of the choice either honourably to discharge a gladiator from combat (*missio*) or to order his immediate execution in the arena, represented a concentration of this formerly group-based, organic authority into the hands of a single individual, and that – assumedly within the surrounding context of the *editor*'s political self-interest – this concentration of arbitrary power over life and death, as a means to political ends, was "atrocious" (*La gladiature* 18).

The significance of Ville's claims regarding the power of the *editor* should be understood against the later nineteenth century's image of the *pollice verso* as the salient element of the moment of decision in gladiatorial combat. Previous interpretations of gladiature, and specifically the articulation of abhorrence, had hinged upon the notion of the crowd as an irrational mob, whose 'turning of the thumb' in judgment upon individual gladiators was represented as a dense signifier of the crowd's essential incapacity to be trusted with political power through the franchise; it was upon this basis that the lower-class crowd was inscribed as existing outside of civilization, and as inadmissible to that group distinction. Conversely, the early twentieth century's emphasis upon the bare instrumentalization of the crowd as the means of the political ends of the aristocracy, legitimate or not, had subtly reiterated the un-civility of the crowd as an *a priori*, in a model of socio-political structure within which the image of the *pollice verso* served as little more than a rhetorical flourish. Ville's unprecedented emphasis upon the *editor*, however, encapsulated an inversion of this figuration which had been gradually emerging since the years following the Second World War. Here, the corruption of *agon* into professional gladiature pivoted upon the radical arbitrary power of the patrician *editor* to judge the 'sport' of gladiature, a development correlated to the rise of gladiature's lethality, and thus 'decivilizing', which had previously been closely associated with the threat of the crowd's potentially violent power, was now inscribed as a process of the withdrawal of the crowd's power and its transformation into authoritarianism. In much the same manner that the funeral of Patroclus was represented by Ville as the master image of *agon*, the *editor* was in a sense treated as a metonymic of the republican state, or ultimate representative figure of the nobility, and thus the *editor* was for Ville the focal point of gladiature's descent into barbarism.

Within the fantasized image of proto-historic social cohesion, in contrast, original gladiature was for the first time imagined as in a sense nonviolent; a voluntary staged combat between social equals, subject to the control of a crowd which collectively sought to prevent death rather than demand it with a turn of the thumb, could not but appear almost romantically benign when compared to the form that the practice eventually assumed at Rome, at least as this was construed in the contemporary historical imagination. This observation was, of course, not unrelated to the academic discourse of the earlier twentieth century, with its anxieties over the affinities between the transition of republic to empire in Rome, and contemporary movements in totalitarian government. The critical distinction lay in two related lines of argument which were unique to this period: on the one hand, the suggestion that the authority of the crowd was to be not only recognized but also associated with an 'original' civility which had been eroded by the Roman aristocracy; on the other, the parallel, mirroring discourse surrounding the south Italian cultures, particularly the Samnites, as the creators of gladiature as a practice originally associated with non-lethal sport, in a form organically analogous to warfare, which had been perverted by the Roman establishment into an 'atrocious' practice that took these rustic, noble non-Roman peoples as its first preferred victims.

As in all historiographic periods examined above, gladiature was at bottom inscribed as a richly meaningful site of the discourse of struggle; what differed in this period of *embourgeoisement* was the notion that gladiature's gradual appropriation into the political sphere at Rome was a corruption of a practice which originally had expressed a far greater social cohesion, whether this was imagined to have existed among the Greeks of the heroic period, within the tribal democracy of the Samnite *touto*, or even among Romans of the middle

Republic. Moreover, the bourgeois version of the later 'corruption' of original

gladiature was inscribed as the work of the patrician group, in contrast to the

nobiliary history of the nineteenth century which had firmly blamed the mob; and

contra the earlier twentieth century, the nobility's exploitation of gladiature to

political ends was not logical instrumentalization, but an atrocity – the new object

of abhorrence. The crowd's old bloodlust for gladiature – the abhorrent

intersection of violence with pleasure – shifted to the aristocracy, whereas the

'barbarian' relation to gladiature, linked with entirely different notions of the

State, began to create a parallel discursive space wherein the pleasure of

gladiature could signify civilization.

Rome, decivilized

Insofar as Rome, particularly after the middle Republic, was situated by

Ville and others as 'decivilized' in relation to the strategic claim being mounted

for the civility of the barbarian democracy (whose initial early twentieth century

trappings of primitivism, incidentally, were no longer discursively in evidence),

contemporary historiography was careful to annex Roman history's primary

narrative structure: the trope of the 'fall of Rome', which had defined the

historical imagination since Gibbon and which had lapsed within the nobiliary

strategy only when the bourgeois perspective was first beginning to make itself

apparent (again, in the early twentieth century).

One tactic that the bourgeois history of right adapted for its own purposes

was the origin story associated with the fall – the choice, in the narrative of

Rome's history as a process of decivilizing, of 'the moment when the rot set in'.

Scholars of this period maintained the narrative of Rome's fall, but sought the source at an earlier moment in Rome's history. Bourgeois strategy went further back in time than the well-trod ground of the late Republic, wherein the speaking subject of the nobility had sought its own self-image in the troubling tale of the republican oligarchy and its transformation into an empire perceived by turns as either the republic's descent into tyranny or triumphant ascent to totalitarian power. Instead, the new speaking subject of history sought a 'more original origin' than that which had organized the nobiliary history of right, and found it in the early Republic, specifically in the Struggle of the Orders.

The Struggle of the Orders – a term which covers the period from the beginning of the fifth to the early third centuries B.C., and refers to the political and juridical attempts of the Roman plebs to attain political and juridical equality with the patricians, with constitutional protections - offered two important possibilities to the articulation of the Third Estate's history of right. First, it briefly returned the central trope of the myth-historical narrative to struggle, as one would expect in the opening stages of a political project "going back to a constitution or demanding a return to something resembling an equilibrium of forces" (*SMBD* 208). Second, the use of the particular 'struggle' of the Orders as an origin story enabled the narration of Rome's 'fall' to be dramatized not through the civilized aristocracy's defeat by the barbarism of *imperita multitudo*, as had marked nineteenth century historiography, but through the representation of an unequal contest between patricians and plebeians, wherein the plebs' attempts to attain parity of power were oppressed by a corrupt ruling class, and the legitimate violence of popular justice, held up as a key signifier of civilization in the hands of the plebs, was gradually frustrated and eventually misappropriated by the *populares*, who themselves were now seen as a group numbering as many 'turncoat' wealthy plebs as opportunistic patricians.

The influential work of Brunt defined this period's conviction that the fall of the Republic had occurred as the direct result of corruption in the ruling class as a whole, and the spread of that corruption to the upper echelons of the plebeian class, which was imagined during the Struggle of the Orders to have been characterized by a high degree of political solidarity.[xliv] The founding claim of *Social Conflicts in the Roman Republic* (1969), reiterated numerous times within the text, was that the Roman Republic was a house essentially divided; the abyss into which the Republic eventually fell was the gulf between rulers and ruled, and the history of the widening of that social separation was a slow descent from a relatively cohesive sociality into a massive, socially anomic state whose program of territorial expansion had been mismanaged by private and group interests into five subsequent centuries of autocratic government. Brunt's moral condemnation of the ruling class was rather restrained (41); nonetheless, citing Sallust, the "avarice of the ruling class was reflected in the misery and discontent of the masses ... and it was in this context of discontent that the ambition of men such as Marius and Sulla, Pompey and Caesar, was to wreck the established order" (76).

In Brunt's view, the Roman historical memory of peace and social solidarity which fuelled late republican nostalgia for earlier centuries was not a by-product of superficial cohesion produced by external conflicts, as Salmon had accorded to the Samnites, but rather a veneer of solidarity engineered by the collusion of the patrician class with the wealthiest plebeians to suppress popular discontent; he felt that if "popular agitation at Rome almost ceased for a hundred and fifty years after 287 [the creation of the tribune of the plebs], the reason may partly be that there were few potential leaders for the masses, once the aspirations of the richer plebeians for office had been satisfied" (12). A hundred and fifty years after 287 was, of course, the period of the Gracchi, whose championing of land distribution to the advantage of the lower classes "exposed all the divisive forces in Roman society, and their reforms and ruin set in train the events that culminated with the fall of the Republic" (92). What was obscured by the artificial peace between the creation of the tribunate of the plebs and the Gracchan reforms was a political system which was only nominally democratic, Brunt argued, as the ruling group controlled access to political office, the convening of popular voting assemblies, and the submission of proposals to popular vote (9, 46). After the Gracchi, all subsequent champions of *populares* political causes, once castigated as demagogues, were universally insincere in their aims; these individuals were democratic in their defence of the sovereign right of the *populus* to decide any question that might be referred to it in assembly, but "none of them claimed that the people at Rome, as at Athens, should control all policy" (Brunt 94).

What lay on the far side of this swamp of political corruption, in the early Republic and especially the years immediately following the culmination of the Struggle of the Orders, was something that Brunt's text suggested was comparatively much more like civilization. This was argued on the basis of the existence of greater social parity between the classes within the mutual constraints of the original system of clientage, and further upon the "truly democratic character" of the early political assemblies, wherein the wealthy did not enjoy superior voting power within the system of tribal voting (Brunt 49-52). Brunt's image of Roman civilization, then, was a tragic one, which had experienced a brief flowering of a relatively equal distribution of political power - an early period of 'barbarian democracy' - before the 'established order' was wrecked by patricians and wealthy plebs. Conversely, what lay on the near side, in the rise of imperial autocratic government, was a sociality exhausted by its own internal struggles and prepared to exchange freedom for security (Brunt 153-4); moreover, the transition to empire did not in itself address the gap between the wealthy ruling class and the impoverished masses, as evidence from the late empire suggested to Brunt that at that time the "gulf between rich and poor was at least as wide and deep as ever, misery and oppression as great" (155).

Brunt's contemporary, Lintott, continued the theme of excoriation of the Roman aristocracy, inscribing the end of the Republic as a failure to be laid firmly at the patrician doorstep much as Brunt had done; however, Lintott's work also represented a significant development for two reasons: Lintott was an early voice for cultural relativism, and he attempted to apprehend Roman social and political violence from that perspective. *Violence in Republican Rome* (1968) directly approached the ancient accounts of the social and political upheavals that presaged the transition from Republic to Empire, and sought to interrogate the legal as well as cultural conditions of possibility which had shaped and supported the reorganization of political structure during that period. Lintott claimed

outright that "Roman tradition tolerated and even encouraged violence in private

and political disputes, and both the law and constitutional precedent recognized

the use of force by private individuals" (4), and interpreted this traditional legal

tolerance within the "Roman cult of expediency" wherein interpersonal violence

and the use of force were socially coded as acceptable means provided that their

associated ends were politically defensible (52). In a clear sense, 'expediency'

functioned as a strategic inversion of what the high point of nobiliary historico-

political discourse had inscribed as (hyper-) rational instrumentalization; where an

earlier generation of scholars from Warde Fowler to Ross Taylor had argued

straightforwardly that the ends had justified the means, Lintott objectified and

implicitly critiqued the Roman ruling group's instrumental rationality as a key

factor in the decivilizing of Rome.

Within this analysis, the series of historical events that precipitated the end

of the Republic – class conflicts associated with socioeconomic shifts, the

agrarian problem, and the growing concentration of military power in the hands of

individual generals as well as political power in the hands of demagogues – were

linked to a 'lack' or 'weakness' in the Roman constitution (legal, not spiritual),

which "denied adequate executive powers to magistrates who had the will to

exercise them" (4). In effect, the infamous upheavals of the end of the Republic

were the product of crucial gaps in the legal system, which were themselves

expressions of deeper Roman cultural attitudes towards violence as a political means. These legal aporias, however, were themselves traceable to a deeper 'un-civility' of Roman culture.

In his attempt to assess the 'Roman attitude to violence', Lintott maintained a strict distinction between the range of attested attitudes of the aristocracy and a monolithic representation of the disposition of the lower classes; moreover, the historical evidence cited as the embodiment of this division drew heavily from gladiature. Lintott conceded that the Roman aristocracy, as the literate class, had exerted a disproportionate influence upon surviving historical evidence regarding the end of the Republic, yet he further argued that "it is the mind of the politician that provides the ultimate answer to the fall of the Republic. For it was his will which was the origin of the most atrocious and politically dangerous violence" (35). In examining the mind of the republican politician, primarily via Cicero and Sallust, he felt that a "satisfactory case could be made for the Roman upper class being callously indifferent to physical suffering than for their being actively sadistic ... insofar as they are distinguished in their attitudes from other nations, it is because they followed policy not passion" (44); thus the 'cult of expediency', forming an attitude to violence that was half moral and half instrumental in character, cast the Roman ruling class as a group which did not feel the abhorrence of violence that they had been accorded in the nineteenth century, and whose instrumentalization of violence, in a refinement of early twentieth century approaches, sprang not simply from the apparent logic of political expediency, but from political expediency as an actual element of group identity.

The aristocratic cult of expediency, in Lintott's view, was the basis of their range of attitudes to gladiature, none of which were now read as expressive of anything like outright abhorrence. An illustration was Cicero's claim (*Tusc.* II. 41) that the sight of blood and death in gladiatorial combat was salubrious for the masses in maintaining a properly Roman warlike character: as Lintott paraphrased, young men among the spectators "must be blooded at second hand if they cannot have first-hand experience, and, if only criminals suffer, there can be nothing wrong" (41). Of gladiature as a whole, however, Lintott interjected an authorial statement of abhorrence, considering that the religious pretext of original gladiature was acceptable in comparison to the secularization of the practice; this was a "serious reproach to the Roman character ... [as gladiatorial combats] were simply intended to satisfy a desire for excitement of a morbid kind" (40).

Within this framework, Lintott explicitly dissociated civilization from violence, with one crucial exception: he argued for the legitimacy and importance of the tradition of popular justice as a substratum of political violence, in Rome as in other states both ancient and modern. The legitimate face of the violence of popular justice, which "[c]ivilization and political development will suppress or divert into legal channels" (6), was exemplified nostalgically by the *secessio plebi*, the general strikes or mass protests of the plebeian class which occurred intermittently between the first decades of the Republic and the establishment of the plebeian tribunate in 287. Where Rome as a whole had fallen short was in the failure to suppress, divert, or otherwise incorporate populism into the governing structure, such that the legitimate violence of the *secessio plebi* had its decivilized echo in the rioting of the first century B.C. Rome's failure in political development, in Lintott's view, was linked to the legacy of the Struggle of the Orders in the early republican period, as the plebeian access to political office was won in the context of an abiding opposition which was consequently established between the senatorial order and the tribunes of the plebs. This legally mediated conflict, which logically reduced to an opposition between the *imperium* (legal right to employ force) of senatorial magistrates and the sacrosanctity (legal right to exception from acts of force) of the tribunes, was an old tree that would bear evil fruit in the later Republic. Through this perspective, Lintott deconstructed the shared ancient Roman narrative of the valourization of early republican 'moral virtues', which had informed and influenced so much of the modern narrative of decline in the historiographic scholarship of the end of the Republic and, further, of gladiature; he argued, instead, that the late republican historical memory of an idealized social concord was a nostalgic inscription of an artificial solidarity produced by external conflicts with other states:

> "Although Rome was free from civil war and bloody revolution
> during the first four centuries of the Republic, and before 133 most
> disputes ended in concord, this does not imply a utopia of restraint
> throughout Roman society. There was a greater group solidarity in
> the close community of the early Republic, while it was menaced
> by outside enemies. But group solidarity led not only to patriotism
> but to faction, as the struggles between the patricians and plebeians
> shows. The techniques of self-defence employed by a group,
> whether based on family, tribe, locality, or client-patron
> relationship, are a doubtful asset to the spreading metropolis of a
> complex civilization" (6).

Despite Rome's increasing complexity, at an early point in its political development the shift towards greater political parity between social groups had at the same time legally enshrined a fundamentally violent conflict between the means by which different social groups could legally pursue political ends. Consequently, the Roman project of civilization was, in Lintott's view, flawed at its core, as a direct consequence of the legal calcification of violence as a political means in the context of the Struggle of the Orders. The implicitly natural course of civilization to suppress or divert such violence was choked off at that point precisely because of the ruling class' response to the plebeian claim for political access, which arose directly from a specifically aristocractic exercise of the 'cult of expediency' that permitted violence.

Gladiature, bourgeois myth-history, and social cohesion

The castigation of the nobility was ultimately a transitory phase in the *embourgeoisement* of gladiatorial historiography, which arguably had been foreshadowed a generation earlier by Robert, whose analysis had cast Rome for the first time in the position of the barbarian. The strategic inversion of historical tropes may have provided the necessary framework for the rudimentary construction of a 'civilized violence' and its consequent alignment with barbarian democracy (initiating the elision of violence into the bargain), but the framework itself would prove to be a provisional moment in historico-political discourse. As the bourgeois speaking subject entered upon gladiatorial historiography, its advent was marked by a re-ordering of imagined socio-political power structures within an overarching continuity of discursive structure, as the discourse of struggle was initially carried over; however, in the context of an emerging scholarly trend which tended to focus directly upon gladiature as a discrete subject, we see the discourse of civilization seek to ennoble, or Romanize, itself once more.

The alignment of 'civilized violence' with 'barbarian democracy' in the image of gladiatorial origin defined the point at which the gradual elision of violence in gladiatorial historiography began; flashing forward a little way, the discursive takeaway from these developments for the next generation, as will be explored in the following chapter, would be the civilizing of violence in its association with a democratizing of power structures beyond the realm of the barbarian, and in the construction of an image of Rome wherein gladiature would come to function as a lynchpin of social cohesion – in stark contrast to its earlier incarnation(s) as a primary site of social conflict. In the meantime, scholarly consensus – in an inchoate, contradictory manner, as evidenced by the sources surveyed below - began to move toward the notion of social cohesion via the deployment of the rhetoric of reflexivity surrounding abhorrence.

The first real intimation of the idea that gladiature and civilization were not mutually contradictory terms is traceable to Auguet's unannotated 1970 monograph *Cruauté et Civilisation*. On one level, Auguet's thought echoed the high notes of nobiliary historico-political discourse from the late nineteenth century; he maintained, for instance, a descriptive model of the development of gladiature which emphasized late republican power struggles between the conservative Senate and ambitious individual members of the ruling class (4), relegating the political affectivity of the plebs to an instrumental afterthought.

Gladiature was in his view a perfect tool of propaganda, acting upon an electoral

base in the republican period and carried over more or less seamlessly into the

governing structure of empire, wherein it was "indispensible to the smooth

functioning of a regime that was at once authoritarian and demagogic" (188). In

Auguet's model, the plebeian class had no real determinative political power:

their votes were essentially for sale while they yet possessed them, their sense of

entitlement to entertainment was the force largely responsible for the scale of

massive conglomerate spectacles, and they were drawn to gladiature "like

children" (195). The most salient socio-political function of gladiature and other

spectacle was to distract the lower classes from actual politics, since "[i]t had

long been known that the more the public shouted itself hoarse at the circus, the

less importance its voice had" (184). Moreover, although Auguet argued

extensively that 'the Romans' ought not to be considered cruel by modern

scholars, he readily conceded that the plebs possessed a "lust for cruelty" which

gladiature satisfied (195).

However, Auguet stepped into the space opened by Lintott, wherein the

Roman elite, at least, commanded the benefit of the doubt regarding pleasure

and violence; there Auguet attempted to incorporate a degree of self-reflexivity

into the discussion:

> "If we are astonished at the attitude of the Roman elite in this
> matter, it means only that we are putting the question wrongly. We
> start from the idea that they should have taken a stand against the
> cruelties of which we disapprove and, to excuse them, we search
> desperately for problematic traces of disapproval. We must, on the
> contrary, start from the idea that such disapproval was out of the
> question. When we consider the gladiatorial combats according to
> our own criteria, we are doing no more than applying a cautery to a

wooden leg. (...) We consider them out of relation, when the
reverse is what is needed to place them in the context of the beliefs
and ideas of the Romans" (197).

The 'beliefs and ideas of the Romans', again reminiscent of Lintott, characterized them as an extremely and relentlessly rational culture, for whom gladiature could have only a pragmatic and logical function despite the modern inclination to attribute gladiatorial violence to "some cruelty in the Roman nature" (1). In Auguet's analysis, gladiature would have been pointless if it existed only as an expression of cruelty or sadism, because it "destroys and consumes without advantage, to satisfy a passion or merely for pleasure. It is a luxury. But the Roman was not only a realist; he was a slave to utility in the narrowest sense. The sacrifice of what could be a source of wealth, made to satisfy a momentary instinct, a partiality or a purely subjective emotion, was for him a serious fault, a slur on the most elementary principle of his morality" (14). The Romans built a "civilization which [granted] nothing to pleasure or to fantasy"; Roman civilization "obeyed the dictates of calculation and not a bloodthirsty instinct" (15).

The rationality of gladiatorial violence specifically lay, in Auguet's view, in the interpretation of gladiature as a performance of exactly that system of Roman mores which precluded the possibility of bloodthirsty pleasures. The question of the moral value, for Rome, of properties or behaviours that modernity would label violent was of course not new, and was under debate both before and after the publication of Auguet's text. Lintott's analysis has been covered above, for example, and even this study had earlier roots pertaining to Roman warfare: Heinze (1938) had argued several generations

previously that Romans did not place moral value upon warfare and military

prowess – were not, in Heinze's terms, '*kriegslustig*'; yet Harris, writing

several years after Auguet, was to argue in turn that Roman bellicosity was not

only a value, but a norm (180). For Auguet, the moral value of gladiature, from

which pleasure could legitimately arise, was attributable not strictly to violent

spectacle but to the experience of Roman group identity, "the consciousness of

oneself as a Roman" (187). The experience of group identification, in turn,

rested upon two related factors: the acceptance at face value of Roman written

evidence which praised gladiature as a practice which instilled *virtus* and

fortitudo into spectators, and the extent to which gladiatorial spectacles could

be read as symbolic re-stagings of Roman civilization's struggles of imperial

conquest, or as "historical romances" (195) of common group heritage. Auguet

claimed that the relevant writings of the Roman elite contained neither post

hoc justifications nor negative judgments of gladiature, but sincere approval of

its morally beneficial effect upon the plebs (190). This patrician approval, in

conjunction with the pan-Roman appeal of the "historical pageants" of the

most elaborate spectacles, were early suggestions of gladiature as a force for

social integration which appeared even in the midst of one of the last studies to

organize itself around the notion of class opposition.

Auguet must also be credited with the kernel of another idea that would

be taken up and developed in later years, specifically the notion of gladiature

as a quasi-magical practice of what he labelled transmutation. On the strength of the claim that written evidence for the values of *virtus* and *fortitudo* were

now to be taken seriously and literally by modern scholarship, Auguet pointed

out that gladiators were almost universally *infamis*, or outside of the legitimate

social order, whether by virtue of their status as slaves (which all gladiators

were), captives, or criminals. On the surface, this presented a paradox wherein

the most socially degraded individuals became spectacles precisely for their

performance and embodiment of what were, according to some scholars, the

highest moral values; for Auguet, the apparent paradox was in fact the key to

gladiature's 'meaning', in the sense that gladiature was thus a site of the

transmutation of social identity, and moreover that this phenomenon lay at the

heart of the pleasure of gladiatorial spectacle (196-7).

This idea, which will be encountered again below, should not be

overlooked now: the notion of transmutation represented a perfect

concatenation of what would emerge as the new central tropes of the

historiography of gladiature. Transmutation was the earliest iteration of an

emerging perception of gladiature as a site which manifested the permeability

of social divisions, which bespoke an image of Roman society that stood in

stark contrast to the far more rigid discourses of class struggle and class purity

which had preceded it. Gladiature rationalized as a transmutation of social

identity contained a dramatization of the *transformation of the barbarous into*

the civilized – and therefore represented the antithesis of the anxiety of

'decivilizing' which had ordered the historico-political discourse of civilizing

since the early eighteenth century. This transformative rhetoric is politically central to the bourgeois history of right. The image of 'civilization' as an open society is, arguably, a particular filter of barbarism, which functions by declaring that the barbarian is not filtered.

Embourgeoisement of historico-political discourse framed itself as the breakdown of multiple boundaries which had been formerly policed: not only did a bourgeois history admit of a certain barbarism into society in support of an alternate history of right, but civilization itself was gradually re-inscribed as a less exclusive entity in a traditional sense. In the next chapter, the full consequences of this development will become clearer, as a truly bourgeois historico-political discourse rests upon the discursive convergence of the nation with the State, in a strategic co-option of the terms of nobiliary discourse of civilization. For the moment, the critical idea to be bookmarked is the close, even definitive association between the profound socio-political realignment implied by transmutation, and the suggestion that transmutation was the real key to gladiature's meaning and pleasure. Such a notion seized upon earlier scholarship, which had begun the work of uncoupling violence from pleasure (witness the decline of the language of abhorrence); more importantly, transmutation began to build an essential, even constitutive association between gladiature – which still bore connotations of violence and pleasure, for all that the relation between those two elements was constantly shifting – and what would come to appear as a bourgeois construct of civilization. In a certain sense – especially in the way that gladiature, as will be seen in the following chapter, would come to be re-positioned at the very centre of Roman civilization, and eventually imagined as a site not of immutable conflict, but of profound (and profoundly civilized) social unity – gladiature, from the moment of Auguet's text, would come to function as a sign of 'bourgeois civilization' itself, particularly in its re-invented capacity to dramatize and embody the constitutive power dynamic that was the ordering trope of the bourgeois self-image as civilized.

The most widely respected scholar of this period was not, as has been stated, Auguet; it was Veyne, the posthumous editor of Ville, who was the first to bring any degree of theoretical rigour to the subject of gladiature in *Bread and Circuses: Historical Sociology and Political Pluralism*(1976).Veyne argued that gladiature, related spectacle and numerous other phenomena of Roman social life were interpretable as manifestations of euergetism, or civic benefaction from private funds. Gladiature was not the focal point of his analysis, and he had virtually no comment to make about violence; any related question of pleasure was consequently similarly disregarded, as incidental to the functionality of euergetism as a whole. Even within this distinct approach, however, Veyne conceded several points about gladiature that accorded closely with contemporary developments in academic thought.

Of the various forms of euergetism in Roman society, Veyne felt that gladiatorial *munera* were among the lowest-ranked and least effective, in the republican period "regarded [by *editores*] as somewhat sordid obligations. The *munera*, as forced contributions or taxes, were imposed by the magistrates; it was the *honores*, awarded by the people's votes, that distinguished one man from another" (207). Veyne thus inscribed the historical development of gladiature as a practice which initially was a funerary ritual of obligation to the dead (221), as *euergesia* encompassed desire for immortality and one's memory as well as social and political patronage (18), but which became increasingly secularized across the late Republic (221-2).

When the progressive secularization of gladiature throughout the Republic confronted the larger political shift to Empire, in Veyne's view, the gradual appropriation of gladiature into the formal ruling structure of the state entailed that gladiature as *euergesia* reached its purest and most abstract form, as the erosion of the popular franchise shifted the negotiation of power between the Emperor and the plebs. The pretext for gladiature which replaced the patrician funeral was the celebration of the imperial cult, thereby channelling the essential meaning of gladiatorial spectacle into a performance of loyalty to the central authority (318). At the same time, however, gladiature as a specific form of *euergesia* had the capacity to simultaneously work against this hierarchical system, and to reverse the flow of power in a limited sense:

> "Between the Emperor, the plebs and a *terzo incommodo*, the
> Senate, a sentimental drama was played out for which the public
> entertainments were the setting and the symbol. Given by the
> Emperor or in his presence, the shows were a material satisfaction,
> but they also allowed the sovereign to prove to his capital that he
> shared popular feelings (*popularis esse*). (...) One could also say
> that there was something democratic in this largesse that the
> Emperor paid to the most representative city of his Empire" (398).

Though his work is accorded a great deal of respect within classical scholarship, Veyne's analysis had little direct impact on subsequent gladiatorial historiography specifically; *euergesia* may have had considerable explanatory capacity as a structuralist approach to Roman social history, but contemporary and subsequent scholarship never warmed to the idea. More directly influential – although less rigorous, with something of a kitchen-sink approach to sociological theory – was Hopkins, who contradicted Veyne's assertion that euergesia, as a form of conspicuous consumption, was inherently 'depoliticizing' – i.e. it transcended the pursuit of specific political objectives (Veyne 18, 398). Hopkins' 1983 text *Death and Renewal* continued the shift away from the inherited approaches to gladiature, which had repeatedly inscribed it (with many local nuances) as a site of social conflict between the ruling group and the lower orders of Rome, and toward the emergent perspective wherein the amphitheatre has been seen as a crucially important site of Roman social integration, and gladiature specifically as a key signifier of Roman social and cultural identity.

In Hopkins' bluntly stated view, Rome was a "warrior state" (1), a "militaristic society" (29) and a "cruel society" (28); the pleasure in gladiatorial violence rested upon the militaristic "myth that gladiatorial shows 'inspired a glory in wounds and a contempt of death, since the love of praise and desire for victory could be seen, even in the bodies of slaves and criminals'" (Pliny, *Panegyric* 33; Hopkins 2), and gladiatorial violence itself ritually maintained an atmosphere which enshrined "[b]loodshed and slaughter joined [with] military glory and conquest as central elements of Roman culture" (2). Hopkins' image of Rome also foreshadowed what would become a new emphasis upon the Empire, as the historical period wherein the 'true' meaning of gladiature could be thought to reside. The little he had to say about republican gladiature (5-6) framed those centuries as a prologue to the fate of the institution under the Empire; imperial gladiature, in turn, was one element of a spectacle programme whose function was to "provide repeated opportunities for the dramatic confrontation of rulers and ruled" (15). Hopkins characterized the amphitheatre as "part of the political order" (9), as "the only surviving assembly of citizens" (19) to persist into the Empire after the end of the Republic, and as an "arena for popular participation in the city of Rome" (14). The 'confrontation' staged in the amphitheatre, however, was tightly circumscribed and politically hollow; the *pollice verso*, which had once appeared as the force which toppled the Republic, and even appeared to Veyne as a pleasant nod to democratization, was for Hopkins merely an empty gesture, which in any case supported prevailing power structures rather than threatened them:

> "When a gladiator fell, the crowd would shout for mercy or dispatch (either *missos* or *iugula*). The emperor might be swayed by their shouts or gestures, but he alone, the final arbiter, decided when the fighting was to stop and who was to live or die. This dramatic enactment of imperial power, repeated several times a day on several occasions a year, before a mass audience of citizens, conquerors of the world, helped legitimate an emperor's position. ... [T]he crowd's potential for legitimation and support contained an inherent risk of subversion and resistance. (...) Yet the dangers of political confrontation were lessened by the crowd's lack of coherence, by its own volatility, and by the absence of an ideology which could bind it together in a sustained programme of action" (18-9).

Arguably, the true influence that Hopkins' work exerted in scholarship arose from his image of Rome as something not unlike a new barbarian. The full impact of this strategy would come to be felt in successive decades, and will be explored in the next chapter.

Auguet, Veyne and Hopkins, though they and others of this period had a range of nominally different interpretations of gladiature, were thus all similarly bent upon the same assertion: that gladiature was a key tool of social order in the Roman world. This claim had, of course, been part of twentieth-century classical historiography in one way or another since the interwar period; the main difference from this point onwards was the de-emphasis upon (perpetual) conflict between groups, whether of different races or different classes, and the gradual re-positioning of violence as a less than fundamental element of the practice of gladiature. Hopkins may have summed up the pleasure of gladiature in antiquity as a "by-product of war, discipline and death"; however, in the practice of gladiature – and, as will be explored in the next section, in the distinctive historiographic claim -"[w]ar had been converted into a game" (29).

Chapter 7: *Pax Romana*

The 'elite crowd' and the myth-history of democracy

In Foucault's analysis, a fully bourgeois historico-political discourse is

fundamentally characterized by a complete re-conceptualization of the once-

definitive boundary between nation and State, in the sense that the two entities

merge:

> "[The nobiliary] concept of nation, which the aristocracy wanted to
> reserve for a group of individuals whose only assets were common
> customs and a common status, is not enough to describe the
> historical reality of the nation. But, on the other hand, the Statist
> entity ... is not really a nation to the extent that it does not exactly
> coincide with the historical conditions that are necessary and
> sufficient to constitute a nation. Where, then, are we to find the
> historical core of a nation that can become 'the' nation? In the
> Third Estate, and only in the Third Estate. The Third Estate is in
> itself the historical precondition for the existence of a nation, but
> that nation should, by rights, coincide with the State" (*SMBD* 217).

The elision of the fundamental boundary between nation and State –

which, arguably, functions within a nobiliary historico-political discourse as the

initial or central boundary which establishes all conflict, and around which the

entire structure of the discourse of perpetual war is ultimately organized –

consequently produces an equally fundamental re-figuring and re-positioning of

the space of violence within the historical discourse of the bourgeoisie, starting

with the condition that the 'defining characteristic of a nation is [no longer] its

dominance over other nations', but rather "its ability to administer itself, to

manage, govern, and guarantee the constitution and workings of the figure of the

State and of State power. Not domination, but State control. The nation is

therefore no longer a partner in barbarous and warlike relations of domination"

(*SMBD* 223). Instead, the organization of discourse around a history of the war for domination "will be replaced by a struggle that is, so to speak, of a different substance: not an armed clash, but an effort, a rivalry, a striving toward the universality of the State" (*SMBD* 225).

When it comes to the representation of such discursive developments within the myth-history of Rome, particularly in the challenging case of gladiature, this push toward the universalization of the bourgeois State took the historiographic form of an image of Roman gladiature as the central emblem of a wider image of the social that might be termed a 'bourgeois empire'. Some elements of this development have already been encountered. The earlier emergence of the 'barbarian democracy' had initiated the elision of violence from modernity's myth-history of Rome, through the suggestion that what had formerly been labelled as 'violent' could be considered civilized in its association with a democratizing of power structures and therefore with social parity and/or cohesion, as was seen in the image of a Samnite origin of gladiature. At the same time, republican gladiature, which had once been accorded a significant space within gladiatorial historiography in its close alignment with late republican political upheaval, was now increasingly relegated to merely prefatory status within the historical narrative; this took place in the context of a wider 'pushback' of the always-uncertain line between Republic and Empire (as briefly discussed in Chapter One) which tended to treat the political ascendance of the Julio-Claudian dynasty as less a 'revolution' than a culmination of developments which could be traced back several centuries. Consequently, the working concept of 'empire' –

particularly within gladiatorial historiography, which by the end of the twentieth

century attained a sort of specialist status which tended to isolate it from

contemporary studies of Roman social history – expanded considerably at this

point, and gladiature was aligned with a notion of empire that more or less

originated in what would traditionally be labelled the middle Republic. In this

most recent phase of *embourgeoisement*, the implications of the scholarship of the

postwar generation coalesced in the production of an academic consensus wherein

gladiature functioned as the great lynchpin of pure social cohesion and

democratizing – a perfect overlap of nation and state, *even in an imperialist*

context – and thereby also simultaneously achieved a perfect inversion of the

violence/pleasure cathexis by declaring gladiature nonlethal and nonviolent, even

under the later Empire, which had always been associated with the image of

gladiature as a massive and widespread institution.

In the wake of such conceptual reorganization, there has followed a shift

in the academic opinions surrounding the origin of gladiature. Although the

Etruscan evidence still holds a place in the discussion, and the Osco-

Samnite/South Italian hypothesis has not been comprehensively unseated,

gladiature's origin has been gradually shifted from beyond the boundaries of the

Roman world to its very centre: Rome itself. The redefinition of gladiature as

'civilized', contingent as this is upon the purging of violence from its image, has

created the conditions of possibility for the origin of gladiature to be arrogated to

the (new) west; the 'other' gladiature(s) of Etruria and Samnium have been

correspondingly redefined among some scholars as proto-forms of a practice that should not be regarded as true gladiature until we encounter it at Rome. Hopkins, discussed above, was arguably the first to begin representing Rome in language that had formerly been reserved in classical scholarship for its designated barbarians; what arose in this most recent period of historico-political discourse was what Foucault termed a 'third tactical operation' in the process of filtering barbarism, wherein the goal was to "make a distinction between two forms of barbarism: (...) the bad barbarism from which we have to be freed; and then there is a good barbarism ... which is the only real source of freedom" (*SMBD* 204).The 'good barbarian', in the fully bourgeois myth-history centred upon gladiature, effectively became Rome itself.

First, the crowd was fundamentally reinvented in a manner that has already been touched upon in the previous chapter: the conflict between social groups, in the discourse of class struggle that had functioned for three centuries as a central trope of historiographic writing, was now replaced by a dominant image of social integration and cohesion in the Roman world. Secondly, the internal pacification of Roman society, as imagined within gladiatorial historiography, was accompanied by a comparable civilizing of the notion of what went on at Rome's outer boundaries. The historical rupture signified by the shift from Republic to Empire, which had long served as the crucial pivot of swinging debate over Rome as civilization, was abandoned as the definitive topos of scholarship, as the threshold of empire was pushed several centuries back into the middle Republic, and the character of that empire was reinscribed to emphasize its benevolent, systematizing, essentially civilizing properties. Concomitant with this change in the broadest conceptions of the path of Roman socio-political

history was the imagined relation of original gladiature to that history; the

peculiar disappearance of the embodied barbarian from all aspects of the story,

either within Roman society or between Rome and other cultures which came

under the sway of its empire, coincided with a new impetus to suggest and

(eventually, for some) to insist that gladiature's origin and innovation was nothing

less than Roman, dismissing categories of evidence related to the other

hypotheses of origin just as these had each successively dominated the discussion

in their turn.

Though there are certainly variation and disagreement among recent

scholars, they are in accord upon one premise which stands behind what is now

regarded as the central importance of gladiature to the Roman world: the

interpretation of the practice of gladiature as an institution which produced,

performed, and ultimately embodied the Roman concept(s) of social, political,

and even cosmological order. Gladiature was the practice through which Roman

civilization confronted and subdued the disordered forces which beset it from the

outside. Emphases vary; for some scholars the crucial point of interest has been

the arena crowd's formal metonymic echo of social hierarchies, for others the role

of the amphitheatre throughout the empire as a unifying force across disparate

cultures. In the flourishing period of the mid to late nineties, most scholars of the

English-speaking world were particularly attracted to the illumination and

definition of a numinous space of meaning that transcended the more mundane

workings of the social politics of empire, which went beyond the sociological laundry list of Hopkins into a full-blown cosmology, wherein the amphitheatre became the primary site of order in the Roman world only incidentally in its higher capacity as the core site of *all* social meaning. In a rather astonishing way, what had once been considered the great shame of Roman history was fundamentally refigured as an almost magical key to understanding the structure and inner workings of the entire Roman world.

Second was the all but total disappearance of violence from the narrative of gladiature. This was more than a question of 'overcoming' abhorrence in modernity, an issue long since raised by Auguet and which, as will be seen below, assumed an elaborate new form during this period. Instead, the reinterpretation of gladiature as an institution of order banished violence to the extreme margins in several senses. Firstly, the violence that had long been held to define gladiatorial combat when the practice was inscribed within a discursive framework that posited a binary conflict between nation and State, was now, within the proclaimed universality of the State, transferred to an abstract construct of 'disorder' that gladiature was now seen actually to address and correct; gladiature's definitive violence now existed beyond the boundaries of the arena, rather than within it. Secondly, the relocation of violence outside of the arena effectively severed the association between violence and pleasure, which had formed the central moral and historiographic problem of gladiature since the Enlightenment: the new pleasure of gladiature in antiquity, indissociable from its new meaning, was the construction and reinforcement of structures of civilized order. The residual violence of gladiature itself thus no longer appeared during this period as a true problem, since gladiature as a means to a legitimate, ultimately civilized end was neatly justified. The contemporary intellectual environment, which was defined however briefly by the seeming disappearance of the barbarian or any other form of the 'second race' at the macropolitical level, also excised the barbarian from the myth-history built upon gladiatorial historiography, where it arguably survived only in the abstract trope of disorder.

A closer examination of exactly how this was achieved within the confines of gladiatorial historiography, however, reveals that the process of this elision of violence, though it appealed to the external term of social order to convert the traditionally imagined antagonism of plebeians and patricians into the neutral workings of an overarching system, was in fact an interpretation that inscribed itself within the near-total dominance of the Roman aristocracy within the re-imagined political structures of antiquity. This appears, at first, to be a contradictory claim – the assertion that a bourgeois historico-political discourse, with a framework predicated upon the universality of the State which is itself understood as continuous with the Third Estate-as-nation, could produce an altered myth-history for itself which resolved a profound aporia within civilization's narrative of power through a historical image *of the nobility*, is perhaps unexpected. Phrased another way, if we accept Foucault's analysis that the universalization of the Third Estate within bourgeois historico-political discourse was no longer focused upon relations of domination between nation and State, it is unsurprising to find violence being written out of the historiography of gladiature within the wider myth-history of Rome; however, the discovery that a bourgeois history of right could organize its narrative around an image of Roman gladiature that is actually dominated by the aristocracy – its structural relation to what had been thought of as 'the crowd', and the nature of its particular pleasure in gladiatorial violence – invokes closer inquiry.

The amphitheatre as civilization

The commitment to gladiature as an institution of social order eventually gave rise to the consensus that the Roman amphitheatre is to be viewed as a site and a symbol of civilization itself, rather than as an avatar of civilization's extreme limit or complete opposite. Gladiature and the amphitheatre are frequently asserted in various ways to have been critically, even definitively important to Roman civilization in antiquity; as a consequence, a common element of recent scholarship has been to begin from the premise that gladiature and amphitheatrical spectacle were the *sine qua non* of the Roman world, and that the centrality of the institution's importance in Roman society, its microcosmic quality, cannot be overstated.

However, the predicating claim that gladiature *must* be reconciled with civilization is not the only shared premise which strongly shapes the most recent field of historiography: a critical additional factor is a heightened preoccupation with the assumed modern abhorrence of gladiature as an intersection of violence with pleasure. In Foucauldian terms, the preoccupation with the present appears as an instance of the "internal dialecticalization" that he claimed accompanied the *embourgeoisement* of historico-political discourse, stating that the " problem we have to understand is this: How, after this displacement (if not decline) of the role of war within historical discourse, does the relationship of war – which has been

mastered within historical discourse – reappear, but at the same time in a negative

role, with a sort of external role? At this point, we see the emergence of the idea

of an internal war that defends society against threats born in and of its own

body" (*SMBD* 216). Consistent with the new centrality of the present, the social

body which examines itself for threats of internal war is the speaking subject that,

in the recent historiography of gladiature, repeatedly and reliably frames any

approach to gladiature within an explicit and almost ritualized excursus on

modernity.

The conceptualization of the boundary of civilization, as this is overlapped

by the relation being written between antiquity and modernity on the point of

violence and pleasure, is repeatedly expressed in the form of paired statements

which achieves a specific rhetorical staging of the discussion of gladiature in

nearly every recent monograph. The first is the invocation of abhorrence of

violence, and specifically of the collapse of violence and pleasure, as a

fundamental distinction of the modern perspective on gladiature. Hopkins had

already stated it bluntly: "The welter of blood in gladiatorial and wild-beast

shows, the squeals of the victims and of slaughtered animals are completely alien

to us and almost unimaginable" (5). A decade later, Wiedemann delicately

pointed out the influence that such insurmountable abhorrence could work upon

the direction of scholarship, while at the same time gesturing toward the anxiety

of affinity: "Scholars have tended to avoid betraying too much interest in

gladiators and amphitheatres. They have perhaps been put off by the popularity of the games, the fact that they fascinated the Romans, and – worse – fascinate

ordinary people today" (xvi). Barton, whose social psychological analyses of

gladiature are unique, fascinating, and an unapologetic manifestation of

contemporary modernity's tendency to see Rome in terms of itself, phrased the

initial claim of abhorrence in strong language: "The Roman fascination with the

gladiator confounds us: we see him as a twisted 'athlete' in a twisted 'sport', the

embodiment of Roman sadism, brutality, and callousness" (*The Sorrows of the*

Ancient Romans 11). As a final example, of which there are many more, Kyle's

pragmatic and lengthy study of the disposal of bodies both animal and human

from amphitheatre spectacles struck the atonal chord of the central paradox,

between the desire to perceive Rome as 'civilized' and the proclaimed imperative

to see gladiature as anything but: "The blood sports and deadly spectacles

fascinate moderns as, on the surface, a glaring contradiction of Rome's image as a

civilizing power. Modern scholars have long pondered how civilized Romans

could condone and even enjoy, make sport of, watching hundreds and even

thousands of humans and animals being killed in elaborate public spectacles" (5).

The second claim repeatedly paired with those above is the injunction to

bracket out, once firmly established, this averred modern attitude of abhorrence

from any ensuing interpretation of Roman history. Hopkins felt that the cultural

divide in the case of gladiature was so vast as to "make the modern historian's

normal tactic of empathetic imagination particularly difficult" (29), but the

development of this angle of discourse seems to have made the attempt appear

easier with practice. Wiedemann located the cultural divide between ancient and modern attitudes to violence and pleasure in the eighteenth century, and felt that if

"we are to try to understand the attitudes of any pre-Enlightenment society

towards the imposition of cruel punishments on evil-doers, we have to set aside

our perception that such punishments would be categorised as sadistic in our own

culture" (70). Welch's 2006 study of amphitheatre architecture and the origin of

gladiatorial practice traced a similar line: "[W]e may get closer to an

understanding of the 'strange' Romans if we think of violent death in Roman

culture as something that was not unusual, and if we try to put aside modern

notions" (*Roman Amphitheatre from its Origins* 4). While all this reads very well

on the surface and appears to uphold the injunctions of responsible scholarship

following what used to be called the linguistic turn, there is abundant reason to

suspect that these attempts at critical reflexivity are on the whole inadequate.

From a Foucauldian perspective, what is arguably in play with regard to

such statements is a shift in the discursive trope of origin, which in a thoroughly

bourgeois historico-political discourse is far more strongly associated with the

civilized than with the barbarous, and which is consequently re-positioned in

relation to the speaking subject of historical narrative. Foucault explained that the

universality of the State necessarily produces "a history that is polarized toward

the present and toward the State, a history that culminates in the imminence of the

State, of the total, complete, and full figure of the State in the present" (*SMBD*

224); in consequence, late twentieth-century historiography of gladiature operates

within "a grid [of historical intelligibility] which, rather than functioning with a

point of origin such as the first war, the first invasion, or the first national duality, works backward and starts with the present. The fundamental moment is no longer the origin, and intelligibility's starting point is no longer the archaic element; it is, on the contrary the present. ... [W]e have ... the inversion of the value of the present in historical and political discourse: the present becomes the fullest moment, the moment of the greatest intensity" (226-7). The function once carried out by 'origin' in gladiatorial historiography is comprehensively transferred to modernity itself, and the myth-historical narrative of the bourgeois speaking subject is grounded not in an implicit image of civilization that is signified through a representation of the barbarous, but in a carefully, explicitly foregrounded account of the civilized which – because it is predicated upon universalization of a monadic nation/State rather than upon a divide between them – then seeks in turn to construct a representation of the barbarous as the 'good barbarian', continuous with and inherent within civilization itself just as the nation is now coextensive with the State. What could formerly be treated as separate issues in this dissertation – origin, conflict, the speaking subject of history, the language of abhorrence and the problem of pleasure, and the theme of decivilizing – are all therefore confounded, and occupy the same site in the prevailing discursive framework.

This discursive arrangement is indicated by the presence of a third element in this complex of attitudes, that arguably exerts a strong influence over the motivated approach to the problem and the resolutions taken: the anxiously perceived possibility that gladiature represents an uncomfortable point of affinity between antiquity and modernity, most importantly that the familiar resonance of mass spectacle, and certain forms of large-scale public entertainment which may be felt to contain various degrees of violence, points to the intersection of violence and pleasure in the present as much as in the past. In a sense this is nothing new, and in a real way this entire discussion up to this point has been intent upon this specific problem; however, what is new here is the extent to which scholarship of this period has attempted to confront the difficulty directly or – to perhaps phrase it better – has embraced self-reflexivity at the very moment in historiography when the prevailing image of that self was most radically defined by an almost-universal 'civilization', and thus most discursively hostile to the violence of gladiature. Frequently, the anxious possibility of an inadmissible affinity between modernity and antiquity on the point of gladiature is invoked by the meta-scholarship of 'classical receptions' and the fin-de-siècle storm of thought that reached its height in the years immediately following the release of Ridley Scott's *Gladiator*. The 2004 collection of essays *Gladiator: Film and History* put it explicitly: "...the depiction of the Roman mob in *Gladiator* offers the ... audience an unnerving mirror-image of themselves, eager to be entertained at all costs and demanding ever more intricate, dangerous, and realistic spectacles..." (Cyrino 140). The question of whether or not the social issue of violent entertainment in contemporary society is to be considered truly a significant problem is not the point; the fact remains that gladiature demonstrably evokes an anxiety of affinity within recent historiographic discourse, and this notion is very much in play within the framework of scholarly interpretations.

Recent scholarship of ancient gladiature as a historical phenomenon (rather than a cinematic subject) is hardly unaware of the difficulty in which it finds itself:

> "...the Colosseum has become for us the defining symbol of ancient Rome precisely *because of* (not despite) the fact that it raises so many of the questions and dilemmas that we face in any engagement with Roman culture. How different was their society from our own? What judgments of it are we entitled to make? Can we admire the magnificence and the technical accomplishments, while simultaneously deploring the cruelty and the violence? How far are we taking vicarious pleasure in the excesses of Roman luxury or bloodlust, at the same time as we lament them? Are some societies really more violent than others?" (Beard and Hopkins 16).

This doubled position of Rome – the conflict between affinity and abhorrence - presents an aporia wherein the perception (or construction) of Rome as civilized is made fundamentally problematic by the violence/pleasure cathexis represented by gladiature. As the present has become the 'fundamental' moment in history, the most recent scholarship has attempted to write over this aporia by dismantling the relation between violence and pleasure itself, in a two-pronged strategy which sought on the one hand to redefine the object of the 'true' pleasure of gladiature as something other than violence, and on the other hand to redefine gladiature itself as not simply contextually, but essentially non-violent. Some societies may or may not be really more violent than others; regardless, classical scholars have collectively re-inscribed the western myth-history of Roman antiquity in such a way that neither the ancestral society nor its modern descendant could be seen to take pleasure in violence, and drove the point further with the eventual suggestive claim that gladiature in antiquity had not been 'violent' at all.

Social order and integration

To begin to understand the shift in scholarly consensus of this period,

particular to the extent that historic-political discourse came to be organized

around the universality of the State and the reorientation of struggle towards that

universalization, perhaps the best place to start is Nicolet's 1976 *The World of the*

Citizen in Republican Rome, a study which attempted to examine closely the

structures of civic life for that portion of the republican Roman social body

outside of the "thin stratum of magistrates, generals, senators, officers and tax-

farmers" (1), which small group Nicolet termed the "political class" in contrast to

the "civic mass". To the discussion at hand, Nicolet's study contributed two

critical points. One was the argument that the 'origin' of violent civic unrest in the

Republic should be fixed to the mid-second century BC, the period of the

tribunates of the Gracchi; Nicolet cited Appian to claim that, at least, the Roman

historical tradition itself held this to be true (344). The second point was that what

arose in the second century BC was the beginning of "alternative institutions" of

civic politics, including the amphitheatre and gladiature:

> "After the second century BC... we find emerging what may be
> called parallel or alternative forms of civil life, outside the
> traditional domain of public law, and offering fresh *opportunities*
> *of integration and participation to one group of citizens or another*
> ... In some cases there was a positive change in the scene and
> object of the conflict. There came into being a new language
> involving new methods, new techniques of communication, a
> different way of approaching men, securing their support and
> manipulating them. Public life of course continued largely to run in
> traditional channels, but other settings came into view, new
> ceremonies and a different ritual which gradually tended to rival
> and even obliterate the old ones. *At the end point of this evolution,*
> *the circus and the amphitheatre take the place of the Forum and*
> *the Curia*; instead of a dialogue between the people and its elected

magistrates, punctuated by the proclamation of election results, the interchange is between the *princeps* and the urban plebs, and it takes place to the accompaniment of largess and public games" (345, emphases mine).

Violence, then, was here aligned with social integration on several planes: the 'new order' arose initially from the violence and political assassinations surrounding the Gracchan tribunates, which had famously involved the then-nascent amphitheatre; the gradual reorganization of political interaction between different social groups became less violent over time, but this was in crucial part due to the amphitheatre as an institution which gave the new order its outward form. The arena became the new politics. Once this claim had been formulated, within the context of the surrounding image of a progressively kinder, gentler Roman social politics, the question remained: within the new perspective of the overall decrease or withdrawal of violence from Roman socio-political life, how to account for the violence of gladiature which defined one of that life's central institutions?

Of gladiature itself Nicolet had little to say; in the main, he tended to subsume it within his far more detailed discussion of the theatre. However, Nicolet's influential study contained two additional, more specific ideas which would bear fruit very quickly within the study of gladiature. He argued that entertainments and spectacles, including republican gladiatorial shows, were the most effective venues for expressions of popular opinion (that is to say, these were more effective than other mass gatherings, such as patrician funerals and consular triumphs). Indeed, Nicolet claimed that the opportunity presented at spectacles for clear expressions of the will of the 'civic mass' was the main source of their popular attraction, over and above the content of any given spectacle (362). (This perception, which would attract considerable attention in subsequent decades, was nearly an innovation of Nicolet's, who sourced the idea to Abbott's 1907 article but asserted that the idea had received no attention in the interim.)

Secondly, in his examination of "alternative institutions", Nicolet laid heavy emphasis upon a series of later republican innovations and laws which traced out the development of the regulation of the distribution of seats in the theatre. Beginning in 194 BC under the consulship of Scipio Africanus (cf. Livy 34.54.4-8), seating in the theatre became increasingly subject to regulation; Livy indicates that prior to this period, seating was indiscriminate – a 'first-come-first-served' approach, wherein a member of the plebs might take a seat next to a senator – but that the *Ludi Romani* of 194 BC introduced the segregation of senators into the orchestra (i.e. the front seats). The ordering of assignments of seats in the theatres eventually encompassed a comprehensive structure of *discrimina ordinum*, wherein the *ordines* (a complex hierarchy of social 'classes', basically comprised of the property-based ranks of senators, *equites*, and plebeians but further sub-divided by criteria such as sex, age, and birth status) were grouped in reserved banks of seating. Nicolet suggested that C. Gracchus in 123 BC introduced the additional segregation of the *equites* into the first fourteen rows behind the orchestra (365); in any case, this regulation was formally made law in 67 B.C., under the *lex Roscia theatralis*. The most famous law in the series, falling outside the scope of Nicolet's study, was the *lex Julia theatralis*, introduced by Augustus ca. 5 AD, which effectively regulated the entirety of any theatre audience into a completely ordered whole (cf. Suetonius, *Div. Aug.* 44).

For the moment, the point to be extracted from Nicolet's study is the influential

assertion that the 'civic mass' was not, in fact, to be regarded as such: "theatre

audiences were far from being an undifferentiated mass" (373) even in the middle

Republic. The abolition from scholarship of the image and concept of the chaotic,

grotesque, mass social body (or at least its relegation to the active fringes of the

historical imagination) and the introduction of systematic, rigidly policed order to

the image of the amphitheatre crowd – a comparative novelty in application,

despite scholarship's long familiarity with the *theatralis* laws – would prove to be

a crucially important central trope in this period, forming the basis of an entirely

different conception of the crowd, both as an entity in its on right and in its

relation to Roman social order as whole.

Therefore, the rise of theatre (and amphitheatre) spectacles as alternative

institutions of civic politics was a response to, or outcome of, the rise of civic

violence between social groups in certain mass gatherings, primarily those which

were focused on the Forum: these included patrician funerals and 'pre-

amphitheatrical' gladiature, which, as we have seen, were intimately related in

any case until the last decades of the Republic. Most importantly, Nicolet

inscribed the development and refinement of mass spectacle, as evidenced by the

system of *discrimina ordinum* in the theatres, as a disciplining of mid- and late-

republican political violence – and, consequently, as the opposite of violence, not

the sign and scene of violence itself. Thus, to extend the implications of Nicolet's

reasoning, the institutionalization of the amphitheatre was coextensive with the imposition of order upon chaos and socio-political violence: these were the grounds upon which subsequent arguments for the civilizing force of gladiature would come to be built. The deeper implication, of course, was that the breakdown of the Republic was to be considered a period of decivilizing; thus, conversely, the rise of a (bourgeois) empire – borne upon the back of essentially benevolent and structurally organic 'alternative institutions' such as gladiature – was an opposing force for civilizing.

The consequences of Nicolet's approach were very quickly transferred to the amphitheatre with greater specificity. Nicolet had briefly pointed out that one of the consequences of *discrimina ordinum* in the theatre was the possibility it afforded to precisely identify which group within any given audience was the source of demonstrations of group opinion (365); Roman historical texts are plentiful with recorded instances of outbursts of criticism, mockery of public figures, and demands upon officials and emperors taking place in the context of entertainments, and these will not be canvassed in detail here. Instead, it is more crucial to observe that very soon after Nicolet's work was published, the suggestion was put forth that the more important effect of the visual identification of social groups within seating arrangements at spectacles was the impact that this exerted on corporate self-identification of such groups, and the possible broad consequences that this held for the understanding of social order in the Roman world. The idea was first tabled by Kolendo (developing the earlier study by Bollinger, 1969), in his short article "La repartition des places aux spectacles et la stratification sociale dans l'empire romain" (1981); this was a close study of epigraphic evidence from the surviving seating structures of the Colosseum at Rome itself, where late imperial inscriptions indicate that places in the *caveae* were by this period reserved for not only social groups, but in some instances even for specific individuals. Kolendo asserted that "small groups of people who were well known to each other could exert perfect reciprocal control to avoid the places that would be occupied by other people" (305, my translation), suggesting that the emphasis of the *discrimina ordinum* should be laid not upon its inception as a regulatory movement of the ruling class (which was possibly Nicolet's point), but as a mechanism that facilitated the self-regulation of conflict between social groups – that is, the systematic, structural pacification of social relations - within the public theatre space of mutual identification.

Moreover, Kolendo saw in the *discrimina ordinum* an ideal embodiment of social order which he argued was key to its understanding in antiquity. In the Colosseum epigraphy Kolendo read a "strict ... image of the social and juridical stratification of Roman society" (301). He asserted that ancient citizens of Rome regarded the city as an entirely independent entity or microcosm of the known world (307), and that the tight regulation of the seating arrangements in the Colosseum "proved that [the microcosm] was deeply ingrained in the mentality of urban dwellers of the Empire" (306). A crucial element of this image of ideal social order, in Kolendo's view, was that it did not *reflect* actual social structures but, rather, *produced* them, in a manner which cast the amphitheatre as a central site of civilization by way of structuring and fostering social bonds, and moreover by rendering them 'emotionally authentic'(Kolendo 315, my translation).

Finally, Kolendo actually exerted a perhaps unintended influence upon the course of later studies of gladiature and the amphitheatre. Although he himself stated that the 'microcosm of the Roman mentality' was the city, not the arena, the idea of microcosm was eventually attached to the amphitheatre itself. The notion of amphitheatre-as-microcosm, and as a social technology based upon visuality, would prove popular; as late as 1996, Gunderson would take the thought so far as to naively label the amphitheatre a panopticon, despite Foucault's explicit statements precisely to the contrary (see *Discipline and Punish* 217: "We are much less Greeks than we believe. We are neither in the amphitheatre, nor on the stage, but in the panoptic machine"). (Gunderson 115; although the confusion of the amphitheatre with the panopticon was something of a misfire, the article still contains numerous provocative insights; cf. also Edmundson 1996.)

Such ideas were carried even further by Rawson (1987), in a lengthy article on the *lex Iulia theatralis*, which exceeded both Veyne's view of the amphitheatre as euergetism and Kolendo's arguments for the amphitheatre as a productive site of deeply ordered social structure, by referring both of these claims to a third term: religious practice.

> "The games in Rome were not simply a supreme expression of euergetism, or a method for their giver to gain popularity with the plebs and impress foreigners with Rome's splendour; they were central to its culture in innumerable ways. They had also always been to some extent, and were even more after Augustus' death, as the people lost its right to elect magistrates and pass laws, political gatherings where public opinion was made known and political demands put forward. But they were more yet; not only where the Emperor met his People, but where the whole of society met to do honour to the gods" (83).

Rawson's perspective did not rest upon this point alone; rather, her close examination of the *lex Julia theatralis* specifically permitted an alignment of the *discrimina ordinum* with the Augustan moral programme of social and juridical reorganization in the earliest years of the Empire. To refer amphitheatre spectacle after the Augustan *discrimina ordinum* to the context of religious practice was to refer it more broadly to the pious discourse of Augustan society, with its emphases upon the *pax Romana*, the benevolence of the state, and the importance of the nuclear family as the core unit of social structure. Rawson's analysis thus ingeniously credited an aristocratic representation of recognizably bourgeois social values, insofar as we might read the semi-official Augustan social code as a historical image of a 'bourgeois nation' within an imperial state. This atmosphere of propriety enforced by the *discrimina ordinum* directly connected, in Rawson's analysis, to the amphitheatre's function as a site of political assembly, for the associated dress code of public occasions visibly underlined the arrangement of social groups within the seats and greatly facilitated the process of politically motivated acclamation and performance (111-3). Echoing Nicolet's model of the transition from Republic to Empire as the benign rise of alternative institutions, Rawson's image of the amphitheatre elevated it from mocrocosm to microcosmology, by weaving political order even more tightly to social order, until the institution represented a mirror of an essentially benevolent and uncannily totalized system, predicated upon the absence of conflict and, in this way, utterly distinct from amphitheatre imagery put forth even fifteen years earlier.

In toto, however, what this sub-group of interpretations held in common –

or rather, lacked in common – was the scope to encompass gladiature itself within

this entirely novel image of the crowd. The order and integration suggested on

multiple levels – the precise ranking of the distribution of seats, the repeated

gestures towards the opportunities for group proclamation, the growing assertion

that the amphitheatre could have functioned as not a populist perversion, but a

stalwart bastion of democratic social politics – added only vague references to

'religious practice' in alluding to the violence of gladiature as an element of this

systematically ordered institution. The reinvention of the binary image of the

aristocracy and the crowd would need to go one step further before gladiature

would resume a central position in its own historiography.

The civilizing of the crowd

The subtle effect which coincided with the flurry of investigation into the

discrimina ordinum, however, was not simply to 'order the crowd'; in fact, the

traditional image of 'the crowd' during this period was gradually reinvented as

'the elite crowd', and thus, not a crowd at all in the traditional sense. The

discrimina ordinum was based upon textual evidence that had been known to

scholars for a very long time; nevertheless, its new and relatively sudden

centrality in academic discourse entailed that, to a degree at least, the image of the

crowd which now prevailed was one which contained a great many more senators

than had previously been thought. (More than twenty years after his highly

influential paper in 1983, Hopkins (in conjunction with Beard, 2005) would assert

that "even though the shows were free, the poor and the very poor were systematically under-represented ... the audience at the Colosseum was more of an elite of white toga-clad citizens than the rabble proletariat often imagined" (Beard and Hopkins 112)).

The dominant image of the crowd in the last decade of the twentieth century was suggestively one of a disproportionate social cross-section, a neatly ordered site of Nicolet's "opportunities of integration and participation to one group of citizens or another" which was heavily weighed toward the Roman aristocracy. The main point lay in the fact that the wholesale entry of the aristocracy into the amphitheatre bore with it the reinterpretation of the surviving evidence of the Roman attitude to gladiature, violence, and pleasure. As might be expected, that 'Roman attitude' was now conceived of as the attitude of the elite (typically of the first two centuries of the Empire), which essentially dominated the written source material and which quickly came to speak for the crowd as a whole; moreover, as might also be expected, that elite attitude was not read as one which took straightforward pleasure in violence 'for its own sake' – pleasure was, instead, referred to an intermediary term of 'order' which rehabilitated violence from abhorrence.

The domination of the image of the crowd by the elite was articulated perhaps never so strongly as it was initially, at the outset of this line of thought. In 1992, there appeared Wistrand's *Entertainment and Violence in Ancient Rome: the attitudes of Roman writers of the first century AD*. The work was marked from the outset by an emphasis upon the attitudes of the Roman elite ("For whom do [ancient] authors speak? Definitely not for the man on the street; what he thought we simply do not know", 60); moreover, the elite's prevailing attitude was one

which did not draw a direct line between violence and pleasure. Wistrand's

examination of first-century texts arrived at the conclusion that elite attitudes to

all forms of public entertainment – whether at the theatre, the circus, or the

amphitheatre – had expressed a discursive continuum of opprobrium and moral

censure across the range of spectacle; the 'average' attitude was one of neutrality

(11), but the spectacles of the amphitheatre were exceptional, in that these alone

were associated with anything like positive remarks in the surviving texts (56).

> "...all types of arena shows might be described as having symbolic
> values: gladiators demonstrate *virtus*, animal shows illustrate
> *numen Caesaris* (the godlike power of the emperor), and the public
> executions are necessary to maintain law and order in society. Seen
> in this light, it is not startling to find that such performances were
> not only better appreciated than the traditional low respect shown
> for entertainment generally would lead one to expect, but even
> looked upon as good" (29).

The 'good' of gladiature, within Roman elite literary discourse, rested

upon the association with and performance of *virtus*. *Virtus* rapidly became a

major trope of gladiatorial historiography during this decade, and Wistrand

provided a perfectly adequate definition although, as will be seen, *virtus* as a

moral attitude which determined the Roman attitude to violence was deployed by

modern scholars in multiple ways. Synthesized from a loose collection of

surviving statements made by first-century Roman writers, who in various

contexts offered interpretations or justifications of the value of gladiature as a

spectacle for the lower classes, *virtus* summed up an idealized moral discourse of

violence, as "[g]ladiators were thought [in antiquity] to demonstrate moral quality

or *virtus* in the form of strength and bravery (*fortitudo*), discipline and training (*disciplina*), firmness (*constantia*), endurance (*patientia*), contempt of death

(*contemptus mortis*), love of glory (*amor laudis*) and desire to win (*cupido*

victoriae)" (Wistrand 56). Wistrand, following Hopkins (who admittedly had

never referred directly to a reified sense of *virtus* in his earlier work), was highly

critical of *virtus* as ideology; he felt that the symbolic qualities for which the

amphitheatre was appreciated were so valued in the textual sources precisely

because they "taught to Romans exactly what their leaders thought essential to the

survival of Rome. The gladiatorial fights demonstrated soldierly values and

effectively illustrated basic military ideas by punishing cowardly gladiators and

rewarding courageous ones. [...] No wonder the Romans, especially the high and

mighty ones, appreciated the violent entertainment of the arena. It served the

regime perfectly as a means of propaganda and indoctrination of exactly those

values the rulers considered fundamental" (68-9).

However, Wistrand's suggestive critique of *virtus* as an oppressive

ideology of the elite never found a receptive audience. Rather than a basis of

critique, *virtus* instead rapidly came to be used, relatively acritically, as a

palatable substitute for violence as the object of the crowd's pleasure. What

Wistrand had seen as an aristocratic agenda was instead accepted literally, and the

pleasure of gladiature was no longer in witnessing acts of violence, but witnessing

performances of *virtus* - which was immediately argued to be understandable not

as propaganda, but as a quasi-magical path to social rebirth.

Order as pleasure

Rather than Wistrand, the preeminent text of classical historiography published in the same year was Wiedemann's *Emperors and Gladiators*. Wiedemann returned to Auguet's injunction of a diametric opposition between ancient and modern attitudes to gladiatorial violence, and delicately pointed out the influence that modernity's insurmountable abhorrence could work upon the direction of scholarship, while at the same time gesturing toward the anxiety of affinity. Wiedemann's text heralded a crucial development in the historiography of gladiature: while it marked a return to the starting premise that modern abhorrence of gladiatorial violence must be somehow suspended within historical interpretation of ancient pleasures, far more importantly, it undertook this return in the context of a doubled and ultimately redirected abhorrence. The new object of true exclusion, as referred to above, was no longer the intersection of violence and pleasure in antiquity, but its contemporary manifestation, or at least the notion that *modern* 'ordinary' people could be fascinated by, and take pleasure in, the violence of gladiature.

Wiedemann's version of the amphitheatre as a metaphor of civilization drew elements from both Kolendo's statements about social order at the civic level, and Hopkins' broader claims for the performance of centralized imperial authority; Wiedemann summarized a system of ordering which held that both intra- and inter-group relations were expressed with equal significance in the practice of gladiature along with other arena spectacles, and moreover that the confluence of these two spheres implied the presence of a deeper epistemological structure crucial to the modern understanding of the Roman world.

> "At the margins of the Roman empire, amphitheatres reminded Roman soldiers far from home that they were part of the Roman community. But the arena did not just serve to integrate into Roman society: it also symbolically divided off what was Roman from what was not. It was the limit of Roman civilisation in a number of senses. The arena was the place where civilisation confronted nature, in the shape of the beasts which represented a danger to humanity; and where social justice confronted wrongdoing, in the shape of the criminals who were executed there; and where the Roman empire confronted its enemies, in the persons of the captured prisoners of war who were killed or forced to kill one another in the arena. (...) The arena was visibly the place where civilisation and barbarism met" (46).

The meaning, and thus the pleasure, of gladiature rested upon the symbolic role of the amphitheatre as the limit of Roman civilization (Wiedemann 46), and upon the amphitheatre as the embodiment and performance of civilization's structured, ordered response to the chaos and disorder by which it was threatened and oppressed. The relocation of 'violent conflict' to the margins of Roman society has occurred in conjunction with the construction of a society that, internally at least, is seamlessly and entirely civilized.

Wiedemann therefore achieved the separation of violence and pleasure by ultimately insisting that the true object of pleasure in gladiature for Rome was in fact civilization itself, emerging victorious from its struggle with barbarism; such struggle, however, through its ritualized essence, was more dramaturgical than actual (or, perhaps, more virtual than real), and the essential function of the 'struggle' enacted by gladiature was to signify that, within a nation-State defined by the absence of relations of domination, there was no real 'struggle' between the civilized and the barbarous at all. Gladiature's relation with death

(Wiedemann 34) was rationalized on all levels: its initial association with

funerary ritual righted the imbalance of the social loss of the deceased, its

institutionalized practice resolved both individual anxieties about the

confrontation with mortality and collective anxieties about the security and

vitality of the social body, and, as a final stroke, the early imperial state's

absorption of *munera* into the religious calendar centred routine gladiature upon

the winter solstice and spring equinox, evoking the deepest cosmologies of the

cyclical relation between death and regeneration (47). Wiedemann's assessment

even addressed the historical moral objection of Christians, both ancient and

modern, to gladiature; he suggested that the immoral intersection of violence and

pleasure was not the true object of Christian critique, but that Christian moral

invective was in fact evoked by gladiature's unacceptable co-option of the

discourse of resurrection (155).

Wiedemann's innovative study took Auguet's dictate of the suspension of

presumed abhorrence, and applied it to the separation of violence and pleasure in

a new way: whereas the scholarship of the previous period had tended to derive its

main explanatory force from violence and to dismiss pleasure as a structural

ephemeron, at most incidental to the meaning of gladiature, Wiedemann (and

others to follow) reintroduced the element of pleasure into the core of the analysis

of gladiatorial spectacle while simultaneously writing violence out of its

previously central position:

> "To interpret [the historical association with funerals] in terms of
> human sacrifice, as Tertullian did, is to emphasize killing, rather

than dying, as the central point of the spectacle ... Gladiators faced
death every time they entered the arena, but they were not certain
that they were going to die on any particular occasion: on the
contrary, there were vested interests in favour of their surviving.
Instead of seeing a gladiatorial combat as a public display of
killing, it might be useful to see it as a demonstration of the power
to overcome death. The victorious gladiator overcame death by
showing that he was a better fighter than his opponent. But the
loser, too, might win back his life by satisfying the audience that he
had fought courageously and skilfully. (...) In that sense, even the
gladiator who died in the arena had overcome death. (...) [H]is
death was certainly a consolation to those who watched it. (...)
Each pair of gladiators brought the Roman audience face-to-face
with death; through their skill in fighting they might escape that
death" (34-5).

From the basis of the claim that overcoming death was the true essential
meaning of gladiature as spectacle (and leaving aside the premonitory suggestion
that even death was not a certainty), Wiedemann proceeded to argue that what
stood behind the 'link between gladiature and death' was an even stronger
association between gladiature and 'rebirth', functioning within multiple spheres.
Most salient was gladiature as a symbolic practice of social rebirth, alluded to in
the above passage; the legal marginalization (*infamia*) of the figure of the
gladiator coincided with his personification of the most precious Roman moral
values (*virtus*), and as such a 'successful' combat was tantamount to winning
some measure of social legitimacy. This notion had, of course, been traced out in
brief by Auguet; Wiedemann, however, extended it considerably further, by
centralizing the concept of social rebirth and couching it in language that alluded
to a total cosmology, well over and above the level of a socio-legal structure.
Wiedemann's ingenious reversal of the terms of emphasis (the exchange of death
for rebirth as the essence of gladiature), embedded as it was within the injunction

to modern self-reflexivity, rather neatly aligned the contextual significance of gladiature with the bourgeois mythos of the orderly, cohesive, and organically self-regulating social body: at its deepest level, gladiature produced social (re)integration for gladiators and spectators alike, and far from representing an inadmissible pleasure in violence, was instead the key to the Roman ordering of the world.

The deeper thinking at play here was the development of carefully argued detachment from violence, and the separation of violence from pleasure as the necessary condition underlying the claim for gladiature as a positive force for social integration. The perfect solidarity and organic unity of Wiedemann's crowd, consolidated in its anxiety about what lay beyond the boundaries of the civilized world and in its joy over the drama of restored order, was a social body so utterly free of conflict that even the oldest tropes of gladiatorial historiography, particularly the discourse of struggle, could be rewritten: specifically, the almost magical conversion of the *pollice verso*, which a century earlier had represented the most grotesque perversion of democratic franchise, into an act wherein the benevolent collective judgment of the crowd restored life in celebration of order, rather than inflicted death for the sake of its own barbaric pleasure. The power of the franchise is here worked up to an almost sublime state, which nearly two decades later is still reflected in the two-storey projection of the 'thumbs-up' sign on the Colosseum to mark state abolitions of the death penalty (cf. Beard and Hopkins 19-20).

Pleasure/*virtus*: legitimate violence in service to the (civilized) State

Among Wistrand's concluding statements was a remark upon the occasional appearance, as attested in numerous ancient sources, of aristocratic Roman citizens in the arena, where they would perform as gladiators; most of the surviving textual evidence which attests to these incidents casts the behaviour of such upper-class individuals in an extremely negative light, and it would appear that such events were considered shocking to the sensibilities of the literati who recorded them. It is perhaps unsurprising that this particular historical detail would arise as something of a sticking point during this period of historiography, when scholars were more or less unanimous in the perception of gladiature as the very avatar of civilization in antiquity. Ville himself had designated that a crucial distinction between proto-historic *agones* of Greece and Rome was that, among the Greeks, citizens participated equally in the combat sports of the *pankration*, while we may extrapolate from the elder Pliny the notion that the Romans, at some point in early republican history, conversely had begun to send down their slaves to compete (*La gladiature en Occident* 16-7; cf. Pliny NH XXI.5). While Ville was arguably the last to evoke the old comparative rhetoric which pitted a democratically enlightened Greece against a relatively benighted Rome, nevertheless the contemporary re-inscription of gladiature as a practice predicated upon social integration and the spread of order was periodically troubled by the seeming anomaly of the descent of patricians into the arena, and the distasteful, condemnatory comments that such moments drew from ancient writers. Wiedemann had emphasized the moral value of the performance of the *infamis* and the demonstration of high cultural values by individuals who had been

excluded from the formal social order; Wistrand took a rather more cynical view,

stating that the "special flavour added to the teaching of *virtus* in the arena was ...

of a profoundly optimistic and uplifting nature: the idea that it was possible to rise

above one's station. That edifying effect would have been totally undermined, if a

Roman aristocrat – *vir ad gloriam natus* as Cicero put it – descended to

performing as a gladiator. Instead, a demoralizing perversity would have been

created: the sorry spectacle of seeing a man voluntarily defaming himself" (78).

This 'sorry spectacle of self-defamation' swiftly formed the subject of an entire

monograph: Barton's 1993 *The Sorrows of the Ancient Romans: The Gladiator*

and the Monster.

Barton's unique analysis attempted to penetrate the social psychology of

the Roman world through a parallel examination of both the gladiator and the

'monster' as figures of the Roman cultural imagination; what Barton sought, to

which end the interpretation of gladiature was allied, was a broader picture of

what might be termed the 'cultural psyche' of Rome in the late Republic and first

centuries of the Empire. The work is thus not a historicist interpretation of the

institution of gladiature so much as an attempt to represent Roman sociocultural

structures using gladiature as an interpretive lens; though such a description easily

applies to most contemporary scholarship of gladiature, the crucial difference

with Barton was a detachment from all but the broadest structures of Roman

history in favour of a close emphasis upon the structures and poetics of written

discourse. These poetics, in Barton's view, centred upon a complex semiotic economy of nostalgia, wherein gladiature assumed its most spectacular form in response to a deeply embedded contemporary conviction that Roman 'civilization' was in decline: "The fascination of Roman society ... with the gladiatorial games is not simply a matter of an idiosyncratic inclination to sadomasochism but a response to an intense and excruciating feeling of humiliation and insecurity and an attempt to find compensation, even exaltation, within this feeling of inescapable degradation" (46).

The focus upon this particular period in Roman history, though explicitly prompted by the relative wealth of surviving textual materials from this timespan, further supported an analysis mounted upon the framework of the transition from Republic to Empire as a decline of civilization, at least as this was represented by certain literate members of the ruling classes upon whose writings Barton's interpretation was primarily based. This view of the republican/imperial transition was arguably unique to Barton during this period, when the vast majority of other scholars saw the advent of the Roman Empire in positive terms; however, despite the decivilizing socio-political backdrop of her interpretation, Barton still brought forth an image of gladiature which gestured towards its relatively civilizing influence. The distinction rested upon a probing deployment of *virtus* as the key to gladiature's ideological content in antiquity: as the 'decivilization' of the Republic gave way to the corruption of empire, gladiature was repositioned as a survival and an evocation of *virtus* as the nostalgic moral code of a nobler Roman past, and as the performance of values longed for by elite Romans who recalled a bygone social and political order. Barton read in the selected source material an acute sense of 'despair':

> "The importance of the social and psychological role of the gladiator among the free and privileged classes in Rome developed apace with the notion that with the failure of the aristocratic republic, *dignitas*, social worth, had become a word whose only content was humiliation. One finds in Roman literature, from Cicero on, a sense that the price exacted for political, social, and economic status (indeed, for life) had become self-abasement and that honour and dishonour had become synonymous. The traditional testimonials of power, freedom, and pride began to signal as well powerlessness, enslavement, and humiliation" (27).

In Barton's analysis, gladiature became in a certain sense a form of resistance to the decivilizing, anomic pressures which patrician Romans were here claimed to have experienced in the shift from Republic to Empire. The terms of analysis common in this period were inverted, but the ultimate connection implied or drawn between gladiature and order/civilization – even when this was coded as 'despair' – was maintained. Moreover, the discourse of despair and abasement, wherein patrician participation in gladiature was an attempt to reclaim the old aristocratic code of honour (called elsewhere *virtus*), was still curiously inscribed in Barton's text as a socially integrating force, despite her otherwise strict emphasis upon the Roman elite both as source material and as subject matter: "The glorification of abasement and pleasure in abasement (...) was not an isolated or sectarian tendency, nor one based (as one might expect) principally or exclusively in the nonprivileged classes. It was, rather, a widespread social phenomenon, which attracted many members of the free and privileged classes in Rome" (25). Gladiature, then, was a specifically elite form of expression of the 'pleasure of abasement' which Barton read as widespread in first-century Roman imperial society as a whole, underlining yet again the strong fundamental consensus that not only was the practice to be considered a force for social unification, but also that its essential pleasure and meaning lay in the dissemination of aristocratic mores through the lower classes of society.

Within a few years of *Emperors and Gladiators*, Futrell's 1997 *Blood in the Arena: The Spectacle of Roman Power* offered further specifications of the core of Wiedemann's line of thought. Futrell similarly felt that the central issue to any contemporary approach to gladiature was the problem of "how to reconcile the bloodiness of the arena and the events it sheltered with the arena's centrality in Roman society", but in her view, the scholarly trend to 'secularize' amphitheatre spectacle and reduce it to 'mere entertainment or sport' was insufficient to account for that centrality; instead, the key to the interpretation of gladiature was to view the practice as a religious institution of human sacrifice (7). Futrell did not claim that the survival of the victorious gladiator was the true object of the spectacle and therefore of spectator pleasure – in this analysis, sacrificial death was very much the point. However, Futrell's version of events did hinge upon the notion that 'sacrifice' was inherently to be understood as ritual death in the service of life in some sense, and to be considered as a response to some external violence or disorder rather than as violence itself.

Futrell's argument pivoted upon Nicolet's idea that socio-political upheavals of the middle and later Republic should be understood as creating sufficient conditions for gladiature and the amphitheatre to emerge as a legitimate 'alternative institution' for the performance of power; her interpretation, however, was comparatively literal in character, as the "contemporary ambience of civic disorder also favoured the use of the *munera*; the violence in the arena replicated in many ways the faction fighting among the gangs of political thugs in Rome's streets. The arena, however, had certain advantages: the impact and outcome of the mayhem could be controlled by its organizers. This was idealized violence, violence in support of order instead of disorder" (Futrell 31). Further, although she did not cite Wistrand explicitly, Futrell hit upon the apprehension that gladiature was a powerful tool of the late republican ruling factions and further specified – in contrast to many of the more familiar iterations of the idea from earlier in the twentieth century – that the real power benefit was reaped not by the *populares*, but the *optimates*:

> "The Gracchus incident also points up particular features of the
> *munera* in terms of their role in manipulating popular behaviour
> and expressing public opinion. The "insiders" of the games of 122,
> those who promoted and produced them and lost by their
> destruction, were opponents of Gracchus, identified by Plutarch
> with the conservative element in the ruling class. The antipopulist
> sympathies housed by the arena are detectable as well in the
> writings of Cicero, who values the expressions of public opinion
> manifested at the games very highly, specifically for this very
> reason. The "popular" leaders were not popular at the shows, in
> direct contrast to the assemblies. (...) Cicero, of course, has his own
> political agenda, tending to favour conservative policy as less
> damaging to the Roman State and as more likely to foster his own
> dream of a consensus among "good men". Likewise, the audience
> of the spectacles could be manipulated by the *editors* as well;
> admission to public games was determined on the basis of who had
> access to the sponsors of the shows. The suggestion, however, that
> public shows were produced predominantly by nonpopulists is
> intriguing, with implications for the development of the institution
> of the amphitheatre as an important tool of the Imperial machine"
> (32).

In Futrell's analysis, the implications which arose from the alignment of gladiature with conservative political policy seemed to merit critique, although *Blood in the Arena* never allowed such critique to rise above the level of implication, buried in suggestive language. Nevertheless, it remains interesting to observe that the trope of 'social order' as an end served by gladiature eventually became so completely, and relatively unproblematically, elided with the increasingly conservative authority of the Roman ruling class.

Futrell's nascent critique, however, was ultimately subjugated to the notion that the 'social order' produced at the site of the amphitheatre was somehow to be bracketed out from social politics; as already encountered with Rawson, the absolving force invoked here was religion, with gladiature as the connecting site between historically embedded politics and a kind of transcendent Roman cosmology. Not unlike Wiedemann, Futrell's interpretation maintained the core idea that gladiature ought to be seen as a practice defined by the symbolic construction of social order, and consequently as a positive force for social integration and the production and reinforcement of social bonds. Her concept of social integration was instead pitched at the space of overlap between the political structure of the Roman state and the socio-political function of Roman religion. Though gladiature was to be seen as an essentially sacral activity, the poetics of sacrificial gladiature were here derived from the religion of state: though gladiature was nothing so literal as a sacrifice offered to Roma or any other specific deity, nevertheless the practice, as a performance of Roman state power, was argued to be aimed not directly at intimidation and social control as it had been fifteen years earlier, but at the sacred duty of all citizens to ensure the continuity of the central authority. Just as the original funerary context of gladiature offered blood to the shade of the deceased to nourish its afterlife, gladiature as a state institution was a "celebration of the continued life of the Roman state" (Futrell 3); gladiature's essential meaning was continuous from its origin throughout its history, and the original funeral was a metonymic for the broader, later social significance of the spectacle. The state here represented a system of order and a context of social identity whose overarching synchronicity with matters of religion provided the basis for gladiature as a particular practice, and which was desired and required equally by all social groups, even though Futrell saw the development of the institution of gladiature as entirely under the deliberate control of the aristocracy at Rome. In a certain sense, Futrell's analysis represented the further possible extension of Auguet's idea of transmutation, extended from the individual gladiator to the Roman state as a whole.

Violence and 'good barbarism'

In Foucault's analysis, the 'distinction between two forms of barbarism' which is central to bourgeois historic-political discourse is a strategy for the filtering of barbarism which "performs two important operation: on the one hand, freedom and Germanity ... are dissociated; on the other, Romanity and absolutism are dissociated" (*SMBD* 204). If we can accept that the third strategy for the filtering of barbarism from the bourgeois discourse of civilization dissociates freedom and absolutism from their traditional historico-political frameworks, this suggestively renders it possible for the bourgeois, in its historically novel position of dominance, to construct for itself a history of right that aligns 'freedom' (i.e. 'good barbarism', an image of essential, immutable freedom which was never subjected) with 'Romanity' (i.e. the traditional narrative tropes/discursive structures of the nobiliary history of right). In a bourgeois historico-political discourse, the posited coextension of the nation with the State unseats the discourses of struggle which has defined the historiography of the nobility: consequently, what becomes significant in a bourgeois historiography is not a division of ancient groups into categories of 'civilized' and 'barbarous' and the inscription of a particular power conflict between them, but is instead the production of a narrative which founds the 'history of right' of a universalized nation/State in an origin story already defined by 'universalization', as opposed to the narratives of invasion and conquest which had legitimized the dominance of the nobility. The discursive collapse of nation into State coincides with the construction of a 'civilized barbarian' that is internal to the social. At the level of classical historiography as a myth-history of the modern west, this can arguably be interpreted to mean that the 'good barbarian' – who was always and essentially free, whose freedom was never disrupted by relations of domination or conflict from outside of itself, and who therefore signifies the essential 'meaning' of civilization – can be, in fact, Rome.

We have already observed the passing of the main 'rupture' that had marked the larger interpretation of gladiature since the eighteenth century: the once-pivotal moment of the transition from Republic to Empire, which for almost two centuries had served as one of the most crucial and determinative topoi in the historiography of gladiature, had during this new period given way to an emphasis upon the relative seamlessness of that erstwhile momentous and revolutionary change, and to a series of claims which saw the empire as a structured, intelligible, and possibly even natural outcome of the specific historical circumstances of the last centuries of the Republic. Since the general model of the middle to later Republic as a period of 'proto-empire' coincided with the posited 'appearance' of gladiature in Rome, as Livy's Epitomator has it, a perceived link emerged between both historical developments: the inception of the practice of gladiature at Rome, and Rome's entry into the politics of imperialism even while yet operating under a republican form of government. Gladiature was no longer the sign of the Republic's fall; instead, it became the sign of the rise and spread of a relatively benign Empire, characterized not by totalitarian mechanisms of ideological control (as seen, for instance, in Hopkins), but by social integration, economic and cultural exchange, and the largest internally pacified territory in human history to date. The narrative of the origin of gladiature became the narrative of the origin of the Roman Empire itself – and functioned, by extension, as a myth-historical narrative within the historico-political discourse of the present, for a 'bourgeois empire' characterized by the absence of the discourse of struggle or of perpetual war.

Universalization of the State

It must be pointed out that the new image of gladiatorial origin has not commanded total consensus among academics. Numerous recent scholars of the subject (Coarelli 2000, Golvin and Landes 1990, Jacobelli 2003, Rea 2000) have not engaged the problem critically; origin, when referenced, is mentioned only

briefly, and is passed by unexamined with a citation of the Osco-Samnite/South

Italian hypothesis. Conversely, the former Etruscan hypothesis retains some

limited purchase in the discussion: Futrell, in an argument essentially founded

upon the premise that Rome would have been more likely to emulate the

sophisticated Etruscans than to "ape the Campanians" (14), attempted to reopen

the case for Etruria and the Phersu images (although see Thuillier 1987). The

image of a Roman origin of gladiature is yet emergent.

What is abundantly clear about the nascent construct of a Roman origin of

gladiature, however, is the extent to which it accords with Foucault's claim that,

in a historico-political framework based upon the universality of a nation

continuous with the State, the "fundamental moment is no longer the origin, and

intelligibility's starting point is no longer the archaic element; it is, on the

contrary, the present" (*SMBD* 226). To some extent, the determinative force of the

present is a self-conscious utterance among scholars of antiquity, as witnessed by

the collection of ritualized statements of abhorrence and reflexivity covered

above. The 'internal dialecticalization of the present', however, manifests deeper

historiographic effects when proclamations of abhorrence give way to the

construction of new origin stories. If we accept the network of suggestions that

'western modernity' exists as a broad speaking subject of history, that this

subjectivity has become dominated by the historico-political discourse of the

bourgeois, and that the historiography of Roman antiquity persists in performing a

myth-historical function within this discourse, then it becomes possible to perceive in the newest historiography of gladiature a representation of what we have been calling a 'bourgeois empire' in which the persistently troubling link between violence, pleasure, and civilization has been completely inverted – and the corresponding account of gladiature's origin carries even further the push to inscribe gladiature as a 'civilizing non-violence' that can be imagined as standing at the centre of a universalized nation/State. The polarization of historical discourse toward the present and toward the State "make[s] it possible ... to write a history in which the relations of force that are in play are not of a warlike nature, but completely civilian, so to speak" (*SMBD* 224).

Those who do take up directly the problem of origin manifest many subtle commonalities in their approach and structure of thought. The impetus to re-inscribe the amphitheatre as a civilizing institution, it will be seen, associated the interpretive framework applied to gladiature much more closely with narratives of origin than had ever been the case; phrased another way, the historiography of this period has pursued an essential continuity of gladiature's cultural meaning for Roman audiences across the centuries of its practice, such that gladiature's 'meaning' in its original context was essentially – or, at least, functionally – similar to the meaning that it held for spectators several centuries later. The conceptual pushback of empire into the later centuries of the Republic, and the generalized de-emphasis of socio-political 'ruptures' that has supplied determinative coherence to most earlier narratives of gladiature, produced an entirely different sort of story.

Hopkins may be credited with initiating this entirely novel approach to the storied historiographic problem of gladiature's origin: he dismissed it, or rather, he dismissed as uninteresting the framework of the question in terms of extra-Roman cultural origin, and focused exclusively upon Rome's own 'origin' of gladiature, in the form of the patrician funeral:

> "Gladiatorial fights originated apparently as an element in funeral games. 'Once upon a time', wrote the Christian critic Tertullian at the end of the second century, 'men believed that the souls of the dead were propitiated by human blood, and so at funerals they sacrificed prisoners of war or slaves of poor quality bought for the purpose' (Lib. Spec. 12). It was also thought that gladiators were originally imported from Etruria or from Campania. Stories about origins are notoriously unreliable. Yet repeated evidence confirms the close association of gladiatorial contests with funerals" (3-4).

The gradual relocation of gladiatorial origin to Rome has occurred in conjunction with a new emphasis upon the patrician funeral as the 'functional' context of that origin, in preference to any notion of origin overtly based upon race. Within a decade this in fact became self-conscious: Wiedemann, for example, meditated at some length on the "Roman ambivalence about the games" which he saw as the motivating force between the contradictions which marked the surviving ancient evidence. Discarding what he politely termed 'geographical' constructs of origin provided a pretext to abandon 'valueless' "[s]peculations about the functional origins of [non-Roman] *munera*" as well, and arbitrarily to relocate the 'meaningful' point of origin as the moment when gladiature seemed to emerge at Rome which, suggestively, did not appear itself to qualify as 'geographical' (Wiedemann 32-3). This subtle shift in thinking, articulated by no scholar more clearly than Wiedemann, was a definitive failure of critique: while the endeavour to transcend what were now identified as intellectually irresponsible biases in the inherited historiography of gladiature sought to escape the categories of thought that had so long shaped the scholarly accounts, it simultaneously denied the reactionary character of the narrative erected in its place.

More significantly, a 'functional' construct of origin acquired a new importance to the interpretation of gladiature, since the introduction of the practice into the Roman sphere could no longer be comfortably attributed either to the perversions or backwardness of their originating peoples, nor to the base and uncivilized appetites and pleasures of the Roman lower classes. Consistency and essential continuity of meaning has been sought between the funerary practices of the third century B.C. and the massive amphitheatrical spectacles which developed hundreds of years later. Culturally specific functionality, which bears out across centuries, has been sought only once origin is moved within the Roman sphere (i.e. within the realm of myth-history of modernity); this has meant that 1) originally Roman gladiature can 'have' social functionality (whereas only moral properties were attributed to Etruscan and even Campanian gladiature), and 2) the pursuit of functional/essential continuity (whether this is achieved by the carrying-forward of the fundamental meaning(s) of funerary ritual into the Empire, or by the pushback of late republican/imperial political performance and process into middle republican funerals) has entailed that gladiature did not undergo (and therefore does not indicate) a 'decivilizing' process; despite its socio-cultural 'centrality' and its undeniable acceleration and increases in scale, such considerations are immaterial next to gladiature's essential consistency of function and meaning. Thus the new origin of gladiature inverts the traditional narrative of history – at least briefly, the historiography of gladiature formed a narrative of perfect progress, wherein Nicolet located the 'real' violence in the political unrest of the mid-Republic, and gladiature as central to the pacification of that violence within the framework of a newly benevolent, humanitarian imperialism, inscribed over the image of Rome in the historical imagination in a fantasy representation of a universalized bourgeois nation/State.

Within this historiographic *embourgeoisement* of the Roman empire, the essential benevolence of gladiature as a civilizing force is closely linked to the Roman context of its origin. A clear example is Welch, whose most extensive contribution to the historiography of gladiature did not appear in print until 2006, with the monograph *The Roman Amphitheatre from its Origins to the Colosseum*; however, the bulk of her arguments had been published well before in the early nineties (1991, 1994). Welch's study was dismissive of the origin of the practice of gladiature as traditionally discussed (*Roman Amphitheatre from its Origins* 17-18), and instead weighed in on the side of Roman origin in terms of architectural history; in her approach, the possible non-Roman origins of gladiature were not only uninteresting but historically suspect, and in any case were eclipsed by the evidently Roman origin of the amphitheatre as architectural form. However, this architectural construct of origin, besides its thoroughly Roman character, was also invoked in her analysis in a manner which ultimately completed the reinscription of gladiature as civilized: here, the practice was not only imagined as having emanated outwards from Rome, but as having emanated outwards from the metaphorical centre of Roman civilization itself.

In essence, Welch's analysis argued for a reversal of the always somewhat vaguely conceived Samnite/Campanian hypothesis of gladiature's origin, which had some additional basis in architectural history on the strength of the fact that, as near as can be presently determined, the earliest permanent stone amphitheatres were constructed in those southern regions in the late republican period (cf. Bomgardner). In Welch's view, this and related evidence from southern Italy should be read not as indicative of a movement of the practice of gladiature from the southern frontier to the Roman centre, but of the reverse. Welch argued at length that the architectural form of the amphitheatre should be sourced to the construction of temporary wooden structures for gladiature, attested in literary sources, in the Forum Romanum, the civic and religious centre of urban Rome (*Roman Amphitheatre from its Origins* 43-71; cf. Golvin 1988); in her analysis, the original funerary context was significant only for its socio-political function as aristocratic performance, which eventually accounted in turn for the central location of gladiatorial contests in republican Rome (*Roman Amphitheatre from its Origins* 51). Welch therefore linked gladiature not simply with Rome, but with the social identity of the aristocracy, the physical and symbolic centre of Roman politics, and the dawn of Roman imperialism, all in a single rather ingenious stroke.

Welch's subsequent image of gladiature was unusually tightly knit to this specific notion of origin. Though the initial (unexamined) popularity of gladiature

at Rome was associated with the social politics of aristocratic group performance,
for Welch it was the locus of architectural incubation in the Forum Romanum
which laundered out any possible political subtext from the essence of
gladiature's 'meaning'. The significance of locating gladiature's origin in the
Forum Romanum specifically was associated in her analysis not with any
historically embedded notion of aristocratic politics, but with a more generalized
idea, that cited the physical proximity of numerous monuments of warfare in the
Forum Romanum to claim that the ahistorical, transcendent 'meaning' of
gladiature had less to do with politics and more to do with 'warfare' (*Roman
Amphitheatre from its Origins* 71). Not only was gladiature's origin accorded a
suitably aristocratic pedigree, but Welch's model then immediately deployed the
value of the nobility in support of the contemporary image of empire, as the
'civilizing force' of gladiature was shifted away from the more abstract
connotations of social transmutation and symbolic rebirth, and instead tied firmly
and literally to the Roman army, whom Welch credited with expanding upon and
spreading the practice of gladiature as Rome's colonial power grew. It was a
rhetorical move that not only reflected bourgeois historico-political discourse in
its shifting of violence to the boundaries between nation/States, but also converted
that colonizing violence to something like its opposite: just as the loaded
symbolism of the Forum Romanum served as the basis for claiming a
depoliticized history of gladiature, the army as a vehicle of gladiature's
dissemination across the Empire forged a mutually civilizing link between the

"two most violent institutions in Roman society" (*Roman Amphitheatre from its Origins* 27).

For Welch, the connection between gladiature and warfare under the Republic was not focused upon the presumed military ethos of the Roman crowd in the urban centres (a suggestion which had arisen from, of course, Hopkins), but upon the (far more demonstrable) military ethos of republican army soldiers, either actively serving in garrison forts on the frontiers or in their capacity as veteran settlers, colonizing lands granted to them on completion of service; legionary forts are known to have included rudimentary facilities for gladiature, and many of the known permanent republican-period amphitheatres of southern Italy are found in what were then Marian and Sullan colonies (*Roman Amphitheatre from its Origins* 88-89). The observation that republican gladiature appears to have followed the army further identified soldiers as a highly specialist form of the crowd, whose pleasure in gladiature could have been in no way aligned with violence, since on the one hand their lives were already likely replete with it, and on the other the relationship of soldiers to violence was broadly presumed by Welch to have been professionally disinterested rather than based upon pleasure of any more sordid variety:

> "Since they appreciated the combat as connoisseurs, soldiers would have been an exacting audience. There is even evidence that army unit under the principate included soldiers who doubled as arena combatants. It is often said that legionary amphitheatres were constructed specifically for military training and exercises. [...] [I]t is clear why ex-soldiers in the age of Sulla would have been particularly interested in gladiatorial games: not only were *munera* good military-style entertainment that they were familiar with from the capital, but the technique of the combat may also have been

familiar to them from their army training" (*Roman Amphitheatre from its Origins* 81-2).

The rather myopically focussed detail of war monuments in the Forum Romanum furnished Welch's claim for a link to the army's affinity for gladiature, and for the dissemination throughout the empire of the practice as a literal, direct expression of a lived military ethos as well as a group performance of Roman identity in a colonial context. As a whole, then, gladiature was interpreted in turn as both instrumental to the benign spread of Roman identity (which in the context of gladiature, we will recall, was originally aristocratic), borne abroad by the army but as an element of the relatively peaceful aftermath of military conquest, and essentially benevolent in its detachment of violence from more sordid conceptions of pleasure. In the impetus towards universalization of a cohesive nation/State as the central tenet of a bourgeois historico-political discourse, not only had the erstwhile discourse of perpetual war been suppressed and diverted into a construct of civilization as an 'internal' struggle from which universality must flow, but the very agents of perpetual war, in the figure of the Roman colonial army, were actually re-inscribed as a locus wherein civilization's seemingly age-old discursive imperative to dissociate itself from violence was at last resolved.

The heavily constrained position that violence retained in association with gladiature was pushed to the furthest boundaries of the Roman world, held there as a vague notion to be gestured at and to provide coherence to the rehabilitated image of the Roman Empire as a western historical avatar of the successful spreading of an orderly, internally pacified civilization, the first such to achieve

such vast size, to hold power for so long, and the last of its kind in western history
for over a thousand years. The popularity during this period of the 'Romanization'
metaphor to describe the progress of empire can be read in this light. As discussed
above, particularly in reference to the work of Wiedemann, the amphitheatre
came within this larger construct of empire to be viewed as a sort of technology
for the conversion of (increasingly abstract) violence into order, on the one hand,
and on the other as a vital, unifying cultural institution whose dissemination
across the far-flung provinces was instrumental to the coherence and pacification
of the empire. In an odd and ultimately uncanny manner, the inversion of the
image of gladiature was thus completed: what had previously been inscribed as a
grotesque sign of decivilizing had now, within a conceptual political merging of
nation and State wherein the spectral possibility of decivilizing had been
provisionally suspended or overcome, been reclaimed as a marvellous instrument
of ultimate civilization. From this point, the only thing that remained to be
overcome was death itself.

Stantes missi/sine missione

No one denies outright that gladiators died in the amphitheatre.
Considerable work has been done on the mortuary epigraphy of gladiators' tombs,
and such developments are not new; Robert's collection of inscriptions has
already been mentioned, and subsequently added to by Sabbatini-Tumolesi (1980)
and Hope (2000). However, there is a new atmosphere of debate about the
circumstances of gladiators' deaths – the frequency with which they died, the
reliability or certainty of death in the amphitheatre and, most importantly, the role

played by that old perversion of the democratic franchise, the *pollice verso* of the crowd and the final judgment of the *editor* or emperor. Wiedemann had already intimated that the popular power of the crowd was employed not to judge death, but to confer life/rebirth upon the 'socially dead'; in the decade following, the figure of death in gladiature attracted an increasing degree of attention. One of the conditions of the perception of gladiature as a locus of civilization has been an altered concept of death, the spectre which has always underlain and ultimately defined the more salient construct of violence; death is often at least de-emphasized either in significance to the spectacle or in simple quantity, and moreover, as appears upon close examination, the role of the reinvented elite crowd as agents of and participants in the death of gladiators in some studies completely changed.

At the broadest level is an ongoing attempt to estimate gladiator mortality, of which the leading exponent is Beard and Hopkins' 2005 study. Beard and Hopkins sought in particular to give clear and rationalized dimensions to the inherited image of "[g]ladiatorial combat ... with left-over corpses strewing the Colosseum's arena" (89); they argued, on the basis of the available epigraphic evidence and some casual estimations, that the average gladiator was likely engaged in combat no more than twice per year, that the mortality rate of gladiators in an average show was likely about one in six, that an average of 16000 gladiators were in existence throughout the empire in an average year (based upon data from the late second century), and:

> "What, finally, of the toll in casualties? In individual contests ...
> slaughter was far less common than our popular image suggests.

But what of the aggregate of deaths in the arena? At a death rate of one in six, we have already estimated 4000 gladiatorial fatalities per year outside Rome. We need to add to that the condemned criminals executed at the shows and the deaths, accidental or not, among animal attendants and hunters; say 2000. ... It may be reasonable to guess that the capital on average saw something like one-third of the deaths in the rest of the empire; say 2000 again. A grand total of 8000 deaths in the arena a year is then our best guesstimate. Not much of a burden, one might initially think, for an empire with a total population of 50 to 60 million people. But, in fact, 8000 deaths per year, mostly of trained muscular young adult males, would be equal to about 1.5 per cent of all 20-year-old men. Seen in these terms, the death of gladiators constituted a massive drain on human resources. Gladiatorial shows were a deadly death tax" (93-4).

A 'deadly death tax' perhaps, but eminently calculable, and reducible to numbers far smaller than the tens of thousands of gladiators spoken of in some ancient sources referring to exceptional triumphal games (eg. Trajan's games after the Dacian wars, or those of Commodus following the triumph in Germania). Key to the thrust of Beard and Hopkins' argument was the claim that the long-imagined carnage of gladiature was an 'expensive rarity', for "most amphitheatres, those iconic glories of Roman cruelty, luxury, and profligacy, must have been empty, or used for something tamer, on 360 days out of 365" (93). Crucially, moreover, Beard and Hopkins further glossed over the implication that earlier, republican gladiature was perhaps a legitimate source for such historical rumours; since "Augustus had banned the luxury (in Roman terms) of shows in which all fights were to the death" (89), this reinforced the suggestion, which had begun with Nicolet, that gladiature 'proper' – the institutionalized mass spectacles far more vivid in the historical imagination than the relatively small affairs held in the early wooden arenas – had functioned in antiquity as a directional narrative of civilization in the Eliasian sense, whose internal history of development away from lethality exemplified, even as it shaped and actively constructed, the pacifying influence of the bourgeois nation-State as it grew toward empire.

Beard's and Hopkins' opinions have not been the most extreme; at least one scholar carried this line of thought so far as to elide the suggestive distinction between republican and imperial gladiature, and to claim that gladiature did not 'civilize' to a point of non-lethality, but actually was from its (Roman) inception, and therefore was in essence, a non-lethal practice. Potter (1999, 2009) reached all the way back to Livy's story of Antiochus Epiphanes, the Syrian king who in the eighteenth century had been read as responsible for introducing gladiature to the abhorring Greeks, to argue the point:

> "The terms under which the gladiators fought for Antiochus, as given by the Roman historian Livy, are interesting. Livy says that 'sometimes they fought until there were wounds; at other times, *sine missione*'. A fight until there were wounds was a fight that ended when one gladiator wounded another, even if the person who was wounded was capable of continuing the fight. The meaning of the other sort of fight that Livy mentions, of a combat *sine missione*, is less obvious. The technical term for the end of a gladiatorial fight was *missio*, which means release – in this context, release from the authority of the person who was offering the combat to the public (the *munerarius*) ... *Missio* does not mean victory. A clear victory was not a requirement of all combats. If two fighters fought long and hard without either being able to obtain the conditions for a victory, the fight would be a draw, and the fighters would be *stantes missi*, 'released standing'. A combat *sine missione* was one where *missio* without a clear victory was not permitted, except under the most extraordinary circumstances. The phrase does not mean, as it has unfortunately been taken to mean in many studies of gladiators, a fight to the death. There was no such thing as a mandatory fight to the death between gladiators" (*Life, Death, and Entertainment* 306-7).

Exactly how this view addresses the intent behind Augustus' attested ban, among numerous other historical details, is unclear. As already stated above, Potter was not attempting to suggest that gladiators never died (although he is to be counted among the growing number of scholars, including Junkelmann and Kyle, for whom gladiature is to be considered first and foremost a 'sport' in which death, though a constant possibility, was neither a commonplace nor an objective). Instead, death is redefined as purely accidental, or at least incidental, to the practice and therefore the meaning of gladiature; it is an analysis that goes even one step further than Wiedemann's insistence that survival was the key to gladiature's pleasure for the crowd, for Potter suggests that even a diminshed risk of unintended death was enough.

Potter's image, in fact, goes as far as to resolve the extremely old problem of the *pollice verso*, which since the Enlightenment has signified the grotesque nadir of democratic power and has been deployed in multiple ways by various nobiliary histories of right. Read as a bourgeois history of right, in contrast, Potter's interpretation actually overwrites the *pollice verso* entirely, as "[i]n... texts we find some gladiators who claim that they never killed anyone, others who claim that they killed everyone, and the occasional grudge match. The key point here is that the gladiators say that the responsibility for life and death lay with them, not with the crowd" (*Life, Death, and Entertainment* 315). This 'crowd' – comprising a representation of the civilized society, which is far more aristocracy than mob, whose pleasure is associated with everything except anything which can be called violence – is thus completely, fundamentally depoliticized, in a history of right wherein barbarism is filtered so entirely, and the nation/State

imagined as so perfectly universal, that the myth-historical narrative of antiquity

presents an unbroken mirror-image of bourgeois civilization.

Chapter 8: *Telos*

Civilization, democratization, reconciliation, and myth

At this point, we can return to the familiar image of Roman gladiature – the massive amphitheatre, the roaring crowd with thumbs thrust out, the armed combat on the sand – and attempt to revisit the major questions initially posed. Does the anxiety invoked by the cathexis of violence and pleasure manifested by gladiature, and the sliding interpretation of the nature and meaning of that cathexis in historiography, tell us something about the inscription and re-inscription of Roman antiquity as a myth-historical, foundational narrative of 'civilization'? Does the moralizing discourse around violence and pleasure reveal anything about the rationalizing discourse around violence and power? What, if anything, does the overarching path of the shifts within these linked discourses reveal about modernity's 'self-image' over time?

As posited in the Introduction to this dissertation, and as repeatedly explored throughout, the historiography of gladiature since the Enlightenment has been driven by a 'rationalizing imperative' that had produced an observable series of attempts to circumscribe gladiature in particular ways. The barbarism signified by gladiature is perennial, returning again and again as a troubling or contradictory element within the image of Roman civilization across numerous discursive strategies over centuries of scholarly thought. However, if we step back from the collection of themes, the dynamic iterations of race and class struggle, the constant tension between the notion of civilization and the equally constant spectre of its opposite, and all the many elements that comprise gladiatorial

historiography, the basic question remains: why does gladiature make 'us'
anxious?

For Foucault, the answer lies in the nature of historico-political discourse as
constitutive and representative of the modern episteme: the centrality of struggle
or 'perpetual warfare' to the order of socio-historical power relations compassed
by such discourse has never, in Foucault's ultimate estimation, been
unproblematic. The essential conflict between civilized and barbarous as a
determinative topos of the discourse of history both positions violence at the
centre of all order and simultaneously pushes it toward the margins:

> "...in a rather paradoxical way, the element of war, which
> actually constituted historical intelligibility in the eighteenth
> century, was from the Revolution onward gradually, if not
> eliminated from the discourse of history, at least restricted,
> colonized, settled, scattered, civilized if you like, and up to a point
> pacified. This was because it was, after all, history ... that conjured
> up the great threat: the great danger that we would be caught up in
> a war without end: the great danger that all our relations, whatever
> they might be, would always be of the order of domination. And it
> is this twofold threat – a war without end as the basis of history and
> the relationship of domination as the explanatory element in
> history – that will ... be lessened, broken down into regional threats
> and transitory episodes, and retranscribed" (*SMBD* 215).

Taken simply at a symbolic level, gladiature's resonance with such a
problem is obvious. The image of the practice, despite the variability of particular
critical details over time, has always been perceived and inscribed by modernity
according to specific characteristics that have been held as fixed: as an urban
phenomenon of Roman antiquity, gladiature was situated in the midst of the
earliest fabric of what has since been framed as western civilization, and it
concatenated multiple representations of the social body – the urban setting, the

mass crowd of the amphitheatre, the staging of socio-political structures between rulers and ruled in various capacities and identities – through the violence of gladiature itself, whether this is represented by scholars as sport, spectacle, combat, or some combination of any or all of those interpretations. A more powerful symbolic representation of the idea, whether considered as threatening or not, that all social relations will always be of the order of domination could hardly be imagined.

When the powerful symbolic signification of gladiature is contextualized within the *longue durée* of classical historiography since the Enlightenment, and this corpus in turn is regarded as a myth-historical transcription of modernity's self-image of 'civilization', the presence of gladiature in the imagined historical landscape deepens and complicates the problem. Rome is not the only appointed ancestor of the west, but it is the one whose relation to the notion of civilization as a sociocultural complex, as Robertson terms it, is arguably the most fraught; leaving aside the equally fascinating and convoluted relation to Greece, it is ultimately from Rome that modernity draws a great deal of the form of the rule of law, the language of politics, and above all the image of empire in the west. Gladiature's intrusion into this historical inheritance disrupts the discursive framing of Rome as an ancestor of what western modernity inscribes as civilization, through a manifestation of violence which resists rationalization through the perception of its unavowable association with pleasure.

As well, the structural shifts that have taken place within historico-political discourse necessarily influence the discursive history of gladiature in modernity.

The eventual retranscription of violence alluded to above is also, in essence, the *embourgeoisement* of historical discourse, and Foucault felt that the 'twofold threat' of perpetual war receded into the background within the discursive shift towards parity between the nation and the State, "not in the sense that we will achieve the good and true equilibrium that the eighteenth-century historians were trying to find, but in the sense that reconciliation will come about" (*SMBD* 216). The internal dialecticalization of historical discourse associated with *embourgeoisement* splits the notion of perpetual war and redistributes it in two directions: on the one hand, there emerges an idea of internal war that 'defends society against threats born in and of its own body' – in the unification of nation with State, the struggle necessarily becomes a struggle with self – while on the other hand, warfare is simultaneously externalized and displaced to the margins of society; its role is "no longer a condition of existence for society and political relations, but the precondition for its survival in its political relations" (216).

What we read in the modern historiography of gladiature is, in essence, an index of the discursive movement toward 'reconciliation' – but it is not a straight or steady path. The movement of the nation and the State toward a higher degree of unification arguably can be traced throughout gladiatorial historiography, although at no stage of discursive formation – even what has here been designated as the most recent stage of *embourgeoisement* - can we assume the continued movement toward the posited universalization of the nation/State. It may be possible, when looking at three hundred years' worth of historical writing, to point to the disappearance or abstract internalization of the barbarian, or to the

shifting conceptualization and contextualization of the conflict between socio-
political groups, and on such bases to suggest that the historiography of gladiature
actually provides scope for Elias' notion of a 'civilizing process' – that what we
read in this history are the traces of a directional continuum, ultimate expressions
of a withdrawal of violence and a quantitative increase of social interdependence
that can in turn be taken as empirical fact, as Elias claimed. In other words, it is
tempting to step back from the historiographic corpus of the interpretation of
Roman gladiature and perceive an entire narrative, a story that begins in the
eighteenth century with an anxiety about a certain violence within a certain
context and that eventually arrives at a place of reconciliation, wherein that
anxiety is apparently resolved. In addition, the ability to associate that apparent
core narrative to a wider framework of social historiography, wherein modernity's
reconciliation of gladiatorial violence moves in tandem with consonant shifts in
the image of the Roman State, presents the deeper temptation to take the Eliasian
final step, and infer that civilization is indeed a directional process toward the
withdrawal of violence and ultimately toward functional democratization. Yet the
claim for the existence of such a unifying narrative depends very closely, in the
case of gladiature, upon the periodization scheme that this dissertation has
adopted; were the historiographic span of inquiry any shorter – and especially if it
had been cut off even a generation earlier than the beginning of the present
century – the strongest arguments in favour of anything like a directional
movement toward civilization, according to the tenets of Elias' definition, would
effectively disappear. From the first, this dissertation has worked from the

approach to history as a plastic series of stories, with multiple possible versions; at the end, the story that this dissertation itself tells has at least two versions contained within it.

However, that tangential point raises a further interesting question of the conceptual reverberation between Foucault's notion of reconciliation as the (at least most recent) strategy of historico-political discourse, and the ambiguous, present/absent position of teleology in Elias' directional model of socio-historical change. As argued in the Introduction, despite Elias' insistence that the civilizing process should be understood as inherently non-terminal, his model of social change implied a continuous progression towards an image of democracy as the inevitable structural outcome of western social order, and simultaneously defined the salient characteristic of such functional democracy as the withdrawal of violence. In a sense, Elias' model placed democratization and violence into a mutually constitutive inverse relation, wherein a 'rise' in democratization correlates to a 'fall' or withdrawal of violence, and the central tension between these two linked factors is the crude mechanism by which the civilizing process could be said to function. The *telos* of civilization for Elias, even as he maintained the assertion that the civilizing process had no real 'end', was an internally pacified and democratized society.

Foucault does not hold up reconciliation as anything like the ultimate end of a teleological process of social change. However, it may fairly be said that both analyses, in different ways, pivot upon the same 'great threat of history': the idea that all social relations will always and inevitably be of the order of domination.

For Foucault, this was an observation of one operative element of a given discursive framework, perhaps particularly powerful in more recent periods but certainly discernable across the entire epistemic framework implied by the break of historico-political discourse from its juridico-philosophical predecessor. For Elias, the great spectre of this threat was Nazi Germany, which always maintained a space of exception within Elias' model (a space for which he attempted to account by the reversal of decivilizing, and which he tried to convert into an object lesson in the force exerted upon civilizing processes by cultural and historical specificities): Germany was literally 'less civilized' in the twentieth century than other western nation-states, in the sense that its culture had retained from an earlier period a certain culture of violence which created the conditions of possibility for the catastrophic decivilizing of the Third Reich (cf. *The Germans*). It is at this point that any reader of Elias begins to sense the possibility that the 'optimism' of the civilizing process as a model of social structure and change can be interpreted as a response to, and an attempt to account for, the Holocaust – that civilizing, as a long-term, directional, essentially fixed system guiding social change, was constructed as such by Elias ultimately to allow 'episodes' of 'decivilizing' to be conceptually contained as exceptions, reversals, breakdowns of a total social system whose inevitable output was greater social parity, interdependence, and pacification. For both theorists, this thought of perpetual war, and its concomitant anxiety, is the constitutive inverse of the construct of civilization as a whole. Foucault may have presented a critique of the discursive strategy of which Elias was a rather less self-conscious direct expression, but both thinkers could be said to agree on the notion that 'civilization' – whether this is taken as a political language of a historical speaking subject or as a socio-historical process – abhors violence and pursues a directional movement toward pacification.

To return, then, to the reading of the historiography of gladiature as an index of the movement toward reconciliation within the wider framework of 'civilization' as a significant *topos* within historico-political discourse: does the strong connection between civilization, violence, and a directional or teleological historical imperative that is identified by pacification (i.e. a certain relation to violence) reveal anything additional about itself, and consequently about how this complex of ideas functions for modernity's self-image, when we examine its representation at the myth-historical level of discourse?

'Civilization' mobilizes a language within which power has historically narrated and represented itself; the representation of power as free from violence, as rational and calculable, is a critical element of civilization's self-image. The critical divergence between Elias and Foucault as theorists of history and society lies in the choice between a sociality understood as discursively defined by perpetual war, with violence inscribed within power relations despite the language of abhorrence of violence, and a sociality whose structure is defined as a 'game' of mobile power-chances from which violence has withdrawn to the margins. The Introduction to this dissertation posed the question: if 'civilization' prefers to speak of the game, how then does it cope with gladiature as a grotesque hybrid of both game and war? Elias' process of civilizing, seen as a directional movement from Primal Contest to game theory, is symptomatic of the anxious denial of

perpetual warfare, and we can immediately see the same pattern of thought writ

large across gladiatorial historiography. Particularly in the twentieth century,

gladiature has undergone a gradual historiographic conversion which has weighed

the choice between 'warfare' and 'game' as the practice's essential framework of

meaning: Robert's claim that the civilizing influence of Greece was sufficient to

transform gladiature into a sport; Heurgon and the sport of savages; Ville, and the

notion of *agon*; and the culminating claims of Potter, for whom gladiature, as a

non-lethal sport, was a game by definition. Civilization's drive to disavow

violence from its self-image is sufficiently strong that, at the point at which

gladiature appears to position the ancient past as the second race of the present –

when something like affinity between antiquity and modernity emerges on the

discursive horizon – the imperative to exclude violence, to push it to the margins,

produces a rewritten history that elides violence as completely as possible.

    As a core category of modernity's self-image, civilization is a sliding

signifier whose content exhibits a certain expected variability. Elias' thought may

be taken as a representative index or guide of some of the more fixed elements of

modern western civilization as a construct – the abhorrence of violence and the

fear of decivilizing being key among these – but in other respects, the

'civilization' towards which Elias' model tends is particular to its own

sociohistorical context of utterance. The utopic position of functional

democratization as the direction (if not the *telos*) of civilizing process, for

example, is a philosophically liberal claim that may be a more or less standard element of the language of civilization in the twentieth century, but it arguably

would not have held the same discursive currency in earlier periods. However, the

real point is that when we move from 'civilization' as a contemporary construct to

'civilization' in the inscription of its origin story – when we turn to myth-history

as a particular form of discourse, which presumably reveals certain deeper

pretexts of the construct of civilization that go unspoken within other contexts of

articulation – the relative constancy of the fear of decivilizing and the abhorrence

of violence is joined by the equally persistent drive to exclude the crowd.

Arguably, if there is a summative statement to be drawn from gladiature as

a facet of modernity's myth-history, it lies in the persistent tendency or attempt to

construct and police a boundary of exclusion between 'civilization', especially as

that notion aligns with the exercise of socio-political power, and the *demos* – that

is, the political dimension of the crowd. As Foucault and Elias can be said to

agree upon, civilization, as a construct that mobilizes an entire connotative

language of historico-political discourse, abhors violence more or less by

definition; the language of civilization is essentially motivated by the fear that

violence or perpetual war can never be transcended or escaped, and as such the

abhorrence of violence – whether as an element of discourse for Foucault, or a

property of socio-psychological *habitus* for Elias – is one of the properties by

which civilization declares itself, and around which its associated language is

ordered. Thus it is possible to interpret gladiature's historiography as an idiom

wherein the civilized abhorrence of violence grapples repeatedly with gladiature

as a very specific representation of the intersection of violence with pleasure, and the discord that this creates within the discursive function of Rome as modern

civilization's myth-history can be said to invoke the apparent imperative to

bracket out or over-write gladiatorial violence from the historical image of Rome.

This much was canvassed in the Introduction. However, surveying three

centuries' worth of the historiography of gladiature reveals that the persistent

strategy for over-writing gladiatorial violence, common to both the nobiliary and

bourgeois speaking subjects, involves a seemingly indelible relationship between

the crowd, socio-politically defined, and a violence that is antithetical to

civilization. The pleasure of gladiature has never necessarily been the driving

issue. Instead, it can be argued that the moralizing language of pleasure in its

illegitimate relation to violence has been repeatedly deployed to represent a

deeper discourse of power and right.

From at least the late eighteenth century, when Ferguson described

gladiature as a corruption which 'rendered the People unworthy of the sovereignty

which they actually possessed', to Niebuhr's 'sovereign multitude', to Syme's

description of the *populus Romanus* as having been granted sovereignty only to

have its exercise forestalled, classical historians have perpetuated Juvenal's trope

of bread and circuses and its associated 'political fantasy' of the *demos* as an

entity which had once legitimately exercised political power but which

subsequently - through corruption from within or without, through revelation or

transformation of its essential nature – forfeited that privilege, or exploited that

political right for illegitimate purposes, or any one of a number of ways in which

the basic narrative can be and has been inscribed. Even the most recent scholarly work, which appears to express Foucault's posited discursive development of the unification and universalization of nation and State by strategically writing out violence from the image of gladiature, is nevertheless dependent upon a subtle transformation of the crowd into, effectively, the nobility; the universalization of a reconciled nation/State relation is less about the extension of the *demos* to include the entire social body, and more about the expansion of the nobility to colonize, civilize, and ultimately displace the *demos*. The relation between the crowd, violence, and power throughout gladiatorial historiography in modernity has always been the history of popular power as a perennial threat to social order; it is in this sense that gladiatorial historiography has always articulated a history of right for the self-appointed 'first race' of historical discourse, and consequently has also always provided an idiom for the deeper structures underlying the discourse of perpetual war. Seen in this light, Elias' construct of civilizing appears almost radical in its attempt to separate the continual fear of disorder, which he labelled decivilizing, from democratization, which he posited as the ultimate utopic outcome of all civilizing processes; the historiography of gladiature, when examined as a symptomatic representation of western civilization's myth-historical narratives of self-image, repeatedly and persistently aligns the feared disorder from which society must be defended with the spectre of the *populus* as an active and conscious agent of political authority. Elias may have dissociated decivilizing from democracy, but for three centuries' worth of classical historians, they appear to resist separation. The language or idiom of civilization within historico-political discourse, particularly when we read this language within its constitutive myth-historical deployment of the historiography of Rome, thus appears to be inherently antidemocratic. The history of right of the subject taken as the 'modern west' is consistent in this regard whether the speaker is nobiliary or bourgeois. The ultimate discursive function of myth-history is to exonerate certain violences and to support modernity's self-image as 'civilized' – a construct which changes in some particulars, but which in others appears to be very stable.